DATE

D0021586

M

D 804 G43 R38 1983
Littman, Sol,
War criminal on trial

WAR CRIMINAL ON TRIAL
The Rauca Case

LUTHER COLLEGE LIBRARY

WAR CRIMINAL ON TRIAL

The Rauca Case

SOL LITTMAN

LESTER
&ORPEN
DENNYS
PUBLISHERS

FEB 18 1985

DOUGLAS COLLEGE LIBRARY

Copyright © 1983 Sol Littman. All rights reserved. No part of this book may be reproduced in any manner whatsoever without written permission from the Publisher, except by a reviewer who wishes to quote brief passages for inclusion in a review.

Material in this book appeared in somewhat different form in *Saturday Night* magazine.

CANADIAN CATALOGUING IN PUBLICATION DATA

Littman, Sol, 1920-
    War criminal on trial : the Rauca case

ISBN 0-88619-037-1

1. Rauca, Albert Helmut.   2. War criminals–
Germany–Biography.   3. National socialism–
Biography.   4. World War, 1935-1945–Lithuania–
Atrocities.   5. Holocaust, Jewish (1939-1945)–
Lithuania.   6. Jews–Lithuania–Persecutions.
I. Title.

D804.G43R38 1983   364.1'38'0924   C83-099169-7

Design by Don Fernley

Printed and bound in Canada by
T. H. Best Printing Company Ltd. for
Lester & Orpen Dennys Limited
78 Sullivan Street
Toronto, Ontario
M5T 1C1

To the courageous Jews
of the Kaunas ghetto—
the few who survived
and the many who were slain

Contents

Acknowledgements

The arrest of an elderly, German-born, Canadian citizen on a charge of war crimes launched a voyage of inquiry that took me from a quiet Toronto suburb to Ludwigsburg in West Germany, East Berlin, Moscow, and Vilnius and Kaunas in Lithuania. It exposed me to policemen, prosecutors, politicians, archivists, lawyers, and legal researchers. It also introduced me to some remarkable people who survived the hell that the Nazis imposed on Kaunas.

I am grateful to Helen Werblunsky for braving the pain of recollection to share her story with me. Abraham Tory explained the cruel choices facing the Jewish Community Council of Kaunas, and his diary was invaluable in reconstructing the timetable of these events. Leah Elstein saw the Jewish leaders for what they were—brave men with human failings. Yaacov Rabinovitch, with his journalist's eye for detail, helped me see events in the ghetto more clearly. Chaim Lipman's memory of events, people, and sequences—along with his own gripping story—made important contributions to the manuscript.

I am particularly grateful to Dr. Joel Elkes of the University of Louisville, son of the revered leader of the Kaunas ghetto, for the material on his father, Dr. Elchanan Elkes; I have borrowed freely from the writings of both father and son. My thanks also to psychiatrist Dr. Henry Fenigstein for his invaluable insights into the psychology of the survivor.

Mark Starowicz, executive producer of CBC's *The Journal*, and Bernie Zukerman, the show's documentaries director, placed their resources at my disposal so I could make a television documentary on the Rauca case. I am particularly grateful to William Cobden, the documentary's producer, for suggesting that I make use of the voluminous material I had collected on Rauca and the events in Kaunas by writing a book. *Saturday Night* editors Gary Ross and Tecca Crosby, who worked with me on the article "Agent of the Holocaust", published in the magazine's July 1983 issue, helped bring my research into focus.

Crown attorney Christopher Amerasinghe was especially helpful in directing me to court records and explaining legal issues that normally baffle laymen. Canadian Jewish Congress lawyer Bert Raphael was also a model of helpfulness and patience. Defence lawyers William Horkins and William Parker were generous with their time and frank with reporters; by undertaking the defence of a man whose cause was distinctly unpopular, and handling it with dignity and perspective, they proved the soundness of the common-law principle that every person charged with a crime deserves competent counsel.

Ben Kayfetz, regional director of the Canadian Jewish Congress, shared the adventure of discovery with me and directed me to Jewish sources that I might otherwise have missed. I acknowledge a special debt to Kenneth Narvey of the CJC's legal committee for supplying many fruitful leads and countless photocopies of crucial court documents. My old friends Shirley and Leon Kumove generously provided Yiddish and Hebrew translations of important documents, and my new friend, Elly Gotz, who was a teenager in the ghetto, checked the manuscript against his own memory of Kaunas.

And to that spunky lady, my wife Mildred, my endless thanks for her patience, quiet encouragement, and emotional support.

Introduction

There were three of us wedged into the small blue car with a large yellow Canadian Broadcasting Corporation logo on its side. The floor was littered with empty film cans, tail ends of film, and tattered extension cords, and a large 16mm motion-picture camera occupied most of the back seat.

We were a typical TV-news crew, rushing back to the studio with a report on the first Canadian citizen in history formally charged with war crimes. As we drove I flipped through my notes, mentally composing the story I would file. "Today, in this court-house, a seventy-three-year-old German-born Canadian was granted bail by the Honourable Justice Griffiths despite the Crown's plea that he be kept in prison in view of the enormity of his crimes." In the following paragraph I would report that "Helmut Rauca was charged with aiding and abetting in the murder of 10,500 persons on or about October 28, 1941 in Kaunas, Lithuania." I would go on to mention that the former Nazi SS officer had been born in Trieb, Germany, that he had emigrated to Canada in 1950 and had become a Canadian citizen in 1956.

As we approached the studio, my camera-man, a young Irish-English-French Canadian, broke into a staccato monologue: "I suppose if it was my parents he'd gassed I'd want him strung up by his thumbs—but it was forty years ago at least—the old codger is how old, seventy-three?—why not let him die on his own? What's the point of prosecuting him? I bet he's suffered agonies of guilt all these years."

My sound man, a young German immigrant—gentle,

round-faced—chose his words carefully, translating from his mother tongue. "What's the point of raking up these coals? It will only start things over again, make people think all Germans are Nazis. Anyway, what was Rauca's rank? Hauptscharführer? That's only a master sergeant. He would have had very little real authority. Why can't we let bygones be bygones?"

Back in the newsroom, I waited impatiently for the day's film to be processed. My film editor, a thoughtful Englishman, said, "Now don't take me wrong, but I wonder what business it is of ours to help punish someone for something that took place so long ago in some bloody country most Canadians never heard of. It seems a bit unseemly to pursue an old man who's never harmed anyone in this country. I've always felt that those Nazi-hunters like Wiesenthal make Jews appear vengeful and unforgiving."

Very little of what took place in the court-room that day found its way into the "one minute, fifteen" news item presented on the evening news. There was no time to set the stage, no time to tell how a minor Saxonian police official came to have the power of life and death over thousands of Jews in Nazi-occupied Lithuania during World War II. Nor was there time to respond to the important moral questions posed by the members of my crew, questions which I soon discovered could not be answered convincingly by abstract appeals to justice, or invocations of the memory of the dead. And the questions they raised were frequently repeated by others with whom I discussed the Rauca case—others who exhibited the same impatience with abstract answers. It was not until I offered a detailed, factual account of the horrors imposed on the Jews of Kaunas that they understood why it was necessary to try Rauca, despite his age, and despite the passage of forty years. The same detailed, factual account is the subject matter of this book. May it serve to arouse understanding in all Canadians.

WAR CRIMINAL ON TRIAL
The Rauca Case

1
The Arrest

Otonabee Avenue was quiet—almost silent—on the morning of Thursday, June 17, 1982. Most of the adults in this plain suburban North Toronto neighbourhood were either at work or at home preparing lunch. The children were still at school. An occasional delivery van drifted by, and once in a while a woman would back the family car down the driveway and head for the nearby shopping centre.

The only other sign of activity was at number 96, where an elderly, white-haired man was diligently painting the sash on his basement windows. His modest, post-war bungalow stood out from its neighbours by the extraordinary neatness of its shrubs and lawns, the brightness of its brick, and the garish orange of its garage door.

As noon approached, there was a slight ripple in the calm. Two anonymous grey sedans drove slowly down the street, hesitating from time to time as if unsure of the address. Finally both cars stopped opposite number 96. The occupants stared hard for a moment at the man bent over his paintbrushes, and one of them nodded. Three large, bulky men got out and, with an air of forced casualness, approached the painter.

"Mr. Rauca?"

The white-haired man looked up and silently nodded.

"Helmut Rauca?"

"Yes."

"We are Royal Canadian Mounted Police officers. I am Corporal Fred Yetter. This is Staff Sergeant Smith and Constable Fracke. We are conducting an investigation and would appreciate it if we could ask you some questions. Could we step inside? We don't want to attract the attention of your neighbours."

"Yes, yes, come inside."

Once inside, they took seats in the living-room. Rauca sat upright in his chair, staring politely at the three Mounties.

"What is your full name?" Yetter asked.

"Albert Helmut Rauca," came the reply.

"On what date were you born?"

"The third of November, 1908, at Trieb; that's in Saxony, in Germany."

"When did you arrive in Canada?"

Without hesitation Rauca reeled off, "On the thirtieth day of December, 1950, at St. John, New Brunswick, aboard the Canadian ship *Beaverbrae* from Bremerhaven. That's in the north part of Germany."

His father, he told the officers as they wrote assiduously in their notebooks, was Albert Rauca, born in Austria. His mother was Alma Wolf, born in Trieb.

The questioning moved ahead quickly as Yetter asked his questions and the elderly man with the heavy German accent gave polite, detailed answers. "He was almost like a policeman on the witness stand giving evidence in a case he had investigated," Staff Sergeant Glen Smith recalled later.

Asked about his employment before coming to Canada, Rauca replied, "A professional policeman, just like you." In the early days he had been in the "order police";* later he had become an instructor of young policemen. In 1935—two years after Hitler came to power—he had transferred to the detective division.

He told the RCMP officers that in 1941, when Germany went to war with Russia, he was in Prague attending a course in counter-espionage. In February of 1942, he was transferred to a place in Lithuania called Kauen by the Germans, Kaunas by the Lithuani-

*The Order Police or *Ordnungspolizei* in pre-war Germany were the equivalent of our state or municipal police officers responsible for law and order, the protection of property, and traffic. The detective branch or criminal investigation division was called Kripo, for *Kriminalpolizei*. By 1938 all Kripo members were obliged to join the SS and were under the command of Reinhard Heydrich, commander of the Gestapo and SD (*Sicherheitsdienst*).

ans, and Kowno by the Russians. He remained in the police until the war ended. His highest rank, he said, listing his promotions, was Hauptscharführer or master sergeant. He was about to launch into a detailed explanation of his duties in Kaunas when Yetter interrupted him.

"Hold it, Mr. Rauca. I must warn you that I have a warrant for your arrest under the Extradition Act. You may wish to continue this conversation but anything you say from this point on may be used in evidence against you. You have a right to counsel and you may wish to telephone your lawyer now."

For a moment Rauca stared silently at the floor.

"Gentlemen, you are professional policemen as I was once," he said. "You understand it would be unwise of me to answer any more questions until I have spoken to my lawyer." Then, shaking his head sadly, he added, "Frankly, I never believed it would come to this."

Corporal Yetter's notes indicate that the questioning ceased at 11:56 a.m., when Rauca telephoned a Mr. Kelly at the firm of Day Wilson Campbell. Mr. Kelly was informed that he could meet with his client later that afternoon at RCMP headquarters at 225 Jarvis Street.

In fact, Yetter had no need for further questions. He was certain now that the man sitting opposite him was indeed the man named in the warrant first issued on September 21, 1961, by the State Prosecutor's office in Frankfurt am Main on a charge of mass murder "carried out with intent and premeditation for base motives and in a cruel manner." Yetter's prisoner bore the same name, was born in the same town, had the same father and mother, attended the same schools, joined the Saxony State Police on the same date, held the same rank, and served in the same war zone.

However, the brief interrogation had served an important purpose. Having been invited into the house, the Mounties were now legally free to search the premises and seize any evidence they might find without applying for a search warrant. Since they were not entirely certain what it was they were looking for, a judge might have been unwilling to issue a warrant.

Once he had placed his man under arrest, Yetter ordered Rauca

3

to surrender his passport. The officers then conducted a brief search of his bedroom. From a bottom dresser drawer they removed a photo album containing a picture of Rauca taken shortly after his arrival in Canada. They also seized the usual paraphernalia Canadians keep in their wallets and desk drawers—letters from the Canadian passport office, driver's licence, Ontario Senior Citizen's Privilege Card, Old Age Benefits card, credit cards, household bills, cancelled cheques, and Social Insurance card. These were variously signed Albert Rauca, Albert H. Rauca, Albert Helmut Rauca, and Helmut Albert Rauca, normal variations hardly constituting pseudonyms. (Minor as they may seem, these differences had seriously delayed the Mounties in their search for Rauca, and the documents were to play a key role in nailing down his identification at his subsequent extradition hearing.)

Next the fugitive was taken to the huge, contemporary fortress in downtown Toronto that serves as RCMP regional headquarters. After being fingerprinted and photographed, he appeared before Associate Chief Justice William Parker of the Supreme Court of Ontario to be charged. From there he was taken to the depressingly shabby and overcrowded Toronto Jail—"the Don"—that serves as a lockup for prisoners waiting trial in local courts.

Staff Sergeant Smith, whose droopy blond moustache, comfortable tweed jacket, and easy way of talking give him the air of a bemused English professor, recalls that Rauca looked old and fragile when they first addressed him. "But once we identified ourselves as police officers he seemed to straighten up, and from then on he acted one hundred per cent professional. He wanted us to know that he identified with us, that he too was a professional policeman, that we understood each other. At one point he complimented us on the correctness of our behaviour. But there was one thing about him that struck me funny," Smith adds. "In every photograph of him that we found, whether it was pictures by our surveillance team or group photos taken with friends in Canada, he was always looking down or away. That's what made me think there was something in his background that bothered him."

The television newsroom of CBLT, CBC's local station, is located above a dingy convenience store a block and a half away from the

4

corporation's main studios on Toronto's Jarvis Street. Because the room is low-ceilinged and drab the corporation has made desperate efforts to dress up the newsroom by painting the walls in garish colours and ornamenting them with giant stencils of the CBC logo. For most of the day newsroom staff seem to loll about, holding clubby meetings and staring blankly into TV monitors, but by four p.m. tension is setting in. Faces become drawn and tempers grow short as reporters and crews return from the "street" with the day's stories.

The afternoon of June 17, 1982, was particularly trying for Ted Bissland, CBLT's court reporter. A TV news veteran, he enjoys the challenge of bringing a late-breaking story to air; he will often linger in the courtroom after other reporters have charged out to meet their late afternoon deadlines, so that he can include last-minute developments in his report. On occasion he will do an item "live", in-studio, because there is no time to go to tape.

But that afternoon he was in a real sweat. It was a slow day with nothing newsworthy on the court's roster, and the trial he had chosen to cover was anything but interesting. Then, while having a smoke in the court-house corridor, he heard one court attendant say to another, "Hey Charlie, they've arrested some Nazi for war crimes. He's being arraigned in Courtroom 17."

Bissland—and every other reporter within earshot—raced down the court-house escalator to number 17. As he ran, Bissland bawled, "Standby!" to a waiting crew-member. (Canadian courts do not permit TV crews in the courtroom, so they generally cluster outside the court-house door.)

Inside the courtroom, Bissland saw a husky, straight-backed man being arraigned. He was dressed in grey slacks, blue blazer, white shirt, and neat tie. His white hair was brushed straight back from his wide forehead. His craggy, thin-lipped face registered both resignation and defiance.

The charge was staggering—"aiding and abetting the murder of 10,500 persons on or about the 28th day of October, 1941 at Kaunas, Lithuania." But the legal proceedings were over almost before they began. Bissland barely had time to make notes before the presiding judge set the following Monday for a bail hearing and the white-haired man was discreetly handcuffed and escorted from the courtroom.

5

The reporters, hungry for details, swarmed around Crown attorney Christopher Amerasinghe's table. Amerasinghe held up the warrant of apprehension and waited patiently while reporters copied out the portions they needed. In the warrant, Rauca was described as a member of an SS security unit called an "Einsatzgruppe" stationed in Kaunas from July 3, 1941, to approximately July 1944—"As an SS master sergeant and a member of the command headquarters of the Security Police and the SS Security Service (SD) for the general district of Lithuania, [Rauca] did, in the so-called Big Operation in the ghetto of Kaunas, single out to be shot 10,500 Jewish men, women and children...the shooting occurring on 29th October 1941 in the IXth Fort in Kaunas."

The warrant further stated that Rauca had emigrated to Canada in 1950 and had become a Canadian citizen in 1956. It did not make clear where he had spent the intervening years, or what he had done since coming to Canada, but said that the West German government had been looking for him since 1961. Now that he had been tracked down, the German state prosecutor wanted him extradited.

The details were dramatic enough to impress any editor, but Bissland cursed the fact that he had no picture, not even a courtroom sketch. He had no film of the accused man and there was no time for interviews with Holocaust survivors or heads of the German-Canadian community. In television you're dead without pictures—and he was damned if he'd let such a good story be disposed of in a fifteen-second item read by a blank-faced announcer.

Quickly he called CBLT's assignment desk to ask that a back-up crew be sent to 96 Otonabee Avenue. "You know, the stock stuff," he shouted over the phone. "Ask the neighbours what kind of guy he is. Did they ever suspect they were living next door to a war criminal? Did he ever express any political opinions? Did they ever see any Nazi flags? How do they feel living next to someone accused of mass murder?"

Then Bissland tried a stunt he had never tried before: he telephoned the station's court artist at his home and described the man he had seen in the courtroom. "See what you can come up with," he said. True, the completed drawing bore only a vague resemblance to Rauca, but it was better than nothing, and more than any other station could produce.

Bissland's story on the six o'clock news that night was the first that most Canadians heard of Albert Helmut Rauca, Canadian senior citizen and alleged wartime "devil" of the Kaunas ghetto. As far as Bissland could determine, Rauca was the first Canadian citizen in history to be charged with what are commonly called "war crimes".

Bill Horkins was tired and looking forward to a long, leisurely weekend on the Friday afternoon when he received a call from Rauca's solicitor, Ralph S. McCreath of Day Wilson Campbell, asking him to appear at his client's bail hearing the following Monday. There was little that McCreath could tell Horkins about his client or the charges, except that he had handled the old gentleman's business for the past fifteen to eighteen years, largely real estate transactions. As far as he knew, "he was a respected citizen who did his job and bothered no one." McCreath rated him as "a good client who knew what he wanted and was grateful for everything the firm did for him." The little McCreath could tell him intrigued Horkins, nevertheless. It's not every day that a Toronto criminal lawyer gets a chance to defend a client charged with murdering 10,500 people. Sheer curiosity made him eager to handle the case.

Horkins spent the next couple of days busily reading up on extradition law, looking up relevant cases, and interviewing his client. As he read and reread the warrant of apprehension, the outline of a defence strategy began to form in his mind.

"They don't conduct legal business the same way in Germany that we do here," he thought. "Their depositions seem to contain a great deal more hearsay information. Their affidavits are in narrative form rather than in the meticulously recorded questions and answers familiar to Canadian lawyers. That would be a point to hammer home."

He could also raise the question of witness reliability. How accurate are people's memories after forty years? Could the court depend on those memories, after so many years and in such a serious matter?

7

Then a more intriguing idea occurred to him: wasn't this essentially a constitutional issue? Didn't the new Charter of Rights guarantee a man the right to confront his accuser? Shouldn't his lawyer have the right to cross-examine the witnesses? Wasn't the reliance on written depositions in extradition cases unconstitutional?

Best of all, wasn't there a clause in the charter that talked of a citizen's right to "enter, *remain in*, and leave Canada"? Horkins couldn't remember the wording. He reached for his law books. It was an exciting approach, and one that he might take all the way to the Supreme Court. But that would come later. The first step was the application for bail, which would be decided on narrower grounds.

The bail hearings opened at 10 a.m. on Monday, June 21. Mr. Justice William Griffiths of the Supreme Court of Ontario assumed his seat on the bench. Rauca was conducted to the dock by two court attendants.

Christopher Amerasinghe appeared for the Attorney-General of Canada and the Federal Republic of Germany. Amerasinghe is a trim, handsome man in his early forties. Born and educated in Sri Lanka, he is known as a tough prosecutor who is frequently called on to handle difficult drug, income tax, combines, and extradition cases. His extreme courtesy conceals a dogged persistence.*

The judge was testy. The lawyers hadn't had time to prepare the usual mountain of papers generated in legal matters; Griffiths had nothing before him except the Notice of Motion, and he clearly didn't like flying blind.

"It seems to me I should know the background on which this man has been made the subject of an arrest warrant if I am to

---

*Christopher Amerasinghe was born in 1940 to a highly educated Sri Lankan family. His paternal grandfather was the first Sinhalese to hold the post of general manager of the railways in Ceylon; his father won scholarships to Cambridge and retired as a professor of western classics. Amerasinghe studied law at the University of Ceylon and was a successful barrister for eight years before emigrating to England in 1972. However, he found England, with its rigid class system, distasteful and decided to emigrate to Canada. Admitted to the Ontario bar in 1976, he was hired by the Ontario Securities Commission. In December 1978, having become a Canadian citizen, he joined the federal Department of Justice as a Crown prosecutor.

determine if he should be released," said His Lordship. "Don't you agree with that, Mr. Horkins?"

Horkins readily agreed, complaining that he suffered under the same handicap: "I haven't seen a copy of the material," he said. "My friend doesn't have an extra copy with him."

The judge turned to the Crown attorney. "Mr. Amerasinghe, you can't keep this material to yourself. If counsel is to represent this man he must have the material."

"With great respect, My Lord, I am certainly open to giving my friend a copy if he wants to look at it," the Crown replied.

"But surely the government can produce another copy for his benefit?" the judge said, with proper judicial sarcasm.

"Indeed it can. . . . "

"Is there just one copy available?"

"At the moment, My Lord." Amerasinghe was clearly embarrassed. An experienced Crown attorney, he was accustomed to rough handling by judges, but the absence of documents made him look ill-prepared, unready for court. In fact the arrest had been hasty, but he hesitated to say so in open court. Only after the extradition hearing did he reveal the reason to reporters; for the moment all he could do was stand his ground and doggedly oppose bail.

The Extradition Act makes no provision for bail, he argued; indeed the Canadian government, under its treaty with the Federal Republic of Germany, has a special obligation to see that the fugitive does not escape custody before he can be handed over. It would seriously affect the relationship between Canada and the requesting nation if the fugitive got away while extradition was pending.

What's more, the offences with which Rauca was charged were extremely serious, and the evidence against him was extremely strong: he had been identified by at least five eyewitnesses now living in Israel. Under the circumstances there was every reason to believe Rauca might try to flee, he concluded.

Horkins, staring down at the bare table in front of him, began, "My Lord, the only issues here are . . . will the accused appear as required for the court, and if released is he any danger to the public?

"Mr. Rauca is seventy-three years of age. He has lived in Canada for thirty years, openly and under his true name. He is a citizen of this country, all of his belongings and property are here. . . . He has always lived here quite peacefully and openly. He has no criminal record."

Under the circumstances, he said, Rauca deserved to be granted bail like any other citizen.

To illustrate that Rauca was a good citizen and a decent fellow, Horkins put his client on the stand. This was the only time, in a long series of legal proceedings, that Rauca said anything in court.

His lawyer led him through a review of his place of birth, the date on which he arrived in Canada, his various occupations and places of residence since his arrival, and some questions about his net worth. Given his half-share in a Georgian Bay cottage and his half of the mortgage on a Huntsville motel, plus some odds and ends of short-term bank certificates, the former Gestapo master sergeant estimated his total worth at $150,000.

Rauca stood straight in the dock. His answers, delivered in a heavy German accent, were brief and cautious—like a well-schooled policeman, he frequently qualified dates and times by adding "on or about". His manner was affable; he behaved like a man who had nothing to hide and was prepared to co-operate to the full with the court.

Amerasinghe's efforts at cross-examination were severely limited by Judge Griffiths. The Crown attorney, eager to explore Rauca's background before his arrival in Canada, began questioning him on his career in Germany. Rauca rattled off the dates of his graduation from elementary school, his apprenticeship in a Plauen textile mill, his career as a state security policeman, and his posting to Kaunas. He arrived in Lithuania, he said, some time in February or March of 1942.

Q. Where were you during the war?
A. Well, when the war broke out in '39 I was still in the same place in Plauen with the State Police. . . . Then I was called to a place, Prague, Czechoslovakia, for a time. It was the beginning of the Russian campaign. I think it was June 1941. It was from June '41 to December '41 I attended a course in counter-intelligence in the State Police

Force in Prague. Then I was another two months in my place of employment in Plauen until I got transferred to East Prussia— Königsberg, this was the capital of East Prussia—and was at the State Police of Königsberg. There I was several months and from there I got transferred in spring about, I can't say exactly the months, but it was February or March, in Lithuania territories; I have been in three places there, one was called Smalininkai, the second was called Marijampole, and the third was called Kaunas. . . .

In effect, Rauca testified that he was nowhere near Kaunas on October 28, 1941, the day on which he was accused of having aided and abetted the murder of 10,500 people. But Amerasinghe was just warming up to his work when Judge Griffiths objected to this line of questioning: "Now where is this going, Mr. Amerasinghe?"

He reminded the Crown prosecutor that, as this was a bail hearing, he was not entitled to explore the validity of the charges or to elicit evidence for use in a later trial. There were—as Horkins had pointed out—only two pertinent issues: whether the fugitive would return on the date fixed for his hearing, and whether he represented a potential menace to the public.

Amerasinghe plodded on for a time, but soon gave up further cross-examination.

Horkins was next, and he called on Mrs. Auguste Machdanz, owner of the house at 96 Otonabee. Rauca had moved in with Mrs. Machdanz and her husband in 1973, and had stayed on after Mr. Machdanz's death.

A small, slender woman in a tweed suit, flowing scarf, sturdy walking shoes, and high-crowned fedora, as worn by older women on the Kurfürstendamm, Mrs. Machdanz stated that she had known Rauca since 1951.

Yes, she was prepared to stand surety for her old friend, she told the court. She was prepared to put up her house, which was worth at least $100,000.

His Lordship. Do you know specifically that he is currently accused of aiding and abetting the murder of 10,500 persons in Kaunas, Lithuania?

11

A. No.

Q. You didn't know that?

A. No.

Q. Now that I have told you he is faced with that charge, does that make any difference to your attitude?

A. No, it doesn't make any difference.

While the questioning went on and the lawyers traded precedents, Rauca sat impassively in the dock, staring straight ahead, never looking at the witnesses. Craggy-faced, with large pouches under his eyes, he carried himself with a peculiar air of authority.

"He looks like a retired cop," whispered one of the newspaper reporters.

Judge Griffiths attempted to reconcile the arguments presented by the defence and the prosecution. He couldn't "help but be overwhelmed with revulsion at the nature and enormity of the crime," he said. Nevertheless, the accused was a Canadian citizen and must be given the same treatment as any other citizen. Rauca, he ruled, was entitled to bail.

The next question was, how much? The Crown suggested one million dollars cash. Horkins thought $100,000 would serve the purpose of the court. His Lordship decided the amount should be $150,000.

Not only was this amount unusually high for a criminal case in Canada, but the judge also attached a number of severe conditions: Rauca's passport must remain in the hands of the RCMP; he must not leave Metropolitan Toronto; he must at all times inform the police of his whereabouts; and he must report daily to RCMP headquarters on Jarvis Street, during regular office hours.

Horkins called for a ban on publication of proceedings—a request frequently granted in sensational cases, to avoid influencing potential jurors—but Amerasinghe vigorously opposed the motion. Rauca would not be tried before a Canadian jury, he argued; he would be tried in West Germany, in a German court. The extradition hearing that Rauca faced in Canada would basically be a preliminary enquiry, where the judge did not have to be convinced "beyond a reasonable doubt" of the fugitive's guilt, but needed only be satisfied there was sufficient evidence to merit a trial.

Griffiths denied the motion to ban publication.

Canada's Extradition Act requires that a fugitive be given a hearing within forty-five days of his arrest. If the Crown fails to proceed within that time, the accused is entitled to claim "unusual delay" and, depending on the judgment of the court, may be set free. September 20, the earliest date available on the court calendar, was therefore set for the extradition hearing.

The courtroom had been relatively empty; Toronto's large Jewish community was as yet barely aware that a man accused of Nazi war crimes had been arrested "right here in Toronto, just a few houses away from a Jewish family." But the Jewish Defence League was out in force.* They strutted about in combat-style berets, and T-shirts bearing the slogan "Never Again". A small corps carrying placards reading "Down with Nazi Murderers" picketed the courthouse, while others, muttering darkly, took seats in the courtroom.

As the bail hearing ended and court attendants escorted Rauca from the prisoner's dock in handcuffs, one of the young Jewish militants pressed forward. Catching Rauca's eye, he shouted, "Rauca, butcher! Murderer of children!"

The former Gestapo Jewish Affairs Specialist turned slightly, eyes blazing. His face grew ugly with rage as he drew back his head and hissed like an old, caged eagle being poked by a boy with a stick.

*The Jewish Defence League was founded by Rabbi Meyer Kahane in New York in 1967. Its slogan, "Never Again", refers to the Holocaust and promises that Jews will no longer suffer persecution without striking back. Kahane believes that anti-Semitism is endemic and that there is no long-term future for Jews outside the state of Israel; nevertheless, he holds that Jews worldwide must follow the example of the Jewish state and be prepared to fight physically for their existence.

2
Hauptscharführer

The Berlin Document Centre, located in a semi-rural corner of West Berlin, is a vast storehouse of official German documents seized by American troops in the last days of the war. In its files are 10.7 million Nazi Party membership documents stored in their original cabinets; individual SS and *Sturmabteilung* (SA)* files crowd its drawers, along with the daily guard rosters at concentration camps, and detailed records of art works confiscated, gold teeth collected, and tons of human hair shipped to the Reich.

When the Nazis saw the end of the Third Reich approaching, they gave orders to have all Party records at their Munich headquarters destroyed. American troops arrived just in time to prevent them from being converted into pulp at a Munich paper mill. Trainload after trainload of documents was deposited under guard in various sites in the American occupation zone in Germany. The

---

*The SA (*Sturmabteilungen*) were Hitler's paramilitary, brown-shirted Storm Troops, who specialized in undisciplined street violence. They were commanded by Ernst Röhm who was later shot, at Hitler's command, in the June 30, 1934 purge of Nazi leaders.

The SS (*Schutzstaffeln*) were originally an élite division of the SA, formed in the 1920s to serve as bodyguards to Hitler and other Nazi chiefs. Composed of the best physical specimens and most fanatic Nazis, the SS remained subordinate to the SA until 1929, when Hitler appointed a colourless former chicken-farmer, Heinrich Himmler, to the post of Reichsführer SS. Himmler worked in Röhm's shadow until the 1934 purge (conducted by the SS); then he rapidly increased his power. By July 1936 the SS was declared independent of the SA. The SS soon became much more powerful than its parent group and by the end of the war it rivalled the army in strength.

most sensitive of the material was taken to Berlin to assist the prosecutors in the Nuremberg Trials. Today the documents remain there, under American control, and only scholars, law enforcement agencies, and officials of friendly powers are permitted access to the centre's voluminous files.

One of the files bears the name of Helmut Rauca—rank Hauptscharführer (master sergeant), SS number 290 335.

The heavy cardboard folder contains the usual bureaucratic miscellany: ID photographs of Rauca in his black SS dress uniform, requests for transfer, applications for promotion, memoranda, commendations, and several copies of his *Rasse–und– Siedlungshauptamt* (Race and Settlement) questionnaire, the genealogical check required of all SS personnel to prove the purity of their Aryan racial background. The ancestral chain had to be traced back to 1750, and the discovery of even one Jewish great-grandparent was enough to destroy an SS-man's career.

The form completed by Rauca reveals that he was the first son and second child of embroidery-machine owner Franz Albert Rauca and his wife Alma, née Wolf. Rauca's ancestors were mainly small freehold farmers and master blacksmiths. The family professed to be Lutheran, but in the space for "Religion" provided on the form Rauca wrote "Freethinker".

Rauca graduated from the elementary school in Trieb with a grade of "very good" and was awarded a "book prize". That fall, he was off to the nearby industrial city of Plauen to begin a commercial apprenticeship; again he received a grade of "very good" in the academic portion of his work. To gain practical experience, he served as a clerk-apprentice with several of Plauen's large textile companies.

But clerking did not particularly please him, and on April 16, 1928—at the age of twenty—the broad-shouldered, full-faced young man joined the state police force and was sent to Meissen, north of Leipzig, for training. Earnest, orderly, and strong, he once more earned a grade of "very good" at the police academy. At the end of a probationary year spent in Zwickau, fifty kilometres west of Plauen, he received an automatic promotion to sergeant. In 1933, after five years of routine police work, he returned to Plauen—population 80,000—to serve as training officer for the local constabulary.

15

On January 12, 1931, two years before Hitler came to power, he joined the Nazi Party (*Nationalsozialistische Deutsche Arbeiterpartei* or National Socialist German Workers' Party).

It was more than a token membership; for over a year he voluntarily and enthusiastically served as party cell-leader for the Third Squad at Zwickau police headquarters.

"In this capacity I was successful in persuading twenty-three police officers to join the NSDAP in 1932," he boasted on his Race-and-Settlement form. "A certificate relating to my activities during this period of struggle, issued by the Zwickau county administration, is in the SD files.*

"In 1933, I was promoted to the rank of staff sergeant on the basis of my services to the National Socialist movement."

Rauca "contracted marriage" on May 9, 1934 with Ella Gertraud Voigt, a simple girl of twenty-two who had studied "plain needlework" at domestic science college and had apprenticed for a year as an assistant "in a ready-made store". Her father was the postmaster in Plauen, and she was eager to remain close to her parents, so—despite Rauca's promising career in Zwickau—he was persuaded to apply for a transfer to the Plauen detachment.

"On July 1, 1934, I changed over to the constabulary in Plauen at my own request, doing service first with the police company for one year," Rauca wrote. "On May 1, 1935, I was transferred to the political department of Plauen police headquarters; as of the end of 1936 this agency was attached to the Secret State Police."

On the same day that he transferred to the Plauen constabulary, he and his bride proudly took up residence at Rhaenisstrasse 136, Plauen IV. On June 5, 1937 their first son, Dietmar, was born.

The transfer to the Plauen constabulary proved fortunate for the young police officer; after a year of general police work he was assigned to the force's political intelligence unit.

Hitler was consolidating his hold on every aspect of German life, and the police were a prime target. Traditionally, German police forces were administered by the various *Länder* or states. But during this period SS Reichsführer Heinrich Himmler, by a series of shrewd bureaucratic manoeuvres, succeeded in federaliz-

---

*The SD or *Sicherheitsdienst* (Security Service) was originally a branch of the SS designed to keep watch on SS members.

ing all state and municipal forces and bringing them under his direct command.

When Hitler appointed Heinrich Himmler as Reichsführer SS in January 1929, the SS (*Schutzstaffeln* or "protection formations") was no more than Hitler's private bodyguard, numbering less than three hundred men. By January 1933 it had grown to 52,000 and formed a *corps d'élite* within the brown-shirted SA (*Sturmabteilungen* or Storm Detachments). In the notorious purge of June 30, 1934, when Röhm, the leader of the SA, was murdered, Himmler's SS was given the job of carrying out the arrests and executions and a month later was rewarded with the status of an independent organization. Within the SS itself a separate intelligence and security service (the SD or *Sicherheitsdienst*) was organized.

In 1934 the SD came under the command of Himmler's protégé and second-in-command, the handsome, ruthless, ambitious "Blond Beast", Reinhard Heydrich. For a time Himmler and the Prussian Minister-President Hermann Göring engaged in a bitter power struggle for control of the Gestapo, or Prussian secret state police. "Here too the formidable combination of Himmler and Heydrich proved successful and from Göring's reluctant concession of control over the Prussian Gestapo to Himmler in April 1934, the latter went on to become chief of the entire German police in July."

The takeover of the nation's police forces by the SS meant that they too became part of the Nazi Party apparatus. Hitler's enemies now became Germany's enemies; opposition to National Socialism became treason to the state itself.

As a staunch Party member, Rauca welcomed the melding of political party and police authority. "It is my aspiration to be able to be active in the National Socialist spirit in a responsible position within the Security Police," he told his superiors in the Race-and-Settlement bureau.

The genealogical investigation was a source of extreme embarrassment and irritation to the ambitious young policeman. Normally it was completed before a man became a member of the SS, and before he was given permission to marry, but Rauca was already a husband and parent by the time Himmler's scheming brought him into the élite corps.

17

However, there was no escaping the demands of racial purity. Apparently prodded by his SS superiors, he sent off a letter on November 23, 1937—almost a year after joining Hitler's black-uniformed security service—requesting the necessary forms.

It took him an additional year to gather up the plethora of birth certificates, marriage licences, baptismal documents, and letters of endorsement to meet the Race and Settlement Office's rigorous genealogical scrutiny. In the interim, the young police officer wrote one plaintive letter after another, pleading for more time.

"I ask you to extend the time by another three months," he wrote, "as the documents cannot be procured until May 1, 1938. Because of ancestors on my father's side, time-consuming correspondence with Czechoslovakia is necessary. *Heil Hitler.*"

He was not yet ready in August 1938; he wrote, "Again I must ask you for an extension of time. . . . I am still waiting for the certificates on the Rauca line. These ancestors have been living, from my grandfather on, in the region of Moravia. As to the grandfather of the Rauca line I miss only the birth certificate, all the other certificates I have. As to my great-grandparents, all I know is their names. . . . *Heil Hitler.*"

On September 1, 1938, for better or worse, assistant detective Helmut Rauca sent off whatever documents he had been able to collect. They were accompanied by a sworn declaration stating, "I hereby state under oath that I have furnished all information . . . to the best of my knowledge and belief. I am aware that any wilfully untrue or insufficient information will bring about expulsion from the SS."

The information must have been sufficient, because on September 11 he was promoted from sergeant to SS master sergeant.

War was only a year away. When it came, vigorous young policemen and staunch Party members like Rauca were logical candidates for special assignments in the occupied territories. Who was better equipped to root out Communists and ferret out rebellion by the native population? Who could be better counted on to carry out the dirty jobs too shameful to be expressed in written orders? Who, other than the SS, was capable of the ruthlessness and dedication necessary to serve as Hitler's instrument in the Final Solution of the Jewish Question?

3
The Final Solution

The Final Solution of the Jewish Problem was the code-name for Hitler's plans to exterminate the Jews of Europe. It was used by German officials after the summer of 1941 in order to avoid the necessity of admitting to each other that such plans existed.

More than verbal squeamishness was involved in their use of the term. To liquidate a whole people it was necessary to lull them into disbelief, to take them by surprise. The Nazis were practised at this kind of deceit. They were skilled in the use of high-sounding terms that concealed their real purpose and played on people's desperate hope that things couldn't possibly be as bad as they seemed, that civilized men were surely incapable of deliberate mass murder. To keep that hope alive the Nazis employed an endless series of euphemisms: deportation to concentration camps was called "resettlement"; extermination in a gas chamber was referred to as "special handling".

If words served to tranquillize the Jews, they also helped mask the horrors of mass murder from the murderers themselves. Ordinary people, called on to inflict pain and suffering on others, must first be convinced they are engaged in a noble mission. To Hitler's minions, the extermination of the Jews provided the National Socialist state with its most exalted imperative.

> The Final Solution . . . was part of a salvational ideology that envisaged the attainment of Heaven by bringing Hell on earth. Never before in human history had one people made the killing of another the fulfilment of an ideology.

In this respect, Hitler was radically different from the long line of anti-Semitic politicians, pamphleteers, and preachers that preceded him in German history. For many of them anti-Semitism

19

had been a tool, a device for exciting the masses and gaining power; at most they had called for the exclusion of Jews from the mainstream of German life and from the privileges of German citizenship. His forerunners may have believed, as Hitler did, that "the Jew is no German"; that Jews were unassimilable, a foreign people whose racial qualities could not be harmonized with the racial qualities of the Germanic people; that they were criminals, thugs, and beasts of prey, driven to their crimes by unalterable racial characteristics, polluters of German life and the cause of Germany's sorrows. Hitler, however, dismissed his forebears as "pre-scientific, emotional anti-Semites" who might stir up an occasional pogrom but were too woolly-headed to rid Germany of its parasitic Jews for once and for all.

His brand of anti-Semitism, he claimed, was logical, reasoned, scientific. "The anti-Semitism of reason...must lead to the systematic combatting and elimination of Jewish privileges. Its ultimate goal must implacably be *the total removal of the Jews*" (emphasis added). And when Hitler was appointed Chancellor in 1933, he wasted no time putting his beliefs into effect.

The world realizes now that Adolf Hitler suffered an obsessive, phobic hatred of Jews. Though not the only European political leader to harbour such feelings, he was the first to translate his obsession into a pseudo-scientific fiction of Aryan supermen locked in a climactic struggle with foul, verminous Jews for mastery of the world. "The pages of *Mein Kampf* give off the stench of naked obscenity:'The black-haired Jewish youth lies in wait for hours on end, satanically glaring at and spying on the unsuspecting girl whom he plans to seduce, adulterating her blood and removing her from her people.'"

Hitler's central concept is an insane world "in which history, politics and the life struggles of people are pictured solely in terms of coupling, fornication, pollution of the blood...violation, rape and harassment of the woman; world history as an orgy of rut in which dissolute and devilish submen lie in wait for the golden-haired female." The press, modern art, land speculation, syphilis, prostitution, capitalism, Marxism, pacifism, and world citizenship were all regarded by Hitler as camouflages adopted at various times to conceal a Jewish world conspiracy. "The last obstacle to

20

the Jewish plans was the German nation. . . . If that champion was vanquished in the mighty conflict, the victory of mongrel man, the end of civilization and the disruption of the plan of creation were at hand."

Hitler saw himself as the great breeder, applying the genetics of the barnyard to human survival. He talked endlessly of selective breeding, hybridization, and mongrelization. From the sterilization of the mentally deficient he advanced to euthanasia of the mentally ill and, inevitably, to the Final Solution.*

Given the thousand-year history of the Jews in Germany, and their patriotism, high level of education, and outstanding contributions to German science and letters, it was hard for the world to believe that Hitler's racist tirades against the Jews were meant to be taken seriously. Ironically, among those who found it hardest to believe were Germany's 500,000 Jews. They felt inordinately proud of what they had achieved in the hundred years since their emancipation from the medieval ghettos; they were no longer a separate people, but Germans of the Jewish faith.

Rabbi Gunther Plaut was a law student in Berlin when Hitler became Chancellor of Germany. "Since [the day Hitler came to power] I have often asked myself why we did not pack our belongings at once and leave the country. After all, in *Mein Kampf* Hitler had detailed his attack on the Jews. It should have been clear that with the Nazis in power there was no future for us in

---

*The Nazi ideology was rife with naive, pseudo-scientific social Darwinist ideas. Besides "positive eugenics" to "improve the breed", Hitler launched several programs to prevent the physically handicapped and mentally ill from procreating. The euthanasia program, begun in early 1939, operated directly from Hitler's chancellery under the seemingly innocent title of Heredity and Severe Constitutional Diseases. After beginning with the destruction of genetically deformed—"racially valueless"—children, Hitler turned to the murder of the adult insane. While the children were dispatched individually, usually by injection, the adult insane were gassed *en masse*. Medical experts experimented with carbon monoxide and Zyklon B gases, and gas chambers were erected, disguised to look like shower rooms; it is estimated that 80,000 to 100,000 insane were murdered. Opposition, particularly by Christian churches, temporarily halted the killings in 1941, but not before the program "visibly demonstrated the continuity between killing 'racially valueless' elements within the German community proper and killing the racial enemy." The personnel and techniques of the euthanasia program were readily adopted by the executioners of the Final Solution.

Germany." Plaut points to the strange symbiosis between German and Jew that reached back more than a hundred years. "In Europe, Germany was the first place where Jews became intellectually emancipated, where they left the ghettos...where they became philosophers and poets, artists and professionals, businessmen and artisans; where they sent their children to primary and secondary school and then to university and where they participated in the great cultural and social explosion that marked the beginning of the nineteenth century in the heartland of Europe....Germany was for all of us our home and we had known no other....In that view Hitler was a passing phenomenon; either he would conform to the responsibilities of a traditional German government or he would be swept out of office by the good sense of the German people."

Even after thousands upon thousands of Jewish civil servants, judges, and lawyers were driven from their professions—after school children were ordered out of their classes, and university professors were driven from their lecture podiums by brown-shirted SA bullies and forced to scrub sidewalks—the Central Association of German Citizens of the Jewish Faith advised its constituents to "stand by, remain calm."

"Germany will remain Germany and no one can rob us of our Fatherland," proclaimed a 1933 editorial in the Association's newspaper, the *Zeitung*. For a time, Jewish leaders in Germany believed they could find some *modus vivendi* with the Nazis; life would be meaner, more restricted, but they would survive. The idea was to hang on until the madness passed. They assumed that their traditional techniques of communal survival, refined through centuries of persecution, would work as well now as they had in the past. They must reiterate their loyalty to the state, remind the rulers of their contribution to commerce, science, and the arts, trot out their bemedalled war heroes, send deputations of prominent Jews to petition for understanding and tolerance, and call on Christian friends to intercede on their behalf.

When faced with persecution, "the Jewish tendency has been not to run from, but to survive with, anti-Jewish regimes. The Jewish reactions to force have always been alleviation and compliance...in the knowledge that their policy would result in the least damage and the least injury. . . . It is a fact, now confirmed by many documents, that the Jews made an attempt to live with Hitler."

Unfortunately, none of these techniques would be of any effect in the face of the Nazis' determination to rid Europe of all its Jews through extermination. Jewish efforts at alleviation and compliance failed to stave off the Nazis. Instead these tactics were welcomed and encouraged by Reinhard Heydrich, who turned them to his own advantage in his diabolical scheme to compel each Jewish community to collaborate in its own destruction.

On November 7, 1938, Ernst vom Rath, a third secretary in the German embassy in Paris, was assassinated by Hershl Grynszpan, a seventeen-year-old Jewish student whose parents had been among the thousands of former Polish nationals forcibly deported from Germany in 1938 and dumped across the Polish border without food or shelter. At a party rally in Munich on November 9—the day vom Rath died of his injuries—Hitler was overheard suggesting to Propaganda Minister Josef Goebbels that the diplomat's death be avenged by "allowing the SS to have a fling." Goebbels then made a fiery speech to the Party membership, calling on them to respond to the anger in their blood with "spontaneous demonstrations".

The appearance of spontaneity was important to the Nazis; it absolved the government of financial responsibility, avoided criticism by foreign powers, and allowed them to claim that they were actually containing the German people's fierce anger against the Jews. The record shows, however, that on that very night, at 11:55 p.m., the following message was sent to all Gestapo stations in Germany.

This teleprinter message is to be submitted without delay:
1.   At very short notice, *Aktionen* against Jews, particularly their synagogues, will take place throughout the whole of Germany. They are not to be hindered. In conjunction with the police, however, it is to be ensured that looting and other particular excesses can be prevented.
2.   If important archival material is in synagogues, this is to be taken into safekeeping by an immediate measure.

3. Preparations are to be made for the arrest of about 20,000 to 30,000 Jews in the Reich. Wealthy Jews in particular are to be selected. More detailed instructions will be issued in the course of the night.

4. Should in the forthcoming *Aktionen* Jews be found to be in possession of weapons, the most severe measures are to be taken. SS Reserves as well as General SS can be mobilized in total *Aktionen*.

Gestapo II Müller

This teleprinter message is secret.

The SA needed little urging. That night—November 9, 1938—the crash, slither, and tinkle of smashing plate glass could be heard throughout Germany. More than 815 Jewish shops were destroyed in an orgy of arson and destruction while the police stood by to ensure that no one spoiled the Brownshirts' fun; 267 synagogues were set on fire by well-disciplined, well-organized young men in civilian clothes while fire departments watched to see that the flames didn't affect adjoining buildings. Thirty-six Jews were killed and thirty thousand carted off to Buchenwald, Sachsenhausen, and Dachau concentration camps. Ironically, the Nazis confiscated the insurance money paid for damage done to Jewish shops and institutions by imposing a billion-mark penalty on them for what Göring called their "abominable crimes".

Between January 1933 and November 1938 more than 150,000 Jews had already left Germany. After *Kristallnacht*, the pace of emigration increased; almost 150,000 Jews left Germany in the next ten months. The opportunity for emigration ended, however, with the outbreak of war on September 1, 1939.

The war gave Hitler the opportunity for which he had been waiting. Hidden from the scrutiny of foreign governments and international agencies such as the Red Cross, he was now free to implement his plans for the Final Solution.

The Final Solution was never talked about openly in Nazi circles. There was no speech, no document in which Hitler personally used the term. The closest he came was a speech he made before the Reichstag, the German parliament, on January 30, 1939—a speech to which he referred frequently in later speeches. "Today I want to be a prophet once more. If international finance

Jewry should succeed once more in plunging nations into war, the consequences would not be the Bolshevization of the world and therewith a Jewish victory, but on the contrary the annihilation of the Jewish race in Europe." Hitler's orders to proceed with the Final Solution were apparently transmitted verbally to his deputy, the richly bemedalled Reichsmarschall Hermann Göring, Commander-in-Chief of the Air Force, Prime Minister of Prussia, and Plenipotentiary for the Four-Year Plan. The Reichsmarschall in turn informed Security Chief Heydrich of the decision in a letter dated July 31, 1941, advising the chief of the *Sicherheitsdienst* to submit "a general proposal...for the implementation of the desired Final Solution of the Jewish Question." A few weeks later, Heydrich summoned Adolf Eichmann to Berlin and informed the bureaucratic genius of the Final Solution:* "The Führer has ordered the physical extermination of the Jews."

Hitler's attempt at a Final Solution was sheer madness, sheer evil. It served no purpose. The Jews were not a viable enemy. Moreover, trains needed to supply ammunition to German troops or evacuate German wounded were frequently diverted to transport Jews to death camps. Yet even in the spring of 1945, when only madmen could fail to realize that the war was lost, the SS was redoubling its efforts to kill as many Jews as possible. By the time they finished, nearly six million Jews—two thirds of the Jews in Europe—had been gassed or shot or had succumbed to the effects of systematic starvation and overwork. A great civilization, the unique, thousand-year-old Jewish Ashkenazic culture of Eastern Europe, had been totally destroyed.

*SS Lieutenant-Colonel Adolf Eichmann, head of the Jewish Office of the Gestapo from 1940 to 1945, was directly in charge of the round-up of Jews in occupied Europe and their transport to death camps. So fierce was his dedication to this task that, despite shortage of transport and the approach of Allied troops, he almost succeeded in wiping out European Jewry. Eichmann fled to Argentina after the war. In 1960 he was captured by Israeli agents and flown to Israel; after a lengthy trial he was found guilty and sentenced to death. On May 31, 1962, he was hanged.

4
The Mother Country

For a thousand years Eastern Europe was the Jews' adopted homeland, their "mother country". On the eve of World War II, over seven million of the world's seventeen million Jews lived in Poland, Lithuania, Russia, Romania, Galicia, Bukovina, Hungary, Slovakia, and Carpo-Ruthenia. Typically, it was *Fiddler on the Roof* country, a conglomeration of small market towns (*shtetlach*) described as "a jumble of houses clustered higgledy-piggledy around a marketplace . . . as crowded as a slum, the streets as tortuous as a Talmudic argument." Here Jewish life centred on the synagogue, the rituals that accompanied birth, marriage, and death, the struggle to earn a living, and the delicate, precarious relationships with local peasants and officialdom. It was an intense, passionate world of poverty, oppression, and sporadic pogroms. This is the life celebrated and mourned in Jewish literature and drama, the setting for many of Isaac Bashevis Singer's novels and the works of celebrated Jewish writers of an earlier generation such as Sholom Aleichem and I. L. Peretz.

God seemed close at hand to most Jews, except for His inexplicable absences at the times He was most needed. Charismatic Hassidic rabbis—some of whom were rumoured to perform miracles—discoursed on the mystic nature of God and urged their followers to celebrate His presence in joyous song and dance. Competing with them for moral authority were the skeptical *mitnagdim*, who insisted that only God could perform miracles and that His will could best be discerned through the close study of Talmudic texts. Close on their heels were the *maskilim*, who held that Jewish persecution would end when Jews set aside their own distinctive culture, language, dress, and manners and adopted those of their non-Jewish neighbours. Dozens of roiling political movements ranging through various shades of socialism, Zionism, anarchism, and Marxism claimed the loyalty of growing numbers of young people.

Largely forbidden to own land, and barred from most professions, East European Jews eked out a living as bakers, tailors, shoemakers, tinsmiths, weavers, porters, carpenters, and small shopkeepers. The unskilled became "handlers", petty businessmen making "a ruble here and a ruble there". A few became *gevirim*, rich traders in grain and lumber, industrialists and private bankers; even fewer made their way into the professions as doctors, lawyers, engineers, and scientists—a *numerus clausus* (quota system) severely limited Jewish access to universities.

Nevertheless, Jews in Eastern Europe enjoyed a uniquely rich cultural life that drew strength from the colour, variety, and flexibility of the Yiddish language. An expressive, dramatic tongue, Yiddish borrowed its basic vocabulary and grammar from medieval German, its idioms from Hebrew-Aramaic, its diminutives from the Slavic languages, and its family surnames from western France and northern Italy. In a variety of local dialects it served as the everyday speech of Jews throughout Europe. (Hebrew was largely a holy language reserved for prayer and the reading of religious texts.) Jewish poets and novelists published their works in numerous Yiddish newspapers, while Jewish playwrights wrote for an inventive, ebullient Yiddish theatre. The great classics of English, Russian, and German drama—Shakespeare, Gogol, Goethe—were translated into Yiddish and played the better for it.

That world has vanished, destroyed in Hitler's gas chambers, buried in crude mass graves, burned to ash in crematoria.

Despite Jewish nostalgia for the *shtetl*, it should be noted that large numbers of Jews also lived in large, heavily industrialized cities such as Warsaw and Lodz, and sizeable provincial capitals such as Kaunas and Riga. In Poland and the Baltic countries Jews made up a large part of the pre-war urban population. There were, for example, 350,000 Jews in Warsaw—as many as now live in the whole of Canada—200,000 in Lodz, 100,000 in Lvov, and 55,000 in Vilnius. Jews made up the greater part of the workforce in the textile and steel mills of these cities, and the bulk of the middle class.

Kaunas, where Rauca was posted in the summer of 1941, was no *shtetl*. The capital of pre-war Lithuania, with a population of 128,000, it was a modern industrial city of fine boulevards, shopping streets, schools and universities. Its Jewish community of 35,000, one of the oldest in the Baltic states, supported five daily Jewish newspapers, two theatres, six Hebrew high schools, a number of elementary schools, a commercial high school, a people's university, a technical school, a hospital, and an orphanage.

Pre-war Lithuania, the southernmost of the Baltic states, was a small nation with just over two million inhabitants. About 154,000 were Jews.* Once a powerful principality ruled by its own kings, it was repeatedly seized, subdivided, joined, absorbed, and reconstituted by its more powerful Russian, German, and Polish neighbours. From the eighteenth century on, Lithuania was part of the greater Russian empire. Under the czars the use of the Lithuanian language was discouraged: Russian was imposed as the only language of instruction in the schools, the publication of Lithuanian-language newspapers was forbidden, and the Roman Catholic and Lutheran churches were persecuted.

For a brief time, after the chaotic events that followed Germany's defeat in World War I and the Russian Bolshevik Revolution, Lithuania succeeded in regaining its independence. In 1920 the Soviet government grudgingly signed a peace treaty recognizing Lithuania's sovereignty. Inspired by a century-long dream of self-determination, Lithuania's new constitution was "radically" democratic: it provided for freedom of speech, press, and assembly, and full cultural autonomy. The president of the republic, elected for a three-year term, was chosen by Parliament. The cabinet included a Minister of Jewish Affairs whose mandate was to spur the development of Jewish institutions; several Jews were

*Lithuania—formally the Lithuanian Soviet Socialist Republic (L.S.S.R.)—is now one of the fifteen Soviet republics constituting the U.S.S.R. Its 1982 population is estimated at 3,500,000. Between the two world wars Vilnius was held by Poland, and Kaunas served as Lithuania's capital; the capital is now Vilnius once again.

elected to Parliament, and two served in the cabinet.

Parliamentary democracy did not survive for long. In 1926 a *coup d'état* by Lithuanian army officers put Antanas Smetona, leader of the small but intransigent Nationalist party, into power. This former professor of Greek philosophy abolished all parties but his own, introduced press censorship, and placed all cultural, economic, and professional organizations under police surveillance. The end of democracy also brought restrictions of Jewish cultural autonomy.

Smetona's right-wing, pro-German government was shocked to receive a registered letter from Hitler on March 19, 1939, announcing that he was about to annex the predominantly German-speaking city of Memel in Lithuania. A Lithuanian envoy was quickly dispatched to Berlin to sign a treaty acceding to the annexation. Sensing that his support was slipping away, Smetona sought to bolster his position by including members of the Christian Democratic and Peasant Populist parties in the cabinet, but the coalition was not to last long.

On August 23, 1939, in a move that astonished the world, Hitler and Stalin signed a non-aggression pact in which they agreed not to attack each other and to remain neutral in case either nation became involved in a war with a third power. Secret clauses in the pact placed eastern Poland and the Baltic states squarely in the Soviets' sphere of influence. In September 1939 the German forces swept through Poland, and in a matter of weeks Warsaw was surrounded. On September 17, 1939, Russia marched into Poland as well, taking up positions on a pre-arranged line. With Poland in ruins and France defeated, the Soviets decided to oust Lithuania's peasant-bourgeois government, which had shown unmistakable sympathy for Germany and National Socialism, and replace it with one of their own choosing. Russian troops invaded Lithuania on June 15, 1940, and within days established a pro-Communist government. Lithuania's neighbour Latvia met a similar fate. Wholesale arrests and the deportation of "class enemies" to Siberia followed. Of the 70,000 deported from Lithuania and Latvia in 1940, no fewer than 25,000 were Jews. (To the new regime's credit, it did not distinguish between Jewish and other members of the "bourgeoisie".)

On June 22, 1941, Hitler tore up the non-aggression pact he had cynically negotiated with Stalin and unleashed the full fury of the German blitzkrieg on the Soviet Union. Taken by surprise, badly prepared and poorly led, the Russian forces reeled back. Within three days the Wehrmacht swept through Kaunas; within three weeks they reached the outskirts of Leningrad.

Hard on the Wehrmacht's heels, fanning out over the countryside, came the Einsatzgruppen. Their publicly stated purpose was to maintain order behind the lines and track down pro-Soviet partisans. Their secret orders were to exterminate all Jews, gypsies, and Communist party commissars.

5
Einsatzgruppen

The last days of May 1941 were sunny and warm in Germany. Brilliant spring flowers blazed in the fields surrounding the village of Pretzsch am Elbe near Leipzig. Each morning, several lorries of camouflage-suited SS officers left the village and headed for the nearby woods where they conducted military exercises: they practised leaping from their trucks and fanning out in a skirmish line, they played at ambushing each other in forest clearings. Most days they returned to the village *Hofhaus* for lunch and remained cloistered for the rest of the afternoon. In the evening they gathered in the *Bierstube* where they sang sentimental songs and endlessly toasted the Führer.

Outwardly the gathering looked innocuous—a typical wartime training session intended to keep young officers busy during a lull in the fighting. In fact it was a grimly serious three-week workshop for the Einsatzgruppen leaders being readied for the Eastern Front.

In a few weeks Hitler would unleash Operation Barbarossa on the unsuspecting Russians. Four German armies, operating on an 1,800-mile front, would thrust into Soviet territory. Einsatzgruppe A under the command of SS Brigadier General Franz Stahlecker would follow Army Group North in its drive on Leningrad. Einsatzgruppe B under Artur Nebe would join the march on Moscow. Einsatzgruppe C-commanded by Otto Rasch would join the push on Kiev. Einsatzgruppe D headed by SS Major General Otto Ohlendorf would accompany Army Group South as it

31

punched its way towards Odessa, Simferopol, and Rostov.

Conceived by SS Obergruppenführer Reinhard Heydrich, the Einsatzgruppen or special action squads were dedicated task forces whose personnel were drawn from the ranks of the Gestapo, the SD, Kripo, and the Order Police. They were first employed to track down anti-Nazi elements in Austria following the *Anschluss*. Later they followed the German troops into Czechoslovakia where they took control of all behind-the-lines security functions. "Six Einsatzgruppen were attached to the army during the military campaign in Poland. Their wholesale murder of Poles and their sadistic atrocities against the Jews shocked some [German] army generals."

Ahead lay fresh challenges, Heydrich told his men in the closed-door sessions at the *Hofhaus*: nothing less than the extermination of the Jewish populations of Poland, the Baltic states, and the Soviet Union. Thirty-four years of age, blond, blue-eyed, Heydrich was the epitome of the Aryan stereotype so beloved by the Nazis. Some historians regard him as "the real engineer of the Final Solution which bore the marks of his genius long after his death."

The evil genius of the Final Solution opened the Pretzsch workshop with a review of the top secret directive "The Jewish Question in the Occupied Territory", which he had forwarded to Einsatzgruppen chiefs, army high command, and chiefs of the German civil administration in occupied Poland. To achieve their purpose, Heydrich explained, it would be necessary to concentrate the Jews of Poland into large urban ghettos. Although he was generally opposed to the isolation of Jews in ghettos as a means of resolving the Jewish problem, in this case it was necessary to distinguish between "short term measures" and "ultimate goals". Ghettos, he emphasized, were a temporary step offering better control of the widely scattered Jewish population and their assembly for later deportation. All Jewish communities of fewer than five hundred people were to be dissolved and moved to nearby cities.

Cities chosen as concentration points, Heydrich instructed, should be located on convenient railway lines so as to facilitate "subsequent measures".

Once concentrated, the Jewish communities must be governed, their wealth confiscated, and their labour exploited until "ultimate measures" could be undertaken. Heydrich prescribed that a Jewish council or Ältestenrat composed of "influential personalities and rabbis" be established in each community to carry out the instructions of the Einsatzgruppe. "The council is to be made fully responsible . . . for the exact and punctual execution of all directives issued or yet to be issued," stated Heydrich's directive. "In the case of sabotage of such instructions, the councils are to be warned of the severest measures." The councils, Heydrich ordered, must undertake a census of the Jewish population broken down by sex and occupation. They must take responsibility for housing the Jews moved in from the countryside and for assigning housing within the ghetto. Jews would be barred from certain sections of the city and a curfew would forbid them to leave the ghetto after a designated evening hour. For the preservation of German economic interests, Jewish industries essential to the war effort were to be kept going for the time being.

But should Germany go to war with the Bolsheviks tomorrow—and those gathered at Pretzsch were among the few privileged to know that it was coming soon—then temporary measures must give way to ultimate solutions. Jewish community councils would become agents of their own destruction under control of the Nazis.

As old party comrades, Heydrich said, he had no need to lecture the men chosen to lead the Einsatzgruppen on the decisive struggle about to be waged between the Nazi and Communist political systems. Nor did he need to remind them that Communism was a tool of the international Jewish conspiracy. It was enough that Hitler had selected the SS as his chosen instrument to effect the Final Solution of the Jewish Problem.

What role would the army play, asked one of the SS officers. What support could they expect for the mission from the Wehrmacht generals? Hadn't some of them interfered with Gestapo activities in Poland?

True, Heydrich replied. A number of the old-line generals, unable to comprehend the ideological nature of the battle ahead and still imbued with old-fashioned notions of honour and "the rules of the game", had been squeamish about the treatment handed out to Jews, Polish intellectuals, and Polish army officers. They didn't want their men to engage in acts of brutality; they didn't like their boys taking snapshots and motion pictures of such actions, as though they were on a picnic. They feared that such behaviour would be bad for discipline, that it would damage the reputation of the army. But the Führer had told them to mind their own business, "to restrict themselves to their military duties," Heydrich said. Either the army would accept such "occurrences" or they would find themselves saddled with a system of political commissars which would place a Gestapo agent at the elbow of every general. Heydrich himself had met with Quartermaster General Eduard Wagner. They had agreed that the SS would, as a matter of courtesy, inform the army of any proposed actions. To protect the army's reputation, "housecleaning" activities would be postponed until the army had withdrawn and the occupied territory had been handed over to the civil administration.

The SS officials selected to attend the three-week training course in Pretsch were drawn largely from the ranks of the RSHA (*Reichssicherheitshauptamt*) or Reich Main Security Office. Mainly desk-bound bureaucrats, policy analysts, political snoops, and professional policemen, few of them had previous military training. Though three weeks was hardly long enough to instil a proper military bearing, twenty-four of them were promptly promoted to the SS ranks of major and colonel. "It was thus a queer intellectual riff-raff which stalked the rear areas of the Russian front in the following months, even if profusely jack-booted and armed with unlimited authority."

Dr. Franz Stahlecker, commander of Einsatzgruppe A, although still in his early thirties, was an old hand at "Jewish Affairs". The black-uniformed police general had been Adolf Eichmann's superior in the Departments of Jewish Emigration in both Prague and Vienna. Interrogated by the Israelis after his capture in Argentina in May 1960, Eichmann described his former chief as "a fine man, educated, full of reason and free of hatred and chauvinism of any kind"—in Vienna he used to shake hands with Jewish functionaries and invite them to sit in his presence. Stahlecker was killed in a skirmish with Red Army partisans in March 1942, one of the few Einsatzgruppe leaders to lose his life as the result of enemy action.

Artur Nebe, commander of Einsatzgruppe B, was chief of the Kripo or criminal police for all Germany. He had resigned to command this 700-man unit in the expectation that he would become Moscow's police chief. He was devoted to his work—finding the kill rate lower than expected, he experimented with an early version of the gas chamber, a clumsy affair involving the exhaust of an ordinary car piped into a sealed chamber. When the German advance stalled and the prospect of taking Moscow dimmed in November 1941, Nebe returned to Berlin but by then 45,476 people had been murdered on his orders.

Otto Rasch, the commander of Group C, was the former Security Police inspector for Königsberg. He did not understand the true meaning of his orders until a higher SS officer visited him on the Ukrainian front at Kiev at the end of August 1941. As soon as it dawned on him that his role was to conduct mass murder on a giant scale he set out for Berlin to protest to Heydrich. When he failed to reach the SS chief he returned to Kiev, arriving just in time for the great September massacre.* He did not stay long: he soon quarrelled with other Nazi officials in Kiev, and received leave to return to Germany. Rasch is pointed to as evidence that one could refuse orders to join in the Final Solution and not suffer punishment.

Otto Ohlendorf, who commanded Einsatzgruppe D in the Caucasus-Crimea, was hanged for war crimes in Landsberg Prison on June 8, 1951. Trained as a lawyer and reputed to be a brilliant economist, he joined the Security Service in 1936. Rising rapidly in the Gestapo, he soon became head of a major national bureau. He was only thirty-three when he was appointed head of the southernmost of the four extermination units. Although he spent no more than a year at the Eastern Front before returning quietly to the Ministry of Economics, in that time, according to his own testimony at the Nuremberg Trials, Ohlendorf succeeded in murdering 90,000 people, most of them guilty of nothing more than being Jews.

*The massacre of Jews in Kiev proceeded so rapidly that no ghetto was needed. In September 1941 over 33,000 men, women, and children were shot and buried in two days in the ravine at Babi Yar, just outside the city.

In contrast to the ambitious, active men who commanded the Einsatzgruppen, the subordinate officers were mostly social misfits. Erwin Schultz...was a trained lawyer but he had to forsake the law to be an ordinary policeman like his father. Ernst Bieberstein, who joined the Gestapo to spy on the clergy, had left the Lutheran ministry to found a "Brotherhood of Love". Vladimir Klingelhöffer, an opera singer...had been reduced to spying on cultural activities....Lothar Fendler was an army dentist without a job.... Strauch, the "Butcher of Minsk", had to become a bank clerk despite his law degree, and Blobel, the expert on exhumation and cremation, was an architect ruined by drink—he joined the Gestapo when he was "down to his last shirt". This lost legion of unemployed intellectuals had glued themselves to the office desks of the SD since 1933, only to find themselves, in the summer of 1941, on the muddy roads of Russia in the uniform of the *black crows*.

[They] were in no sense hoodlums, delinquents, common criminals, or sex maniacs. Most were intellectuals. By and large they were in their thirties, and undoubtedly they wanted a certain measure of power, fame, and success. However, there is no indication that any of them sought an assignment to a Kommando. All we know is that they brought to their new task all the skills and training which, as men of thought, they were capable of contributing. These men, in short, became efficient killers.

Heydrich, who was known to have a sadistic sense of humour, must have laughed uproariously when he assigned these educated bureaucrats to the dirtiest jobs on the Eastern Front. Not only did he implicate them in his personal lust for murder, but he compelled them to prove their own "hardness", the unflinching savagery so admired by the Nazis.

Such savagery does not come easy. Reasonable, rational people do not readily commit mass murder. To perform "properly" they must first be convinced that the men, women, and children they are driving to their graves are something less than human, *Untermenschen*, members of an inferior species. Even so, pity and sympathy die hard. The Jews who were said to be such a dire threat to the German people didn't look at all dangerous as they stood naked and shivering at the pit's edge, soothing their children while waiting for the firing to begin. How do you get a decent lad from Diepholz or Rosenheim to witness such sights without becoming unhinged and incapable of doing his duty? The trick was to turn normal human feelings around. "So instead of saying, 'What horrible things I did to people!' the murderers would be able to say, 'What horrible things I had to watch in the performance of my duties, how heavily the task weighed on my shoulders!'" Murder, precisely because it was hard, was good and was justified.

Reichsführer Himmler is reported to have been hysterically opposed to hunting animals. He once berated his doctor, saying, "How can you find pleasure, Herr Kersten, in shooting from behind cover at poor creatures browsing at the edge of the wood, innocent, defenceless, and unsuspecting? It's really pure murder."

Yet in a 1943 speech to a group of senior officers in Poznan Himmler declared:

> One principle must be absolute for the SS man: we must be honest, decent, loyal, and comradely to members of our own blood and to no one else. What happens to the Russians, what happens to the Czechs, is a matter of absolute indifference to me. . . . whether the other people live in comfort or perish of hunger interests me only insofar as we need them as slaves for our culture. . . . Whether or not 10,000 Russian women collapse from exhaustion while digging a tank ditch interests me only so far as the tank ditch is completed for Germany. We shall never be rough or heartless where it is not necessary; that is clear. We Germans, who are the only people in the world who have decent attitudes to animals, will also adopt a decent attitude to these human animals, but it is a crime against our own blood to worry about them and to give them ideals. . . . If someone were to come to me and say, "I cannot build the antitank ditch with women or children: it is inhuman, they will die in the process," then I would have to say, "You are the murderer of your own blood, for if the antitank ditch is not built German soldiers will die and they are the sons of German mothers. They are our own blood." This is what I want to instil in the SS and what I believe I have instilled into them as one of the most sacred laws of the future: our concern, our duty, is to our own people and our own blood. . . . Towards anything else we can be indifferent.

Helmut Rauca, who served as Gestapo Jewish Affairs Specialist for Einsatzkommando 3, Einsatzgruppe A* under Stahlecker's command, was required to demonstrate these qualities of a "true SS man". He was expected to be loyal, honest, brave, and obedient. He and his comrades were encouraged to care only for those of their own blood and to walk ruthlessly over a sea of enemy corpses for the sake of the *Herrenvolk* (master race). Harshness towards others was justified by the harshness practised towards oneself. "To be harsh towards ourselves and others, to give death and to take it," was one of the mottoes of the SS.

Certainly the four Einsatzgruppen assigned to follow the German armies into Soviet territory in 1941 displayed all the cold-blooded brutality Himmler could have desired. Of the six million Jews murdered by the Nazis in their quest for a Final Solution, close to one million were dispatched by the mobile killing units on the Eastern Front. From Tallinn in the north to Sevastopol in the south they applied the techniques honed in Vienna, Prague, and Warsaw, and further refined in those lovely spring days at the *Hofhaus* in Pretzsch am Elbe. Their ravages are the grist of Rauca's story.

---

*As each Einsatzgruppe, consisting of about 3,000 men, fanned out over the countryside, it was divided into smaller operational units varying from 150 to 300 men, called Einsatzkommandos. Einsatzkommando 3 was based in Kaunas, although from time to time its "flying squad" of skilled mass executioners operated in nearby Byelorussian villages.

6
Pogrom

The first wave of German bombers swept over Kaunas at dawn on June 22, 1941. Wave after wave of Heinkels and Junkers dived low over the city, dropped their bombs with fearful accuracy, pulled out, and swung round to strafe the people running into the streets in fear and confusion. No Russian planes took to the air to engage them; no Red Army anti-aircraft batteries sent shells arcing into the sky to drive them off. The Soviet command had decided to retreat rather than risk having their troops cut off on Lithuanian territory. As a result, large parts of the Baltic states fell quickly before the onrushing German forces.

By afternoon of the first day of the German advance, Soviet officials had burned their papers, gathered up their valuables, and requisitioned most of the taxis and buses in Kaunas—private automobiles were still a rare luxury—to evacuate their families. As the Red Army retreated towards Leningrad and the Russian border, the Communist officials fled with them.

When the Jews of Kaunas realized the Russians were gone and the Germans were on the way, panic set in. Thousands of Jewish families, carrying their bedding and household goods, stormed the railway station hoping to catch a train to Leningrad or Moscow. Only one train managed to leave before the incessant bombing crippled the railway yard. Hundreds of families, not knowing what else to do, remained seated on their suitcases at the railway station. Thousands of others set off on foot for the Soviet border, clutching their children in their arms and bearing their possessions on their backs. Some pulled children's wagons or trundled prams loaded with pots, pans, clothing, and bedding; a few, lucky enough to hire a droshky, tied several of their best pieces of furniture to the carriage bench and piled their children on top.

The roads were perilous. German bombers and fighters descended on the trudging masses, killing many of them and forcing the rest to take shelter in ditches, woods, and fields. Belongings were abandoned or exchanged for food. Families were separated; parents couldn't find their children and refused to go on without them. When the desperate throng reached the Russian frontier, the Red border guards, fearing a fifth column, carefully examined their identification papers. Only Communist Party members were admitted; those unable to produce a red card were turned back. Several days later Moscow did issue orders to admit the fleeing Jews, but by then the German panzer units had overtaken them and were charging over the Russian border.

Lithuanian nights are damp and cold, even in midsummer, and sleeping under the open sky makes one's bones ache. Gangs of hoodlums roamed the countryside, accosting Jewish families and robbing them of their goods. In many cases Lithuanian peasants sheltered and protected Jews, taking them into their homes and sharing their food, but just as often the Jews were threatened with violence, charged exorbitant prices for the privilege of sleeping in barns, or forced to trade a family heirloom for a few eggs. Unable to pass through the German lines, harassed and set upon by hoodlums, exploited by their countrymen, and strafed by the Luftwaffe, the surviving Jews wearily made their way back to Kaunas. Better the Germans, they thought, than the dangers of the countryside.

As the Nazi blitzkrieg advanced towards Kaunas, many Lithuanians—embittered by the Soviet takeover of their country the previous year, and the mass deportation of their countrymen to Siberia—were in a mood to celebrate. In particular, ultra-nationalist and pro-Fascist elements saw the war between Germany and Russia as a long-awaited opportunity to punish the Communists and re-establish an independent Lithuanian state. They greeted the approaching Nazis with wild enthusiasm, giving the Nazi straight-arm salute and throwing flowers in their path. At the same time thousands of political prisoners and criminals held by the Russians in Lithuanian prisons, realizing they were no longer under guard, came pouring out of their cells. Arming themselves with weapons smuggled into the country by pro-Fascist Lithuanian fifth columnists—many of them ethnic Germans—they quickly formed partisan regiments and chased after the retreating Soviet troops.* The retreat was so swift, however, that by the end of the first day there were no armed Russian forces on Lithuanian territory to pursue. Frustrated, they launched a bloody terror campaign against their left-leaning political opponents and against all those they labelled Communist. At the head of this list, whether they supported the Communist regime or not, were the Jews.

In the countryside, the partisans intercepted large numbers of the dispirited Jews making their way back to their homes in Kaunas. Some they shot on the spot; others they hauled off to their barracks, where they tortured them for several days before sending them on their way with a farewell barrage of kicks and punches. By the time the badly frightened Jews reached home, advance elements of the German army were in command of the city and Kaunas was in the throes of one of the most vicious pogroms in history.

The indiscriminate slaughter was conducted by so-called Lithuanian freedom fighters, at the urging of the Nazis, in the name of Lithuanian independence. Soon after the 1940 Soviet occupation of the country, a number of Lithuanian political parties had combined under the banner of the Lithuanian Activist Front to organize anti-Soviet partisan units throughout the country. The Front, whose leaders—Kazys Skirpa and Rapolas Skipitis—had fled to Berlin in 1940, developed an extensive underground network which reached into the armed forces, police, post office, hospitals, and judiciary. Plans were laid to seize local governments, attack Red Army units, and establish a provisional government in the event that Hitler declared war on the Soviet Union. The Front's main goal was to confront the warring countries with an accomplished fact: a free and independent Lithuania which

---

*We would prefer to reserve "partisan" for those fighters whose causes we admire, but the term applies to all those who take part in guerrilla activities.

was neither part of the Soviet Union nor German-occupied territory.

To win Nazi approval, this nationalist underground echoed the Nazis' anti-Jewish mouthings. One of its proclamations declared, "Lithuanian brothers and sisters, the fateful and final hour has come to settle accounts with the Jews. . . . Every Jew without exception is hereby warned to leave Lithuania without delay." As the Nazis marched towards Kaunas, the underground promised amnesty to Lithuanian "traitors" "on condition that they could prove that each of them had liquidated at least one Jew."

Operation Barbarossa, code name for the German invasion of Russia, began in the pre-dawn hours of Sunday, June 22, 1941. In the late evening of that day—after the Communists had fled but before the Wehrmacht marched in—a military unit of the Lithuanian Activist Front seized the Kaunas post office and disconnected all Soviet telephones. The following morning they seized the main radio station. At 9:30 a.m. on Monday, June 23, the Front proclaimed the formation of an independent, pro-German, anti-Soviet, provisional government under the temporary leadership of Jonas Klimaitis, a nationalist journalist. Partisan units took up arms cached by pro-German fifth columnists and attacked the retreating Russian military forces. It is estimated that 90,000 Lithuanians joined in the skirmishes that took place all over the country, and émigré Lithuanian historians claim that Front forces suffered 12,000 casualties—5,000 dead and 7,000 wounded—in one or two days of fighting. The Germans had not yet reached Kaunas when the commander of the partisan forces, Jurgis Bobelis, took to the radio to denounce the Jewish enemy in their midst. Jew-Bolshevik guerrillas, he claimed, were firing at the advancing Germans. For every German life lost, he warned, his troops would execute one hundred Jews.

Within hours, armed partisan patrols sped through the city to round up Jews. Many of the victims were shot on the spot, the rest were marched to pre-arranged assembly points. Kaunas City Hall, not far from the *Altstadt* (Old Town) where most Jews resided, was soon crowded with bewildered, apprehensive Jewish men, women and children. Later in the day they were marched to Fort VII, one of a ring of historic fortresses built around the city by

42

the Czar of Russia in 1814 to discourage Polish and German invasions; the fortresses no longer had any military value, but were employed as prisons for dangerous and treasonous offenders.

The partisans also found it great sport to humiliate the bearded Orthodox Jews who lived in the suburb of Vilijampole—called Slobodka by the Jews*—on the other bank of the Vilija River. On Yanove Street, just beyond the bridge that connected Vilijampole to the rest of the city, the partisans set upon a group of twenty-five men on their way to the synagogue and forced them to dance, recite Hebrew prayers, and sing the Communist Internationale. When they tired of their sadistic games, they ordered the Jews to kneel and then shot them in the back. A photograph of this massacre was published later in an illustrated German magazine. The cutline read, "This is how an enraged Eastern people take their revenge on the enemy."

On the evening of June 24, German troops paraded into Kaunas. The German occupation authorities were anything but pleased with the turn of events. The Nazis had no intention of recognizing the provisional government or encouraging Lithuanian independence: in the new order Hitler planned to impose on eastern Europe, Lithuania was slated to be a minor district (*Generalkommissariat*) in a German-administered colony (*Reichskommissariat*) called Ostland. Unlike Lenin, who was returned to Russia in a sealed train by the Kaiser's government, Skirpa and Skipitis were placed under house arrest and forbidden to leave Berlin.

SS Major Stahlecker arrived on the heels of the first German contingent to enter the city. He quickly made himself known to the members of the provisional government and lost no time telling them that all talk of an independent Lithuania was nonsense. In any event, there was still a war to be fought and won. He suggested, however, that it would bolster their chances of an important role in the Greater Reich in the future if they demonstrated their commitment to the anti-Bolshevik struggle by turning

*Since the area beyond the Vilija bridge had been named Slobodka by the Russian czarist regime, the neighbourhood *yeshivah* was simply called the Slobodka Yeshiva. When Lithuania regained its independence the suburb was renamed Vilijampole, but the Jews continued to call it Slobodka in honour of the *yeshivah*.

their forces loose on the Jews. Bobelis's partisans readily accepted Stahlecker's suggestion.

On the night of June 25, gangs of partisans and Lithuanian students armed with rifles, revolvers, axes, and knives came charging down the streets of Slobodka. They broke into Jewish houses to shoot, stab, and slash the inhabitants. In a night-long orgy of violence they severed limbs and decapitated bodies. Rabbi Ossovsky, a prominent Slobodka scholar, was found bent over his blood-soaked books while his severed head looked on from another room. The inhabitants of a house on Kriksciukaitis Street, opposite the Vilijampole post office, barricaded themselves so strongly that the gangs were unable to enter; frustrated, they set fire to the building and cremated the inhabitants. The following day the slaughter continued unabated. On Friday, June 27, wagons moved slowly down the streets of Slobodka gathering up the bodies of the slain. Some were buried in the ancient Jewish cemetery in Slobodka; the rest were lowered into mass graves on the banks of the Vilija River. In sum, 3,800 Jews were massacred over those two nights.

But even as the Slobodka dead were being gathered up, sixty Jews were seized in the fashionable neighbourhood of Vitovt Prospect. They were dragged into a nearby garage and, according to the accounts of neighbours, battered to death with wrenches, ball hammers, and tire irons. The hose used to wash cars was forced into the throats of some of the men and water poured down their gullets until their stomachs burst. When the massacre was over, the garage floor was littered with human blood and entrails.

Although the Germans looked on, they did not participate directly in that week's slaughter. In a lengthy report dispatched to Heydrich in October 1941, Stahlecker wrote, "It was desirable that the Security Police should not put in an immediate appearance, at least in the beginning, since the extraordinarily harsh measures were apt to stir even German circles. It had to be shown that the native population took the first initiative by way of reaction to several decades of suppression by the Jews, and to the terror recently exercised by the Communists."

In addition to these cruel, wanton murders the partisans, under Bobelis's orders, conducted mass arrests. By the end of the week eight to ten thousand Jews had been confined in Fort VII on the Green Hill just beyond the city. Since there wasn't room for all of them indoors, the women and children were stacked in over-crowded cells and corridors while the men were kept in outdoor stockades. Commander Bobelis made frequent inspection trips. One day he ordered that those Jewish men who had volunteered to serve in the pre-war Lithuanian army should be separated from the rest, and about seventy were identified and placed in a separate corral. Their status, however, did not improve; to humili-ate them, their guards made them dance jigs while singing patriotic songs. Later they were removed to the central lockup downtown, where most of them were murdered. Only a handful managed to get free and rejoin their families.

Each day, in what seemed a monstrous roulette game, Bobelis's men selected several hundred of the men at Fort VII for execution against the fortress's granite walls. There was neither rhyme nor reason to their choice of victims: Orthodox Jews with no interest in any -ism were mowed down along with members of the Socialist *Bund*; workmen met the same fate as their bosses. The savagery of the attacks, the unpredictability of the attackers, and the failure of any responsible Lithuanian elements to speak out against the *pogromchiks* created unbearable anxieties in the Jewish commu-nity. Almost anything was better than allowing the horrible, promiscuous bloodshed to continue.

Anti-Semitism was endemic in Lithuania—for almost seven hun-dred years Jews had served as middlemen between peasant and city-dweller and had provided the bulk of the country's skilled workmen. As the cities grew, they became the owners of many of the main-street shops and introduced most of the modern indus-tries. The greater their contribution to the Lithuanian economy, the more they were resented. But never had there been such wholesale violence and cruelty.

Both Jewish and Lithuanian accounts of this period place much of the blame for the intensification of anti-Jewish hostility on Soviet policies during the 1940-1941 Soviet occupation of Lithua-nia. With Poland smashed, France beaten, and England driven off the continent, the Soviets feared they might be next on Hitler's roster, and as a result they grew increasingly nervous about the Baltic states and their pro-German dictatorial regimes. On June 12, 1940, Moscow had accused Lithuania of conspiring to form a military alliance with Berlin against the Soviet Union, and two days later the Russians had marched in and established a pro-Communist government, claiming it was necessary to stem these anti-Soviet activities. A similar series of accusations and ultimatums had brought Latvia and Estonia under Moscow's rule that same week.

Many of the officials installed by the Russians were Lithuanian Jews whose pro-Communist convictions had caused them to flee to the Soviet Union to escape prosecution by Lithuania's arch-conservative pre-war government. Now that they were back, and in the saddle, they sought to remake Lithuania in their own image by deporting some 30,000 Lithuanians to Siberia. These same officials didn't hesitate to arrest and deport thousands of their fellow Jews as well, on the grounds that they were hopelessly "cosmopolitan", bourgeois, and Zionist. One of the first arrested had been Jacob Goldberg, a lawyer and soldier who had organized a regiment of Jewish volunteers that fought hard for Lithuanian independence in 1918. Deemed too dangerous ideologically for deportation to Siberia, he had been confined in the Kaunas prison.

In 1941, when the Red Army retreated, Goldberg was among the political prisoners released. But the very next day he was re-arrested, this time by rampaging Lithuanian partisans who, knowing him to be a Jew, took him to be a Communist. Fortunately, as he was marched back to the "Yellow Prison" he recognized the newly appointed prison warden standing by the prison gates. An officer in the former Lithuanian army, he and Goldberg had graduated from the same military academy. He too had been arrested by the Communists and confined, for a time, in the same prison, and he too had gone free the previous day when the Red Army retreated. Goldberg called to him and was immediately recognized. Within minutes, Goldberg and his family were set free.

Freedom was precarious, however, in a city where Jews were being arrested and killed by the thousands. Desperate to put an end to the slaughter, Jewish community leaders urged Goldberg to seek out his former Lithuanian army comrades—some of whom held prominent positions in the provisional government—and ask them to put an end to the violence. Confident that he need only ask their help, Goldberg visited Bobelis.

Goldberg was cordially received, and for a while the two old soldiers talked of the past, but when Goldberg turned the conversation to the pogrom and the horrors perpetrated at Fort VII Bobelis replied, "The matter is not in my hands, not in my jurisdiction." "But you are directly responsible for maintaining law and order in the city," Goldberg argued. "The Lithuanian military forces are still under your command." He pleaded with Bobelis to save the honour of the Lithuanian people by ordering the violence to cease. Bobelis's only reply was, "Not in my hands, not in my jurisdiction." Despite the failure of his conversation with the Lithuanian commander, Goldberg continued his efforts. He next visited Janus Villeisis, a former mayor of Kaunas and long-time leader of the Christian Democratic Party. "Don't you see what's happening?" Goldberg asked him. "Innocent people are being slaughtered and you, the leaders of the nation, remain silent." Villeisis replied, "My speaking out wouldn't help. Our young people want to have a bit of fun, to make some noise and act wild. What can I do about it?"

Goldberg was shocked by the attitude displayed by this widely admired Lithuanian leader, and quickly took his leave. Never before had he experienced such a deep sense of isolation. The Communists had jailed him. His old comrades in the Lithuanian war of independence were indifferent to his fate. The Nazis were on their way to Kaunas. Goldberg reported to the Jewish community's leaders that little help could be expected from the Lithuanian population in the difficult days ahead.

7
"You Must Withdraw Into a Ghetto"

SS Brigadeführer Dr. Franz Stahlecker, eager to stay close to the headquarters staff of Army Group North, had moved Einsatzgruppe A headquarters to Riga. He left SS Standartenführer (Colonel) Karl Jäger, commander of Einsatzkommando 3 (Operational Group 3) of Einsatzgruppe A, in charge of "cleaning up" Lithuania and parts of White Russia. On Jäger's staff were SS Hauptsturmführer (Captain) Heinrich Schmitz and SS Hauptscharführer (Master Sergeant) Helmut Rauca. A month later they were joined by Municipal Police Captain Alfred Tornbaum, commander of the Second Company of the Third Police Reserve Battalion.

Schmitz and Rauca were the unit's "Jewish Affairs Specialists"—they controlled the destiny of the Jews of Kaunas on a day-to-day basis. Jäger did most of his work at headquarters and rarely visited the ghetto. Schmitz was seen more frequently, usually driving a staff car with the letters POL for "police" painted on the side. Rauca was the enforcer, the administrator of the terror that held the ghetto in subjection, the security agent charged with smelling out sabotage and subversion. It was Rauca who appeared at the ghetto gates, made surprise visits to Jewish Community Council headquarters, planted informants in ghetto workshops, approved or disapproved the delivery of food and fuel to the ghetto, and decided which of the ghetto's residents should live and which die. Tornbaum's police unit turned out for all operations involving the round-up and extermination of Jews, supplementing the three hundred Lithuanian partisans chosen by Jäger for service as

48

auxiliary police officers. The execution squads, the men with their fingers on the triggers—almost all of them Lithuanian—were commanded by SS Obersturmführer (First Lieutenant) Hamann, chief of Einsatzkommando 3A's flying squad.

Proud of their ability to touch off a pogrom and have others do their killing for them, the leaders of Einsatzgruppe A were reluctant to call a halt to the violence in Kaunas. However, several of the Wehrmacht generals, despite "cordial relations" with Stahlecker, regarded such spontaneous violence as unprofessional, bad for discipline and their men's morale. The raging crowds in the street, the random killings at Fort VII, struck them as so helter-skelter and disorganized as to be un-German, and they demanded that Stahlecker restore order. Stahlecker agreed: from here on things would be much more orderly. The first phase in the implementation of the Final Solution in the Baltic region, he reported to Heydrich, had been successfully concluded. It was now time for phase two, the concentration of the Jews into ghettos.

On July 7, 1941, a German officer knocked on the door of Abraham Kahane Shapiro, Chief Rabbi of Kaunas, and ordered him to come along to Gestapo headquarters. The rabbi, old and bedridden, protested that he was too ill to leave the house. Satisfied that Kahane was indeed ill, the officer ordered the old man to appoint three prominent Jews to take his place. The rabbi, whose patience and wisdom made him a revered figure in Kaunas, nominated Leib Garfunkel, a former member of the Lithuanian parliament, Jacob Goldberg, the old friend of Bobelis, and Dr. Ephraim Rabinowitch, a prominent gynecologist. The rabbi had selected his candidates carefully: Rabinowitch had taken his medical degree in Germany and spoke German fluently. Both Garfunkel and Goldberg had been arrested by the Communists, so the Nazi occupation authorities were not likely to suspect them of being pro-Russian. Within half an hour Gestapo agents were knocking on their doors and the three surprised men were being escorted to Gestapo headquarters.

While they waited apprehensively in the anteroom to be ushered into the commander's office, an aide came out to enquire if any of them were rabbis. Their answer apparently disappointed the Gestapo chief who, after some whispered consultations, sent his aide to say that two rabbis must be found to join the delegation. Gestapo vehicles were immediately dispatched, and returned before long with Rabbi Shneer, a former chaplain in the Lithuanian army, and Rabbi Smuckler, spiritual leader of one of Kaunas's larger synagogues. Again there was a lengthy wait. None of the men had any idea why they had been summoned or what would be required of them. As they stood about they speculated on what they could expect from the occupation authorities. Rabbi Shneer, shaken by his unexpected ride in a Gestapo motor car, recited the *kaddish*, the prayer for the dead.

Ironically, incredibly, these Jewish leaders knew almost nothing of the horrors inflicted by the Germans on the Jewish communities of western Poland. Stalin, anxious to avoid giving Hitler any cause for hostility, had forbidden the publication of any news of Nazi atrocities. The Communists had also prohibited any form of Jewish community organization, closed the Jewish schools, and banned the Socialist and Zionist political movements, so that traditional channels of information were cut off. As a result the Jewish communities on Soviet territory were totally unprepared for what was to come. Tragically, many of them still expected more of Germany than of Russia, for they remembered that in World War I German troops had treated them with greater civility and kindness than had the czarist armies. An Einsatzgruppe report of July 12, 1941, reflects a German officer's surprise at this lack of awareness:

> The Jews are remarkably ill-informed about our attitude toward them. They do not know how Jews are treated in Germany or for that matter in Warsaw, which after all is not so far away. Otherwise, their questions as to whether we in Germany make any distinctions between Jews and other citizens would be superfluous. Even if they do not think that under German administration they will have equal rights with the Russians, they believe, nevertheless, that we shall leave them in peace if they mind their own business and work diligently.

After a lengthy wait the Jewish representatives were ushered into a huge office, where they were addressed by two high-ranking SS officers who didn't bother to introduce themselves. Later they learned that the tall, heavy-set man behind the desk was Standartenführer Jäger, while the huge man with the heavy jowls seated on the sofa was SS General Pohl, head of the Waffen (military) SS in Lithuania.

"You may sit as far as there are chairs," Jäger said with a polite wave of the hand. Since there were only two chairs for the five of them, all the delegates remained standing throughout the interview. "You certainly see what's going on in the streets," Jäger began. "The Lithuanians hate you, they don't want you living among them. They blame you for bringing on the Soviet invasion and the expulsion of thousands of Baltic people to Siberia. The Lithuanians want to be rid of you and we Germans, naturally, understand their mood. Nevertheless, we came here to create order and we can't allow this situation to continue. There is only one possible solution. You must withdraw into a ghetto where we can protect you. We will surround it with a barbed-wire fence. If it serves to keep you Jews in, it will also serve to keep the Lithuanians from your throats."

With that, Jäger turned to a large map of Kaunas on the wall and said, "Here is the suburb of Vilijampole, which will be reserved for your exclusive use. There you will have your own community, administer your own municipality, and lead your own life. No one will interfere with you there."

The delegates sensed they were being given no choice. Nevertheless they protested that Slobodka was too small, too old, and too dilapidated to accommodate the whole of Kaunas's thirty thousand Jews. This unkempt, neglected suburb, tucked away in a bend of the Vilija River, had no sewers, no running water, and very few paved streets. In any event, they argued, why Vilijampole? Most Jews in Kaunas lived in the *Altstadt*, in the heart of Kaunas—why not set that section aside for their use?

"For my part," Jäger said with a cynical shrug, "you can take the whole of Kaunas, but you'll have to work it out with the Lithuanians." Garfunkel, sensing that Jäger was laughing at them, said, "You talk of the Lithuanians fearing and hating us. I can't accept that. Let us talk to the Lithuanian leadership." Jäger gave Garfunkel an amused smile and said, "None of the Lithuanian leaders wants to set eyes on you, let alone talk to you." Garfunkel, who had not yet learned of Goldberg's futile conversations with Bobelis and Villeisis, could not believe that responsible Lithuanians could be utterly indifferent to the fate of the Jews. "We Jews have lived in Lithuania for more than seven hundred years," he said. "We've been in Kaunas for four hundred years. We fought against the Russians for Lithuanian independence. We established the Lithuanian economy. We established Lithuanian industry. We developed foreign trade. We can't believe that not one of the Lithuanian leaders is willing to talk to us."

Jäger smiled broadly. "You are daydreaming. You had better wake up to the fact that you have no choice. Either you accept my advice and go into a ghetto, in which case the massacre in the streets will stop and we'll release the three thousand people being held at Fort VII, or you reject my advice and I won't be responsible for the actions of the mob."

The five delegates asked for more time. They had no authority, they insisted, to speak for the Jewish community. "We were scooped out of our homes without warning this afternoon," Goldberg said. "We had no idea why we were being brought here or what was expected of us. We've had no opportunity to consult our colleagues." Jäger drew himself up to his full height. "Go home," he said impatiently. "I want your reply no later than tomorrow at ten hundred hours."

That evening the Jewish spokesmen met briefly at Rabbi Shapiro's home and decided to convene a broader meeting of community leaders early next morning. When the delegates reported Jäger's parting words to the larger group—*"Sie haben keine Wahl; Sie müssen ins Ghetto gehen!"* (You have no choice; you must go into the ghetto!)—they all agreed there was no alternative but to accept German protection. The assembly, which included heads of major Jewish organizations, members of the rabbinate, and leading Kaunas businessmen, authorized the delegation to give Jäger a positive reply. However, they set two conditions: first, that the slaughter in the streets and at Fort VII must stop, and second, that the proposed ghetto area must be considerably enlarged.

At ten a.m. sharp on July 8 the five returned to Gestapo headquarters and were promptly brought before Jäger. Again they argued that Slobodka, with an existing population of seven thousand, could hardly be expected to house all of Kaunas's thirty thousand Jews; conditions in the suburb would be intolerable, and the severe overcrowding could lead to dangerous epidemics. Jäger shrugged off their objections and said, somewhat ominously, "Don't worry. We'll fit you in." The move to the ghetto must be accomplished quickly, he told them, "and I nominate you to be the committee for the transfer of the Kaunas Jews to Slobodka."

The logistics for the *Umsiedlung*, or transfer to the ghetto, were complex and required careful planning. The three thousand Christians who lived in Vilijampole had to be evacuated and housed in other neighbourhoods. Somehow space had to be found for thirty thousand people in a dilapidated suburb that normally housed no more than a quarter of that number. Moreover, the move had to be accomplished quickly, for Jäger had ordered that it was to begin on July 15 and must be completed no later than August 15. After that date, he warned, any Jew found living beyond the ghetto's boundaries would be dealt with severely.

The only concession made by the Nazis was the inclusion of several blocks on the far side of Paneriai Street in the area of the ghetto. Since Paneriai Street was a major thoroughfare required for military traffic, and could not be permanently blocked, the Nazis hemmed the Jews in by lining both sides of the roadway with a barbed-wire fence. Access from the main ghetto, known as the Large Ghetto, to the area on the other side of Paneriai Street, which came to be known as the Small Ghetto, was by a small wooden footbridge which became a famous ghetto landmark.

A secretariat consisting of two municipal employees and two appointees of the Jewish community was appointed to draw up an orderly evacuation plan under the direct supervision of the mayor of Kaunas, Kazys Palciauskas, and the military governor, Bobelis. One of the Jewish appointees was a young lawyer who had volunteered his services to the embryonic Jewish community council—Abraham Tory.

In 1941, the year Germany launched its attack on the USSR, Abraham Tory was a young lawyer struggling to be admitted to the hostile Lithuanian bar. Although he was a brilliant student and law clerk to a former member of the Lithuanian Supreme Court, Tory's application was repeatedly turned down—the bar society wanted no more Jews.

Tory's position on the council gave him a front seat at all important conferences, allowed him to take notes on the conversations between German commanders and ghetto leaders, and required him to maintain a record of all Nazi edicts and decrees. From June 22, 1941, when the first German bombs fell on Kaunas, to March 23, 1944, when he fled the ghetto, Tory made daily entries in his diary. This was not a personal document reflecting private hopes and fears, but a terse, accurate summary of each day's events: the orders of the Nazi commander, work assignments, round-ups, selections, food shortages, overcrowding, reductions in the size of the ghetto, and above all, the relentless, systematic extermination of the Jewish community.

The night before he escaped by slipping past the guards at the ghetto gate disguised as a Lithuanian drayman, Tory buried his diary in a bunker dug beneath the concrete basement of a three-storey building. After the war he made his way back to Kaunas to find that, although the building had been destroyed by shell-fire, his diary was miraculously intact beneath the ruins. The text, meticulously typed in Yiddish and German, remains crisp and clear today. Even the elaborate binding, designed by a skilled graphic artist trapped by the war in Kaunas, is well preserved.

Meanwhile, Jäger had issued a second order. The Jewish community was to appoint an Oberjude (Top Jew, or Chief Jew) to administer the ghetto with the help of an Ältestenrat (Council of Elders).* To keep order within its boundaries and ensure that all Gestapo edicts were promptly obeyed, the Jews were also required to create a Jewish police force.

*Terms such as Judenrat, Ältestenrat, Hauptjude, and Oberjude are archaic titles dating back to the Middle Ages, when a German prince would appoint a Hauptjude or Oberjude to serve as his agent in the ghetto and a Judenrat (Jewish Council) or Ältestenrat (Council of Elders) to exercise authority within the ghetto's walls. The prince might, for example, summon the Hauptjude and announce that the town's Jews must make him a gift of a thousand guilders to finance his participation in the Crusades: the money would then be raised by the council through taxes on their Jewish brethren.

There was unusual activity at the Jewish schoolhouse at 24 Daukshos Street on the evening of July 8, 1941. Seated in the small auditorium were the most trusted of the community's physicians and rabbis, its most respected jurists and professors, its most prestigious businessmen and industrialists, as well as its toughest-minded organizational leaders. At the head of the room sat seventy-year-old Dr. Gregory Volf, veteran leader of the Lithuanian Jewish community, Director General of the Volf industrial empire, and head of the Central Jewish Bank. The Volf family had helped finance Lithuania's shift from a predominantly agricultural economy to a modern industrial nation. "This is a historic gathering for the Lithuanian Jewish community," Volf said in opening the meeting. "Never before have we faced such tragic circumstances. Never before have we suffered such tragic losses. Never before in Lithuanian history have we seen our children slain, our wives raped, and our property set on fire. As you know, we are forced to turn the clock back several hundred years tonight and choose a Hauptjude. . . ." Obviously overwrought, Volf faltered, put his hand to his head, and had to be helped back to his seat.

A number of candidates for the position of Oberjude were suggested. Former officers of the Lithuanian army, former members of the Lithuanian parliament and former judges of the Lithuanian bench were nominated. None of them won general approval. None of them seemed to have the strength and stature to stand up to the Gestapo, or to merit the trust of the whole community in what was clearly a life or death situation. (By now, the Jewish leaders of Kaunas had begun to hear rumours of the massacres conducted by the Einsatzgruppen in Vilnius and Cracow.)

Abraham Tory recalls the pall that settled over the room as candidate after candidate was suggested and rejected. It was as if the Jewish community, previously proud of the quality and abundance of its leadership, had suddenly been left leaderless.

Then the candidacy of Dr. Elchanan Elkes was proposed. Tory explains, "Why Elkes? If you will have patience, I will tell you. It was because he was a well-known physician inside and outside Lithuania. He was the personal physician of all the foreign ambas-

55

sadors accredited to Lithuania. He was himself educated in Germany [at the University of Königsberg]; he was very well acquainted with the German ambassador and was his private doctor. So they thought this was the man who could best maintain contact with the German officials." Elkes, however, demurred. The ghetto, he said, would be a municipality unto itself; it would be required to levy taxes and to create its own police force, fire department, labour exchange, commissary, and industry. He was a physician, he reminded them, not an engineer and administrator. He knew nothing of running a municipality. He would be a poor choice for Hauptjude. He refused, he absolutely refused.

The leaders despaired. Little time remained and still no man-of-the-hour had emerged. "Everyone was oppressed by what would happen if we didn't appoint the people demanded by the German authorities," Tory says. "It could only mean further bloodshed." After a lengthy silence, Rabbi Smuckler rose and said, "Dr. Elkes, we know that you don't want to be an Oberjude. We know that you don't know administration. But we know your Jewish heritage and your Jewish devotion. For the Germans you'll be an Oberjude, but for us you'll be *Rosh hagola*, the respected leader of our community. You'll be the head of a ghetto which is a community within a community, an exile within an exile. You will lead us from this exile to Israel, to the Promised Land. There you will be our mayor in a Jewish city. We will be with you, we will follow you, we'll back you." Quoting an ancient Hebrew proverb, Rabbi Smuckler added, "Remember, those who are on a sacred mission can come to no harm." He closed with, "Dr. Elkes, we beg of you, rise up and take over the leadership."

Everyone in the room wept.

Pale and serious, Elkes stood up and said, "If you are all of the opinion that it must be so, then I offer myself in your service." The tension in the room immediately dissipated. A feeling of euphoria overcame the leaders. They clapped each other on the back and congratulated each other for having made such a fortunate choice. They shook Elkes' hand and embraced him, they linked arms and sang the Zionist anthem *Hatikvah*. Facing Elkes, arms raised high and palms extended, Smuckler delivered the ancient Hebrew benediction. "Go with our blessing," he said in closing.

56

After a few minutes of reflection, Elkes appointed Leib Garfunkel his deputy. Michael Koppelman, the representative of Lloyd's of London in Lithuania, became his police commissioner. Lawyer Jacob Goldberg, gynecologist Ephraim Rabinowitch, former army chaplain Rabbi Shneer, and Rabbi Smuckler were chosen to serve on the Ältestenrat.

Three young lawyers, Israel Bernstein, Elemelech Kaplan, and Abraham Tory, were appointed council secretaries. Their duties were to keep the minutes of meetings, handle correspondence, arrange transport, provide housing, and keep track of food supplies for the ghetto. "They were all people of the greatest integrity," says Tory.

Elkes in particular proved worthy of the community's confidence. A man of great intelligence and courage, he fended off the Gestapo for three years as best he could, sometimes pretending to submit to the Nazis while secretly supporting efforts of the Jewish underground. He played his role as Oberjude with dignity and refused to be cowed by Jäger and Rauca. He saved lives, where he could, without regard for his own safety. When threatened, he showed no fear.

Elkes had realized early that the rise of the Nazis meant a bleak future for Europe's Jews—"These people will not compromise, and neither will we"—and he had sent his son and daughter abroad to the relative safety of England. As for himself, he made his decision to stay.

> He was a man of slight build and clear features. His movements were small, graceful and measured. . . . He rarely raised his voice; his sentences were short, reflecting the same inner economy. . . . There was a warmth and humour in his voice when he spoke of people; human frailties were to him part of the richness of the human condition. Only in the face of cruelty or injustice did his demeanour change. He could then become devastating in his impersonal directness, often putting a question which would leave the other fumbling and ashamed.

Elkes became a legend in the ghetto. It is reported, for example, that SS Commandant Goecke asked Elkes what he should do to relieve the dizziness and arterial throbbing that plagued him. "Do less shouting," Elkes replied quietly. On another occasion, the whole Ältestenrat was arrested and taken to Fort IX for interrogation. They were guarded by a submachinegun-toting Nazi who shouted, "Hurry, I'm an expert in head wounds." Elkes turned calmly to the officer and said, "I value all skills." The man blushed and lowered his gun.

Within days of Elkes' appointment, the trek to the ghetto began. Since the Germans forbade Jews the use of trucks, carts, or droshkys, families loaded their possessions on their backs or hauled them to Slobodka on children's wagons, sledges, and wheelbarrows. As they arrived in Slobodka they were greeted by representatives of the council who assigned them housing—five to eight people to a room, an average of three square metres per person. No sooner had they shoe-horned their way into Slobodka than the Gestapo demanded the services of one hundred strong men to erect a high barbed-wire fence around the ghetto. When the fence was completed Jäger presented the bill to the Ältestenrat. The ghetto was "closed"; the Jews were sealed in.

Leah Elstein had just turned nineteen that beautiful June when the bombs first fell on Kaunas. She vividly recalls standing in the street watching the Luftwaffe fly over to bomb the military airport a few kilometres outside the city. She remembers how they turned and swooped to strafe the people in the streets.

The attack was not entirely unexpected. She had spent the previous evening with a group of students huddled around a short-wave radio tuned to the German military network. They were startled when, after a brief patriotic speech on the German need for *Lebensraum* and the bitter ideological struggle between Nazism and Bolshevism, a voice announced, *"Um drei Uhr morgens kommt der erste Schuss"* ("the first shot will be fired at three o'clock tomorrow morning"). Some of the students headed home at once to warn their families; others stayed on, arguing it must be a ruse of some sort, manoeuvres perhaps. If an invasion were imminent, why would the Germans tip their hand?

The exploding bombs resolved all doubts. The only question that remained was how soon and in which direction to flee. "Crowds—big, big, huge crowds—tried to get out," Leah recalls.

"There was a terrible panic because they bombed day and night, for hours and hours and hours." People rushed about seeking advice from their friends. No one knew what to do, no one had planned for such circumstances. The Elsteins made hurried plans to leave. "Since my father had died the year before, there were just the three of us, my mother, my brother, and me," she says. "And we decided we would walk out of Kaunas towards the border. It was a very silly decision." But they encountered thousands of others on the way. They came to a small town not far from Kaunas where they were warmly greeted by the people and given food. "Everybody said the war would last a day or two," she says; "It was unthinkable that the Russians would continue to retreat." Tired, frightened, strafed from time to time, they struggled on to the next town only to be told there was a German column ahead of them already. "We saw the Germans and decided that, whatever might happen, we would go home."

When they returned home they found their house intact and everything in its place. Their next concern was to enquire after the other members of their family. "We had a large family in Vilijampole—my grandfather, grandmother, uncles, aunts, and cousins," she explains. On the way to that suburb, just short of the Vilija bridge, they saw blood on the streets where the Lithuanian partisans had cut Jewish throats. Some of the corpses were still lying in the street.

The Gestapo had also arrived in Kaunas. "They were already imposing restrictions on the Jewish population. Every day there were new orders. From the first day we were not allowed any newspapers. Then we had to turn in all our radios—in those days they were big, massive things. Soon we were not allowed to hire any non-Jewish help. Jewish doctors were no longer allowed to treat non-Jewish patients and Gentile doctors were prohibited from treating Jews. Before long we were required to wear a Jewish star on our breast, and then on our backs as well, and it had to be exactly eight centimetres wide and sewn on firmly—you were not allowed to pin it—so it couldn't be removed. We were forbidden to shop for food except in special shops at special hours. All this was done so we shouldn't mix with our Gentile neighbours, to isolate us.

"Then came the order to evacuate our homes. Since Jews were not allowed the use of horses or wagons, people took the doors off their closets and used them as sledges to haul their furniture. Some people took many things, but with three metres per person they couldn't fit in all their furniture."

The restrictions imposed a new way of life on the Jews of Kaunas. People had to find new ways of earning a living now that they could no longer practise their professions, operate stores, or work in factories outside the ghetto. Leah asked her neighbours, "What are you doing? Where are you getting food?" They told her about the canteens that had been set up to sell food, the long queues for the scarce supplies and the inconvenient shopping hours. They also told her of some sort of committee at City Hall that was rumoured to be hiring people. Since it wasn't far, she and her brother walked over to see what was happening. There she encountered Abraham Tory who, with his Lithuanian counterparts, was supervising the transfer to the ghetto. "Leah, you know how to use a typewriter," Tory said. "Could you give us a hand?" Preferring to keep busy rather than have time to dwell on her fears, Leah readily accepted Tory's offer, though he warned her there was no money to pay her. When the relocation was largely complete and the ghetto was about to be sealed, Tory moved his office to Jewish Community Council headquarters. There he and Leah allocated scarce living space, kept track of the ghetto's inhabitants, and served as the ghetto's statistical bureau. In time, she became the Council's chief stenographer.

Life had not been easy for the Elstein family. Leah's father had died, leaving her mother to support two teenaged children. Fortunately they had owned a pleasant house in the *Altstadt* section, and had enjoyed a warm, close relationship with numerous aunts, uncles, and cousins in Slobodka. But when the Russians marched into Lithuania in 1940 the Elsteins were no longer permitted the luxury of a whole house to themselves; classified as "bourgeoisie", the three of them were ordered to move into one room. The rest of the house was turned over to families assigned by the newly established community housing bureau.

Leah had been a gold medal student at university, but here again her class status counted against her. The commissar on the admissions committee was blunt: it was impossible to admit two members of a family with such bourgeois antecedents to the university, it was out of the question. Room must be made for the children of the proletariat. There was room for either Leah or her brother, but not for both. Leah gave way so that her brother, two years younger, could continue his engineering studies. As this left her in urgent need of a marketable skill she enrolled in secretarial school, and in a short time she became a highly skilled stenographer, able to type and take shorthand in three languages, Lithuanian, Yiddish, and German.

Soon the Russians were gone and the Germans were in command. The Elsteins had to give up the luxury of a room to themselves and move in with their relatives in Slobodka.

Despite Jäger's promise that the pogroms would stop, sporadic violence continued. On August 6, 1941, more than twelve hundred Jews were brutally murdered. One of that day's victims was Elemelech Kaplan who, like Tory, had volunteered to serve as a member of the Council's secretariat; in fact Kaplan was killed on his way to attend a Council meeting. One of Leah's uncles was seized by Lithuanians, and his son was killed at Fort VII. Life, nevertheless, had to be lived. "I personally was not very optimistic," Leah says, "but I had a very optimistic mother and that helped. My brother didn't talk about it. He just went to work every day. People used to meet in our house. Everybody was certain that the war would be over within days. There were all kinds of rumours. This one heard the cannon of the Russians here, that one heard the cannon there. We had one man who used to listen to the BBC in a cellar somewhere—he would tell some people what he heard, and of course they would tell others. He was very optimistic and that helped."

However, as time went on, optimism was replaced by a stubborn determination to survive, to hold on, to hold out. The slogan was: "Outlast them—if only by one day." "We wanted to see the day they were beaten and punished," Leah says. Working at the Jewish Community Council headquarters she encountered both optimists and pessimists. "Both seemed silly and unrealistic at times, but the pessimists were harder to take," she says. "We used to throw them out of the office."

In those days Leah was regarded as a "real Jewish beauty". The boys at the university admired her dark hair, grey eyes, and trim figure, and the cute beret and raincoat that became her trademark. But mostly they admired her quick intelligence, her helpfulness, and her discretion. She was never one to gossip or give away a secret. These qualities, along with her stenographic skills, made her invaluable to the Ältestenrat. In time they would also make her indispensable to one of the Gestapo's senior officers.

Leah spent long hours at the Council office typing letters, memoranda, proclamations, and minutes of meetings. After work she would type material for her friends. "I did it gladly," she says, "because I didn't want to go home. I didn't feel secure there. My mother went to work at night, she worked in a stocking factory. My brother went to an *Entlausungsanstalt* (delousing centre): when the German wounded came from the front they were brought to a place where they were deloused, and my brother worked in this place. It was warm there and they had a 'good German' who didn't beat them up. And they liked to see the wounded German soldiers—when they came home everyone asked, 'Well, how many did they bring today?' The more wounded, the sooner the war would end, they thought."

The Jews in the ghetto found it almost impossible to believe that the Germans meant to kill them off. "It was illogical," Leah says, "but somehow people kept pushing the thought away. There was the idea that it wouldn't happen to you, though it happened to your neighbour and the closest of your family." A peculiar callousness, a self-protective indifference, crept into people's minds as the death toll mounted.

8
Operation Intellectuals

July faded into August and the ghetto dwellers prepared to "live their own lives" as promised by Jäger. For the Jews, the ghetto held no terrors: they had lived in them before, they had long ago learned to live apart from their neighbours; indeed "the very word had a soothing ancestral ring. . . . A ghetto implied certain squalors, a crowding in tenements, a sharing of bathroom facilities. . . . Yet it also consecrated the Jews to their own specialness, to a richness of shared scholarship, to songs and Zionist talk. . . . " But they were soon to find that the Gestapo permitted little autonomy within the ghetto's barbed-wire borders.

Hitler's grandiose plan for a "Thousand-Year Reich" required the creation of a series of vassal states on conquered Polish and Russian territory. According to this plan, western Poland was annexed to the Reich and became an integral part of Germany; eastern Poland, including Warsaw, became the Government General of Poland, a fiefdom ruled by Hitler's crony Hans Frank; the Baltic states became part of the Reichskommissariat Ostland governed by Alfred Rosenberg, Reichsminister for the Eastern Occupied Territories. With the German passion for over-organization, the territory was further subdivided into *Generalbezirke* (general districts), *Kreisgebiete* (districts), and *Stadtgebiete* (city commissions).

By July 22, 1941, the rapidly advancing German forces in the north had advanced to Lake Ilmen on the outskirts of Leningrad, more than four hundred miles from their starting point in Poland a month earlier. This left Lithuania so remote from the fighting that it could no longer be considered a war zone, and it was turned over by the military to a tiresome array of civilian Reichskommissars, Generalkommissars, Gebietskommissars, Stadtkommissars, and their deputies, each with his own prolongated title.

In mid-August the newly arrived City Commissioner Cramer informed the Ältestenrat that he needed five hundred well-dressed, well-educated young men to put the shabbily kept Lithuanian government archives in order. The Jewish Council, still inexperienced in the ways of the Gestapo, suspected nothing. Indeed, it regarded the request as an excellent opportunity to provide light, safe work for some of its people, instead of the heavy labour that would soon be obligatory for all Jews. Eager also to show its co-operation and demonstrate its efficiency, the Ältestenrat drew up lists of candidates and posted notices on ghetto walls.

Leon Bauminger, twenty-eight, handsome, blond-haired and blue-eyed, had been a lecturer at a Warsaw university before the tides of war brought him to Kaunas just ahead of the German army. Eager to be among the five hundred chosen to do archival work, he was one of the first to present himself at the ghetto gates on August 18, 1941. As he waited, the streets leading out of the ghetto filled with young lawyers, engineers, chemists, journalists, teachers, and technicians—some with their university diplomas tucked under their arms in case their status as "intellectuals" was questioned.

Twenty-six-year-old Baruch Direktor would also have welcomed working in the archives. Soon after moving into the ghetto he had several times been forced to join labour gangs working to extend the military airdrome's runways. The work was crude and hard. Gravel was manufactured by breaking rocks with sledge hammers; there were no bulldozers to smooth the surface, so that was done by a small army of workers hauling and shovelling dirt with spades and wheelbarrows. By comparison, work in the archives, no matter how musty, would be like paradise.

Fearful that he might be late, Direktor pushed his way to the front of the crowd. There, standing on the other side of the ghetto gate, he recognized Helmut Rauca, a heavy whip tipped with wire cable in one hand, the leash of a straining Alsatian in the other. Next to him stood Tornbaum, commander of the Lithuanian police battalion recruited by the SS. Flanking the two stood a squad of armed Gestapo and Lithuanian auxiliaries.

A shudder went through the crowd. Rauca's reputation for ruthlessness was well established—wherever he appeared, it was said in the ghetto, death and destruction followed. Anyway, one didn't need to be an intellectual to know that men reporting for work in the archives had no need for a Gestapo escort. Something bad was in the offing. Like a tide reversing its flow, those jammed next to the gate began to work their way to the rear, while those on the periphery began to drift off into the side streets.

Yaakov Rabinovitch stood at the edge of the crowd, waiting with a journalist's skepticism to see what would happen. Formerly a writer for one of the half-dozen Yiddish dailies closed down by the Nazis, he had registered for heavy labour to avoid the Gestapo's attention. Suddenly Rabinovitch heard people mutter, "It's Rauca. Oh, God, it's Rauca." Looking in the direction that people were pointing, he too could see Rauca: vigorous, hefty, dressed in Gestapo uniform. Bauminger heard them too but, being new to Kaunas, he didn't quite understand what they meant. A Jewish policeman, noting his confusion, whispered, "Get the hell out of here, you jerk. Can't you see something is up?" Bauminger failed to move quickly enough. Before he could reach the edge of the rapidly melting crowd the gates were opened and the Lithuanian police unit moved in. They quickly surrounded the remaining intellectuals and counted them off—only three hundred. When this was reported to Rauca he grew visibly angry. He bellowed that his orders called for five hundred intellectuals and five hundred it must be. He ordered Tornbaum to round up an additional two hundred men, to arrest them in the streets or drag them out of their houses. There was a moment of confusion during which Bauminger slipped away; Direktor had already taken to his heels.

Before the day was over five hundred and thirty-four men had been rounded up, loaded onto lorries, and driven away. The extra thirty-four, the Gestapo announced, constituted a fine or penalty for Jewish non-cooperation. None of the five hundred and thirty-four was ever seen or heard from again.

The following day, a Jewish labourer who had been on a work gang in the vicinity of Fort IV appeared at the Ältestenrat office with a small packet of identification papers and passports. The labourer told the Council he had received them from a Lithuanian peasant who, sidling up to him on the work gang, had whispered that there had been a lot of shooting at the fort the previous day. Then, making sure they weren't observed by the guards, the peasant had slipped him the pack of soiled documents, saying he had found them in the grass in the vicinity of the fort. "One of those documents belonged to my good friend Badasch who had studied with me," Tory later testified. "I took the passport to Badasch's wife Sonia and asked whether this was in fact the passport of her husband. She confirmed it." The other documents also belonged to various members of the five hundred and thirty-four.

Despite this evidence, people in the ghetto couldn't bring themselves to believe that the group had been annihilated; it was inconceivable that innocent people, randomly detained, could be taken away and shot. The Ältestenrat, not knowing what to think, asked for a meeting with Gestapo chief Jäger. Jäger refused to see them, however, and sent a message through Rauca that there was no need to fret, that the young men were well cared for. Unsatisfied, Elkes invited the City Commissioner to visit him at Ältestenrat headquarters so he could enquire into the fate of the young men. Cramer too assured Elkes that there was no cause for concern; the men were being well fed and well housed and would return home in a few months "all roly-poly", he said.

Elkes stood his ground. He told Cramer not to take him for a fool; the Council had evidence the five hundred and thirty-four had been liquidated at Fort IV. So far the council had kept the information to itself because it wanted to avoid spreading fear and rumours, but now Elkes was convinced the information received by the Council was accurate. He had no alternative but to inform his people of the truth.

Unable to go on denying their deaths, Cramer changed his story. All five hundred and thirty-four had been shot for committing sabotage, he claimed; they had poured gasoline over a supply of sugar in order to contaminate it. Elkes saw there was nothing to be gained from further conversation. A few days later, a bundle of picture postcards arrived from Riga, in Latvia. All bore the same message: "Feeling well. We are well fed and well clothed." The cards were obviously written, by order of the Gestapo, on the same day the writers were murdered. If the peasant hadn't found their papers in the grass, the Jewish community might never have known of their fate. The liquidation of all these fine young men is remembered by ghetto survivors as "Operation Intellectuals".

Similar operations aimed at young intellectuals were conducted by the Gestapo in hundreds of other Jewish communities. They all followed soon after the forced enclosure of the Jews in the ghettos, and their purpose was clear if one understood Heydrich's plan for the Final Solution. The head of the Reich's Security Service was not fond of ghettos. He saw them as a necessary evil—a means of concentrating the Jewish population so that they could be disposed of more efficiently, a device for warehousing them until their labour was no longer needed. But there were also risks in concentration. It gave Jews the opportunity to meet and plot unobserved; it created a breeding-ground for resistance movements. One way to head this off, to nip resistance in the bud, was to eliminate the young intellectuals who were most likely to be the leaders of such rebellion.

The Jewish ghetto police were another of Heydrich's inventions. "The Jewish police force was an institution improvised by the Germans when they locked the Jews into the ghetto. . . . Like its parent organization, the Judenrat, the Jewish police force came to serve dual and incompatible purposes; to protect the Jewish community while it was required to enforce German orders."

In most communities the Hauptjude and the Chief of Police were chosen by the SS. This led to many grave problems. In Berlin and Vienna the Jewish police helped to seize Jewish property and guard Jews at deportation collection points, and in Bialystok the *Jüdische Ordnungsdienst*, as the ghetto police were called, helped the undermanned German Order Police by supplying thousands of men for seizure operations. In Warsaw each Jewish policeman was told to bring seven people for deportation every day or face deportation himself; when the Warsaw ghetto rose in heroic battle against the Germans on April 19, 1943, the first Jewish shot fired felled Jewish Police Chief Josef Szerynski, and the ghetto fighters' next targets were Jewish policemen, informers, and collaborators. But in Kaunas the Jewish ghetto police, appointed at the behest of the Gestapo to keep order in the ghetto's fetid streets and enforce the orders of the Einsatzkommando, became a centre of Jewish resistance. Police Commissar Koppelman took great care to avoid swaggerers and bullies when he chose his men. He recruited athletes, men with military training, school teachers, and responsible youth leaders. On their breasts and backs they wore the yellow star, and on their arms a blue band imprinted with the Star of David and the words "Jewish Ghetto Police". Moshe Levin, who served as Koppelman's police chief, kept in close touch with the underground and protected its members.

"They were excellent people from various student organizations," says Leah Elstein about the force. "Some were people my age, some had received training in the Lithuanian army, some were sportsmen. There were only a few who didn't fit and caused trouble for the Council. The police were actually well liked in Kaunas, but sometimes they had to punish people in order that the Germans shouldn't do it. When the Germans caught people coming back from work with food, the best solution was when they handed them over to the Jewish police. They had some kind of prison they put the people in. When the Germans said, 'Give them twenty-five lashes,' it was okay if the Jews did it; they would say, 'Yell loud, Yossel, so they'll think you're getting a real good beating.' There were few problems...[the police] were helping."

Even so, it was remarkable that a police force which was a tool of Nazi oppression could preserve its determination to help the people of the ghetto—and could continue to be recognized as friends by the community. Much of the credit was due to the moral tone set by the members of the Ältestenrat and the personal example of Dr. Elkes.

9
The Silver Fork

The Germans regarded the Lithuanians as fools who shot people without first exploiting their labour and confiscating their goods. "What kind of nonsense is this," they said, "just shooting people on sight without first registering them and finding out where they've hid their valuables."

A fortnight after Operation Intellectuals, the Gestapo launched Operation Valuables. The Jews of Kaunas were ordered to turn in all their gold, silver, diamonds, furs, art collections, and other treasures. The edict was accompanied by the threat that anyone holding back or concealing anything of value would be shot on the spot. Leah Elstein remembers that her mother couldn't bear to relinquish the family's silver sabbath candlesticks and wanted to hide them under some loose planks in the kitchen. "Are you crazy?" Lucy shouted at her mother. "Do you want to get us all killed for a pair of candlesticks?"

Helmut Rauca, in his capacity as Jewish Affairs Specialist for Kaunas, designated the Ältestenrat as the assembly point. By midday the street in front of the former schoolhouse was heaped high with fur coats, feather quilts, silver utensils, and gold wedding rings. The Gestapo loaded the booty on lorries and drove off. All at once, as if to take the ghetto by surprise, they came roaring back, stopped at designated houses, and began tearing up floorboards, knocking holes in walls, and probing the soil in the garden with their bayonets. "The Jews of Kaunas weren't rich, but they took pride in their possessions," says Chaim Lipman, the ghetto's plumbing and heating expert. "Many things, having been in the family for generations, were hard to part with. Every night for a week you could hear families digging away in their backyards, dropping things down wells, lowering them into backyard privies. But the Gestapo had a number of informers who lurked in the dark and made note of the house numbers, so when they returned they knew exactly where to go."

Baruch Direktor, having barely escaped Operation Intellectuals, tried to keep out of Rauca's way that afternoon. Hiding in the attic of his house, he saw a squad of Gestapo agents enter the garden of the house next door. Trampling the bushes and tearing back the sod, they probed for hidden valuables. Suddenly a shout went up as one of the searchers spotted a silver fork lying in the grass. Rauca strode up and ordered the occupant of the house into the yard. "So you thought you could conceal things from us," he shouted, drawing his rubber truncheon and beating the terrified man over the head. Bruised and bleeding, the man insisted that he was concealing nothing, that the fork wasn't his. Rauca, angered by such effrontery, struck him again. This time the man fell to the ground.

Through a gap between the wall and the tile roof, Direktor was able to see directly into his neighbour's yard. He was no more than five metres away when, in his words, "Rauca ordered [the neighbour] to get up and walk in the direction of the outhouse in the garden. He complied with this order and, at that moment, Rauca drew his revolver and shot the man in the back of the head."

Operation Valuables robbed the Jews of more than their beloved heirlooms and hard-won possessions. It deprived them of the means to trade for food outside the ghetto, to bribe a Lithuanian official, to ransom a husband or child from the clutches of the Gestapo. For Jäger and Rauca, Operation Valuables was standard procedure, a means of enriching the SS and drawing the noose tighter around the necks of the Jews of Kaunas.

On September 15, barely a month after the Jews had been enclosed in the ghetto, SS Hauptsturmführer Jordan—Jewish Affairs Specialist in the German civil administration of Kaunas*— presented the Ältestenrat with five thousand work cards which he

*The Nazis frequently created parallel organizations with competing objectives. Thus Jordan was Jewish affairs Specialist for the German civil administration of Kaunas, and supervised the labour exchange which assigned Jewish workers to various ghetto industries, work at the airdrome, etc. The murder of Jews was not his direct responsibility, although the deaths of many Jews were a by-product of overwork, exposure, and starvation. On the other hand, Rauca was Jewish Affairs Specialist for the Gestapo in the same city, and his primary task was annihilation; any other dealings he had with Jews were no more than temporary measures to prevent flight and resistance.

ordered distributed to the ghetto's skilled craftsmen. Each work-man, he instructed, would be permitted to add the names of three members of his immediate family to the card. The Council had hardly begun its distribution of the *Jordanscheine* ("Jordan's per-mits") when it received a call from a German official in charge of one of the ghetto's industrial enterprises demanding that "his" workers be issued with these *Lebenscheine*, or "life permits" imme-diately. The members of the Ältestenrat were galvanized into action: apparently the cards were much more than a sign that the bearer was a skilled, productive person useful to the German war effort; they were tickets to life itself.

Elkes summoned the members of his Council. What should they do with the cards? Should they be returned to Jordan with a firm note saying the Council could not be a party to some undisclosed Gestapo scheme? Should they burn them? If the Nazis planned to kill all those without cards, wouldn't it be best for all of Kaunas's Jews to die together?

While the Council debated, thousands of Jewish workmen gathered in the street before the Council headquarters. As members of the working class they had no great love for the *balabatim* (upper-class bosses) on the Ältestenrat who made life-and-death decisions ("their life, our death") without consult-ing them. There was angry talk, and accusations that the Council members were reserving most of the cards for members of their own families. Pushing the ghetto police aside, the crowd swarmed into the Council office and tore the cards out of the hands of the secretaries, shouting "The cards belong to us."

The next morning the residents of the Small Ghetto woke to find themselves surrounded by German and Lithuanian troops armed with machineguns. Orders were shouted to assemble with their families in the public square, in rows determined by their work assignments. A selection was made—the holders of *Jordanscheine* were sent to one side, those without cards to the other. For most of the morning they were ordered to hold their positions while the Gestapo officer in charge waited for orders. At last a messenger drove up and gave the officer a piece of paper. The officer read it, shrugged, and ordered his men back to their barracks. The Jews were free to return to their homes.

Several days later the Gestapo announced that the *Jordan-scheine* were no longer valid. They were replaced by a yellow card with a special stamp, which was itself to be superseded in a week or so by a pink paper with two stamps. As Yaacov Rabinovitch explains, "They were playing games with us—trying to keep us confused, not knowing which way to turn, what to expect, how to behave."

The next tragedy to strike the ghetto is remembered as Operation Kozlowski.

On September 26, 1941, a Lithuanian policeman named Kozlowski was strolling down a ghetto street when he heard a loud report. Convinced that he was the target of snipers lurking in the narrow lanes between the houses on Veliuona Street, he raced to the ghetto gate to inform the Gestapo. Within an hour the entire street was sealed off by a convoy of lorries. Rauca and his assistant, Sergeant Stutz, came roaring up in a staff car. They ordered their troops to rout all the people out of their homes down the entire length of the street.

Word of what was happening on Veliuona Street was flashed to the Council of Elders. Tory and ghetto police commissioner Koppelman rushed over but were warned by Beno Liptzer, boss of the work crew assigned to Gestapo headquarters, to lie low. This was Rauca's show, he informed them. It was well known that the Hauptscharführer brooked no interference.

Tory and Koppelman took shelter in a house on an adjoining street. From the second-storey window they had a clear view of Veliuona Street. They watched helplessly as all eighteen hundred of the street's residents—men, women, and children—were hauled out of their homes, marched out the ghetto gates, shoved onto waiting lorries, and driven away. The cries of the women and children still ring in Tory's ears.

Liptzer's men—the Jewish barbers, painters, plumbers, tailors, and carpenters that serviced Gestapo headquarters—soon learned the fate of the unfortunate families; the following day they saw Gestapo personnel unload mounds of used clothing, and in the pockets they found the identity documents of the residents of Veliuona Street. They had all been taken to Fort IX, ordered to undress, lined up before an open trench, and fusilladed. Beno Liptzer reported that Rauca and Stutz had pocketed all the valuables found in the victims' clothing. "This operation was commanded by Rauca," Tory says. "He was standing out in the street with Stutz. Rauca issued the orders to Stutz and the other Gestapo personnel."

The ghetto police investigated the incident and came away convinced that no one had fired at Kozlowski. They concluded that the Gestapo had taken advantage of the frightened watchman's panic to terrorize the ghetto dwellers, to demonstrate that the least sign of resistance would be ruthlessly crushed.

10
"The Big Operation"

On Friday, October 24, 1941, a staff car bearing Rauca and Hauptsturmführer Heinrich Schmitz entered the ghetto. The two Jewish Affairs Specialists drove slowly through the drab streets, stopping to look about occasionally but addressing no one. Hundreds of eyes watched warily as they stopped before a large open field, dotted with a few ramshackle houses, known as Democracy Square. They strode about, pointed here and there with their swagger-sticks, and drove off.

Rauca's saunter through the ghetto heightened the anxiety of its residents. For some weeks there had been reports of large ditches being dug by Russian prisoners of war in the hills surrounding Kaunas. The optimists argued that they were tank-traps being readied in anticipation of a Soviet counter-attack; the pessimists claimed they were mass graves prepared for the Jews of Kaunas. When Rauca returned the following day and drove directly to Ältestenrat headquarters, small knots of curious, apprehensive people gathered on the street, eager to learn what was going on inside. Seating himself at the head of the table while the Council members stood at attention before him as ordered, Rauca announced, "Great tasks lie before the ghetto, to fulfil on behalf of the Wehrmacht. The people will have to do very hard work. We on our part, of course, must feed those who work hard, and their families. But there are people in the ghetto who cannot work hard, and we are not in a position to provide them with the same rations as those who do heavy labour. Therefore those who cannot work

74

hard must be moved to the Small Ghetto, while the hard workers and their families remain in the Large Ghetto. We'll choose who goes where."

He ordered the Council to post proclamations throughout the ghetto ordering the entire population to assemble for a mass roll call in Democracy Square at six a.m. on October 28. He warned them that this meant everyone, without exception; anyone staying home would be shot. With that he rose, turned on his heel, and left.

The Council members were stunned. They recalled how they had been duped into collaborating with the Gestapo in Operation Intellectuals, and they were certain there was much more at stake here than the distribution of ration cards. What was the Council's moral responsibility? Should they post the notice or refuse the order? Their indecision did little to still the panic that was sweeping the ghetto. The handful of people clustered in front of the Ältestenrat headquarters swelled into a crowd; the rumours grew more and more fearsome.

The Council members argued for hours but were unable to come to a conclusion. If they posted the notice and it resulted in the death of ghetto residents, they would be guilty of collaborating with the Nazis in the murder of their own people. If they refused to post the notice, the Gestapo might punish them by destroying the whole of the ghetto population.

Exhausted, unable to see clearly what lay ahead, they decided they needed more information. They must find out what the Nazis had in store for them. Elkes was instructed to seek a meeting with Jäger, but the Standartenführer refused to meet with him; Rauca was the best he could get. Through an intermediary, he asked for a meeting.

On Sunday, October 26, Elkes and Goldberg met secretly with Rauca. The ghetto leaders voiced their suspicion that the order to assemble in Democracy Square signified some sort of disaster for their people. If the German authorities were truly concerned with rations, they pointed out, wouldn't it be more efficient to have the Council distribute the ration books? Didn't they know their own people best?

Rauca made light of their suspicions. There was nothing to fear, he said, it was purely an administrative matter. The Germans just wanted to have a look at the ghetto's residents, to assess its human material. "In considering the question of how to select the hard workers," Rauca went on, "we did discuss handing over the responsibility to the Council of Elders. But we know you Jews. We know how you stick together. If we left it to you, everyone would receive the same rations and production would suffer. That certainly wouldn't serve the purposes of the Third Reich." Several times Elkes and Goldberg pleaded with Rauca not to deceive them. "We begged him to speak to us openly and honestly," Goldberg reported. "We appealed to his human feelings. But Rauca assured us that there could be absolutely no question of any bad intentions against us. He repeatedly described it as purely administrative."

The Council was not reassured by the report of their leaders, and the discussion continued well into the night. Some insisted that in the face of uncertainty the wisest, most moral course was to do nothing, while others argued that the failure to act would be taken as defiance by the Gestapo and would only invite severe punitive measures. About eleven p.m. they agreed that further debate was useless. They decided to put the issue to the community's revered Chief Rabbi, Abraham Kahane Shapiro.

The Council members were educated men, proud of their secular training in law, medicine, engineering, and commerce, and they were not in the habit of turning to their spiritual leaders for answers to difficult moral questions. But now—faced with a situation for which they had no precedent, cut off from other Jewish communities, and unsure of German intentions—they fell back naturally on the compendium of rabbinic law and opinion, the *Halakhah*, to learn what was required of them as leaders. Jewish persecution was not new; the Holocaust was not entirely without precedent; for more than two thousand years Jewish communities had relied on the *Halakhah*'s accumulated wisdom to "confront, deal with, and transcend" the attacks of petty tyrants, rampaging Crusaders, and religious inquisitors. What guidance, they asked Rabbi Shapiro, could *Halakhah* offer them now?

The rabbi, a frail, sick old man, was already asleep when the Council members knocked on his door. After hearing them out he protested, "Why do you come to me? How can I tell you what to do? You are men of experience. You have dealt with the Germans before. If you don't know, how should I know?" They answered, "Rabbi, we are at a standstill. There is no other authority to which we can turn. There is no other precedent we can follow."

Shapiro was distressed at having such a heavy burden placed on his stooped shoulders. "There are similar cases in Jewish history," he said. "A famous passage in Maimonides' Code of Jewish Law concerns two men lost in the desert with only a small store of water. If they both drink, both are likely to die. If only one drinks, that one may survive. Over the centuries, the majority of the rabbis have held that the men must share the water even if the lives of both are endangered: one man does not have the right to condemn the other to death. A minority has argued that it is better for one man to survive than for both to perish." The issue was too complex for a quick answer, Shapiro decided. He agreed not to return to his bed, but to spend the rest of the night reviewing biblical commentaries. Perhaps by morning he would have an answer for them.

The Council members slept badly, and by six they were at the rabbi's door again. They found the old man surrounded by heaps of open books. "He drew his dignified head with his stately beard out of the book," Goldberg later wrote. "He look dreadfully tired. He said, 'No, I am not ready yet with the answer. Try coming at nine.' A member of the Council came back at nine and Rabbi Shapiro asked for another two hours. At eleven [the Council members] returned." This time, he was prepared to give them his answer. He had found an obscure passage in one of the commentaries that set down the principle that if an evil decree threatened disaster for the entire community, Jewish leaders must summon the courage to save even a remnant of their people.

The notices should, therefore, be posted.

The Council fretted over the wording of the decree, striving to make it clear to the Jewish populace that the call to assemble in Democracy Square had been ordered by the SS and not the Council. It finally read:

Order of the commander of the SD, October 27, 1941
All ghetto residents, regardless of age or sex, must leave their houses

on October 28, 1941, and assemble in Democracy Square at 0600 hours in the morning. Any who are found in their houses will be shot on the spot.

Council of Elders

October 28 dawned grey and cold. A chill, damp wind carrying the season's first snow blew in from the Baltic Sea. By 5:30 a.m. a steady stream of people, hunched in their overcoats, trudged through the ghetto's narrow streets to Democracy Square. Leah Elstein's mother puttered in the kitchen, in no rush to leave the house, and Leah, fearing that they would be late, urged her to hurry. "Are you afraid you'll miss the funeral?" her mother asked.

Once in the square the Jews assembled according to their work brigades: tanners, fur workers, road builders, airport workers, plumbers, and tinsmiths. Close family members stood next to the chief breadwinner. Each brigade carried a banner signifying its employment. Many wore their work-brigade armbands and pinned their *Jordanscheine* to their overcoats in a desperate effort to identify themselves as productive workers.

No one dared stay behind. The crippled hobbled in on crutches, the sick were carried to the square in their beds, the old were brought in wheelbarrows, mothers arrived clutching newborns— over 26,000 people crowded into the square that morning.

At 8 a.m. a convoy of troop carriers surrounded the square. Tornbaum's Lithuanians and several squads of SS Gestapo agents dismounted and set up machineguns at every entrance to the square. Minutes later, Rauca arrived, whip in hand, a fierce Alsatian at his heels. The people in the square fell silent as he mounted a small earthen mound at one end of the square, his grey-green uniform looming dark against the grey sky. He looked about for a moment; then, satisfied that everyone was in place, he gestured with his whip for the macabre parade to begin.

The first to march past were the members of the Ältestenrat, accompanied by the Council's employees and their families. With a slight gesture of his whip, Rauca directed them to the left side of the square. Next came the ghetto police, their boots polished, their peaked caps on square. They too were waved left. Liptzer's Gestapo brigade was also directed to join them. But as the pathetic march-past continued, Rauca, with a curt gesture of his gloved hand, sent some brigades right, others left. He divided brigades, separated families, tore husband from wife and children from parents.

Rabinovitch recalls that those waiting their turn to march past the mound scurried back and forth asking their neighbours, "What do you think? Which is the good side? Which is the bad? How should one look? How should one behave?"

By noon it was evident that the left was the "good" side and the right the "bad". The old and weak were directed to the right, the young and healthy to the left. Widows with children, children without parents, pregnant women, were placed on the right. Neatness and cleanliness were apparently important to the man on the mound; those who were well dressed received a nod of approval from Rauca while the thinly clothed, the ragged, were directed to the right with a flick of the whip. Minutes before the selection began the night-shift workers from the airport were marched into the square directly from twelve hours of heavy labour at the airdrome. Unshaven, muddy, bedraggled, they had had no opportunity to clean up before taking their places in the square. Apparently disgusted by their grubbiness, Master Sergeant Rauca ordered all five hundred to the right, while the still-neat day-shift workers were directed to the left.

Those sent to the right were quickly rounded up by the Lithuanian police unit and herded into the Small Ghetto, while those sent to the left stood about in huddled groups in the square. Meanwhile Rauca, unwilling to interrupt his sacred duty for lunch, munched on a thickly buttered sandwich as he continued to direct groups to the left and right.

The Jewish Affairs Specialist brooked no interference with his decisions. Alex Feitelson was a young electrician in the ghetto. When he and his family approached the mound, Rauca waved him left and his parents right. "I understood that the situation was bad, and I wanted to fight my way over to the side where my parents were in order to help them," Feitelson says. "Rauca noticed this and started to hit me over the head with his whip. Some other policemen came to his aid. They also beat me and pushed me over to the left side."

Elkes remained standing close to Rauca for most of the day. From time to time he tried to intervene, to save this one or that one, to claim this group or that person as essential to the operation of the ghetto. Again and again Rauca waved him off, saying, "You will be grateful to me, Elkes, for ridding you of this pile of manure."

It was late afternoon before all 26,000 had passed in review; 9,200 people, "2,007 male Jews, 2,920 Jewesses, and 4,273 infant Jews" had been declared redundant and transferred to the Small Ghetto. "Rauca himself chose who should live and who should die," says Leon Bauminger. "He was very calm. He was doing it quite elegantly, pointing to this one and that one with the handle of his whip, sending people left or right with a wave of his black-gloved hand."

Those who had been sent left returned home in the late afternoon gloom of a Lithuanian winter, hungry, numb with cold, physically and emotionally exhausted. They wandered the ghetto streets like lost sheep looking for the rest of the flock. "People returned to empty houses and empty streets," says Leah Elstein. "In our house only my mother, my brother, and I were left. All my uncles, cousins, and aunts disappeared into the Small Ghetto. We tried to take up life where we had left it. We realized that eventually we would all be killed, but for the present we were still alive. It hadn't been our turn—yet."

Those consigned to the Small Ghetto feared the worst, yet acted as if life was bound to continue—on a reduced scale, but life nevertheless. They tried to persuade themselves that two ghettos were being organized, a "better" one for the young and healthy and a "worse" one for those who were older and weaker. They scattered through the cold, deserted houses and sought to make them livable again; they quarrelled over living space, and worried about the furniture they had left behind in the Large Ghetto.

That evening Elkes somehow persuaded the Gestapo to let him bring back to the Large Ghetto a hundred of the Jews sent to the right. But no sooner did he arrive at the Small Ghetto gate than he was surrounded by a frightened, angry crowd demanding that he intercede with the authorities for every one of them. A Lithuanian guard, trying to hold back the crowd, accidentally struck Elkes in the head with his rifle butt, knocking down the elderly physician. Bleeding and half-conscious. Elkes was hauled back to the Large Ghetto for treatment; he had lost his chance to rescue anyone.

Early the next morning—October 29—the temporary residents of the Small Ghetto were awakened by the pounding of rifle butts on their doors. Lithuanian police auxiliaries shouted, "Out, out! Get ready for a march!" The frightened people asked, "Where? Where are we going?" but the only answer they received was "You'll soon find out." The Lithuanians pushed and kicked the Jews into a long ragged column, the men in front, the women and children in the rear. Soon after they left the ghetto they realized they were being conducted to the Gestapo's favourite killing ground: Fort IX. Some of the men bolted and were immediately shot down. Those who straggled or cried out were brutally beaten.

As the cortège passed within view of the Large Ghetto, friends and relatives rushed to its barbed-wire fence. They called to each other and held out their arms to each other in frantic appeal. Children sobbed as they waved farewell to parents, and the ancient mourners' prayer, the *kaddish*, rose like a cry of anguish from all sides.

When the column arrived at Fort IX the marchers were divided into groups of a hundred and ordered to strip naked, stack their garments in neat piles, and lie down next to each other in the large open trenches dug the week before by Russian prisoners of war. At one end of the trench, his feet dangling over the edge, sat one of Tornbaum's executioners, a bottle of vodka at his side and a submachinegun resting on his lap. When the trench was full, he took a swig of vodka and started firing. The more fortunate victims were killed outright; others, severely wounded but still alive when the firing stopped, were dispatched by two or three Gestapo men who walked along the ditch firing their pistols point-blank at those who still showed signs of life. Lime was sprinkled over the dead bodies, followed by a thin layer of earth, and the next hundred were ordered to lie down on top. The process was repeated until the trench could contain no more corpses.

The killing went on all that day. When it was over, the bloody ground continued to stir and heave, a sign that many of the wounded had been buried alive. Only one person who entered the pit survived the massacre, which is remembered by the ghetto survivors as the *Grosse Aktion*, or Big Operation. A twelve-year-old boy was shielded by his mother when the firing began. Her dead body covered his and he wasn't noticed. Fortunately he was in one of the top layers; for several hours he lay among the twitching corpses, afraid to move, but after dark, when it had grown quiet, he cautiously dug his way out, found some abandoned clothing, and crawled back to the ghetto and the Ältestenrat headquarters. The blood-smeared boy told Abraham Tory his grim story, and the Council secretary took him into the adjoining room where the full Council had been meeting most of the night. He repeated his story again for Elkes and the other Council members. The Council agreed that the boy must be hidden and his escape kept secret, for his life was in dire danger: the Gestapo could not afford live witnesses of their handiwork. Some say the boy's surname was Bloch, but no one remembers what happened to him, or whether he survived the war.

Rauca before his arrest. *Above*, his 1973 passport photograph; *below*, an RCMP surveillance shot.

Rauca during the Nazi years. Survivors of the Kaunas ghetto picked out his photos (*centre, left, lower left*) from an album of a hundred similar shots.

CANADIAN PACIFIC

Escape to Canada. *Above*, post-war refugees arrive from Europe on the SS *Beaverbrae*; *below*, the Huntsville motel Rauca managed for fourteen years.

SOL LITTMAN

In 1941 the Nazis drove the Kaunas Jews into a ghetto and ordered them to appoint a Council of Elders, *above*. Under its leader, Dr. Elchanan Elkes (*below, left*), the Council struggled to protect the community without provoking Nazi aggression.

In 1944, when the Germans dismantled the ghetto and sent the remaining Jews to extermination camps, the underground offered to rescue Elkes. He chose to stay with his people. He died in Dachau; a monument there, erected by the Kaunas survivors, marks the mass grave where he lies.

Der Befehlshaber der Sicherheitspolizei u. des SD
Einsatzkommando 3

Kauen, am 1.Dezember 1941

5 Ausfertigungen!
4.Ausfertigung.

Gesamtaufstellung der im Bereich des EK.3 bis zum 1.Des.1941
durchgeführten Exekutionen.

Übernahme der sicherheitspoliseilichen Aufgaben in Litauen
durch das Einsatzkommando 3 am 2.Juli 1941.
(Das Gebiet Wilna wurde am 9.Aug.41, das Gebiet Schaulen am
2.Okt.41 vom EK.3 übernommen. Wilna wurde bis zu diesem Zeitpunkt
vom EK.9 und Schaulen vom EK.2 bearbeitet.)

Auf meine Anordnung und meinen Befehl durch die
lit.Partisanen durchgeführten Exekutionen:

Datum	Ort		Anzahl
4.7.41	Kauen - Fort VII - 416 Juden, 47 Jüdinnen		463
6.7.41	Kauen - Fort VII - Juden		2 514

Nach Aufstellung eines Rollkommandos unter Führung
vom SS-Ostuf.Hamann und 8 - 10 bewährten Männern
des EK.3 wurden nachfolgende Aktionen in Zusammen-
arbeit mit den lit.Partisanen durchgeführt:

Datum	Ort	Beschreibung	Anzahl
7.7.41	Mariampole	Juden	32
8.7.41	"	14 " und 5 komm.Funktionäre	19
8.7.41	Girkalinei	komm.Funktionäre	6
9.7.41	Wendsiogala	32 Juden, 2 Jüdinnen, 1 Litauerin, 2 lit.Komm., 1 russ.Kommunist	38
9.7.41	Kauen - Fort VII -	21 Juden, 3 Jüdinnen	24
14.7.41	Mariampole	21 " , 1 russ. 9 lit.Komm.	31
17.7.41	Babtei	8 komm.Funktionäre (6 davon Juden)	8
18.7.41	Mariampole	39 Juden, 14 Jüdinnen	53
19.7.41	Kauen - Fort VII -	17 " , 2 " , 4 lit.Komm., 2 komm.Litauerinnen, 1 deutsch.K.	26
21.7.41	Panevezys	59 Juden, 11 Jüdinnen, 1 Litauerin, 1 Pole, 22 lit.Komm., 9 russ.Komm.	103
22.7.41	"	1 Jude	1
23.7.41	Kedainiai	83 Juden, 12 Jüdinnen, 14 russ.Komm. 15 lit.Komm., 1 russ.O-Politruk.	125
25.7.41	Mariampole	90 Juden, 13 Jüdinnen	103
28.7.41	Panevezys	234 " , 15 " , 19 russ.Komm., 20 lit.Kommunisten	288

-Übertrag: 3 834

Page 1 of the Jäger Report, which documents the atrocities of
Einsatzkommando 3A, the extermination unit in the Kaunas area. The
tally begins:
  Executions carried out by Lithuanian partisans under my directive
  and by my orders:
  4.7.41 Kaunas—Fort VII—416 Jews, 47 Jewesses   463
  6.7.41 Kaunas—Fort VII—Jews   2,514

YAD VASHEM

SOL LITTMAN

Above and below. The extermination escalates; Lithuanian Jews are assembled by the hundreds and gunned down on the edges of mass graves in pits and quarries. Others were taken to Fort IX, *left*, and were never seen again.

YAD VASHEM

SOL LITTMAN

After all the brutality and death, a few survive. *Top*, Yaacov Rabinovitch, who led his family from one hiding-place to another, through the smoke and flames of the burning ghetto, until the Russians broke through. *Bottom, l. to r.* Abraham Tory, whose ghetto diary has already helped convict several war criminals; Leah Elstein, who worked in Gestapo headquarters and secretly passed information to the Jewish Council; Dr. Joel Elkes, son of Council chairman Dr. Elchanan Elkes.

SOL LITTMAN

11
Witness

"I was the kind of guy," Leon Kupferberg says, "who landed on my feet no matter how hard they threw me." War had come, his wife was pregnant, food was scarce, their house in the Slobodka ghetto was crowded and narrow. Every day, Kupferberg recalls, there were new *Bekanntmachungen* and *Befehle* (proclamations and ordinances). One day there would be an order from the Stadtkommissar forbidding Jews to walk on sidewalks or roads—"The only place we were allowed to walk was in the ditches beside the roadway," he says. "Then there was a *Befehl* that we had to wear hats at all times so that we could doff them properly in the presence of Germans, military or civilian." Yet Kupferberg didn't despair. Living with him and his wife were a young woman doctor, her brother, her elderly mother, her aunt, and her aunt's sister and her son. "We lived better than most people in the ghetto because we organized ourselves better, planned better, and showed more initiative. For example, I registered with the labour exchange as a plumber. I was no more a plumber than you are, but it was safer to be regarded as a skilled worker."

Kupferberg's work brigade, consisting of carpenters, electricians, plumbers, tailors, barbers, and printers, was regularly assigned to the Luftwaffe headquarters on the far side of Kaunas. "The sixty-five of us reported to the ghetto gate each morning, and were escorted to work by a squad of Gestapo men. It was considered a very good job, because it allowed you to slip off your armband, cover your yellow star with the word *"Jude"* printed on it, and trade with the townsfolk for food. It was risky but necessary." Another advantage of working at Luftwaffe headquarters was that it prevented being drafted for heavy work at the airdrome. "The airdrome was bad, very bad. I tried to stay away from that."*

In late September, 1941, Kupferberg and his comrades began to hear rumours of large ditches being dug by Russian prisoners of war. "We also heard that Dr. Elkes had been handed some very bad *Bekanntmachung* which the Ältestenrat was expected to enforce, and that it was making the doctor sick," he says. "Then the Gestapo emptied all the Jews out of the Small Ghetto and closed the little wooden bridge that connected the Small and Large Ghettos. It looked bad. But when you are determined to live, you look at the good things and ignore the bad."

His optimism gave way to intense anxiety, however, as he stood in Democracy Square surrounded by his friends and family on October 28. "No one can adequately describe the cold, the feverish talk, the tears, and the agitated cries of the people in the square. We waited in the half-light of dawn until eight o'clock, when the jeeps, the trucks, and the half-tracks appeared and set up their machineguns. They were all SS; there were no Luftwaffe or Wehrmacht among them. Their commander, Helmut Rauca—all dressed up in his uniform, with the skull-and-crossbones symbol on his hat and a little stick under his arm—straightened out the brigades." It didn't take Kupferberg long to see that the young were being sent to one side and the old and weak to the other. To wait, he decided, was dangerous. His wife was visibly pregnant, the doctor's mother and aunt were old. They would have to act. Moving slowly, pausing frequently, they edged over to the "good" side. "Nobody stopped us, nobody noticed us. It was a good thing we did it early, because later they posted armed guards in the middle of the square so you couldn't sneak back."

All that night they heard screams from the Small Ghetto, where those sent to the right had been taken in small groups. The next

*Work at the airdrome was heavy, brute labour—shovelling dirt, hauling rocks, carrying back-breaking loads—and getting to and from the site involved a daily march of seven kilometres each way. Only the strongest could survive continuous work there. Those too exhausted to keep up were shot.

morning Kupferberg's work brigade, most of whom had survived the selection, reported for work as usual. But no guards met them at the ghetto gates to escort them through town. Since it was too risky to go unescorted, they returned to their homes. The next morning they reported again, and this time they were met by two guards who told them they had been too busy to come for them the previous day. "They laughed and said they had spent all night shooting Jews at Fort IX," Kupferberg remembers. "Most of them had gotten so drunk afterwards that they couldn't get up to escort us to work."

Chaim Lipman was regarded as something of a roughneck in the ghetto. Sturdily built, an amateur boxer, he would just as soon give a fellow a bloody nose as argue with him. It was rumoured that he carried a couple of pistols in his belt, and that he was the underground's chief source of smuggled weapons. Although considered a crude chap by some, he was known to be totally loyal to his friends and a tiger in defence of his family: during the scrimmage at the Ältestenrat for *Lebenscheine*, the precious "life" papers, Lipman hadn't hesitated to draw his pistol, point it at the head of a reluctant clerk, and walk off with enough cards to supply all his relatives.

Trained as a civil engineer, Lipman had helped erect many of Kaunas's finest pre-war government buildings. He was familiar with all the tricks of electrical wiring, plumbing, heating, excavation, hydraulics, and scaffolding. An intensely practical man, he was impatient with the intelligentsia's attempts to divine German intentions, and their shallow talk of armed uprisings. As far as he was concerned the situation was clear: the Germans intended to kill them all. The Jews' only hope, he insisted, was to build "bunkers", to hide, to burrow into the earth underneath every building, to dig tunnels connecting all the backyards, to build false walls in every closet and double ceilings in every attic.

Lipman's bunkers became a bit of a joke in the ghetto. "Why are you digging so hard, Chaim?" a neighbour asked. " What do you expect to find under your outhouse—pearls? Diamonds?" Lipman and his friends paid them no heed; they continued to build hiding-places. "Getting rid of the dirt was one of the biggest problems," he says. "We sewed large pockets into our coats and carried the dirt to the river bank. We stole bits of lumber from abandoned houses, ripped out radiators, collected iron pipe, and saved bits of concrete and broken brick." But none of the early bunkers he built was successful. "The Germans eventually uncovered all of them. We were really kept hopping, moving people from place to place. I must have built a dozen bunkers before I discovered the true secret of bunker building: don't let *anyone* find out what you are doing. You mustn't let your neighbours know, your friends, even your mother, until you are ready to move in. Then they must stay hidden until it is safe to come out."

One day Elkes summoned Lipman to Ältestenrat headquarters and asked him to undertake a special task. The heating system at the Third Lithuanian Police Company headquarters had failed; would he fix it?

The following morning Lipman cautiously approached the punitive unit's headquarters, in one of the university buildings in the heart of Kaunas, and asked to speak to its commander, Captain Tornbaum. Ushered into the office, he found Tornbaum, a tall, elegant man, playing Beethoven sonatas on a grand piano. "I'm freezing my ass off and I can hardly keep my fingers limber enough to play the piano," Tornbaum said. "Go down to the basement and see if you can fix the bloody furnace." It didn't take Lipman long to get the furnace going. However, he explained to Tornbaum, the boilers were in bad shape and needed replacing. He could bring in a crew the next day and complete the repairs. Tornbaum was pleased, and surprised Lipman by ordering his housekeeper to bring bread and milk for his "furnace brigade". He then ordered Lipman to organize a building-maintenance crew that would work exclusively for Tornbaum. "We were a privileged group like Liptzer's Gestapo brigade," Lipman says. "We went to and from work each day unescorted. We had access to better food. The work was safer and easier." While the rough-hewn Jewish engineer worked at the Third Police Company headquarters, a strange relationship developed between him and the artistic commander of the SS execution squad. Tornbaum would occasionally draw Lipman into conversations, ask him if he had ever heard anything as sublime as Beethoven's *Pathétique* sonata. But if any

86

of the crew inexplicably displeased him, he could turn ugly and order the man taken out and shot.

Privileged or not, though, Lipman and his family were in Democracy Square with everyone else on October 28, the day of the *Grosse Aktion*. As he stood surrounded by his parents, sister, aunts, uncles, cousins, nephews, and nieces, he realized they stood little chance in the selection. Nevertheless, it was too late to hide.

The day wore on, and still the family was waiting its turn to parade before Rauca on the mound. Then, around three in the afternoon, Tornbaum strode up and ordered the remaining Jews to close ranks and make themselves ready to march towards the mound. Catching sight of Lipman, he called, "Hey, plumber, what are you doing here?" Lipman shrugged and replied, "What we are all doing." "Come with me," Tornbaum snapped. "Bring your family." Removing his pince-nez, the captain led them towards the left side of the square. Lipman wasn't sure where Tornbaum was heading, but he was unhappy at leaving behind some of his good friends and their families. While his family followed Tornbaum, Lipman fell back and slipped a fake Ghetto Police armband on his sleeve. Boldly he approached the dwindling crowd, gesturing like a man in full command, and conducted a dozen people to the "good" side.

By four o'clock the selection had ended, and those whose lives were being spared were sent home. Lipman returned home to wait for his family, but no one came. He ran through the dark streets, desperately looking for them. Just when he had given up hope he saw them coming down the street towards him. Tornbaum had conducted them to a small house at the edge of the square and had told them, "Stay here, you'll be safe. We've already searched these houses, so no one will look for you here. But you mustn't leave until after six o'clock."

"But I had no illusions that Tornbaum would happen by to rescue me the next time I was in danger," Lipman says. "The day after, I was digging harder than ever."

Helen Werblunsky was only nine when the war came. A bright, curious youngster, she had found life in pre-war Kaunas secure and exciting; she had wandered safely all over town, read voraciously, gone to movies with her friends, and attended the Yiddish theatre with her father.

"June 22, 1941, was the beginning of the end for my parents, my little brother, and me. I remember how the windows shook as the Germans bombed the airdrome; our family grabbed everything we could carry on our backs and headed for Russia on foot." Like thousands of others, the Werblunskys wandered the countryside until cut off by the Wehrmacht's rapid advance, harassed and robbed by hostile Lithuanian partisans. But those two hard, dangerous weeks away from Kaunas probably saved their lives. Their neighbourhood, just over the bridge in Slobodka, was the scene of vicious murders during the pogrom which accompanied the German invasion of Lithuania.

The ghetto was sealed soon after their return and the Werblunskys sewed *ghetto lattes*, yellow stars, to their clothing and slowly eased into ghetto life. Their small two-room house became crowded with relatives evacuated from the *Altstadt*, and they also sheltered a student who had fled his village.

"How was it for me as a child?" Helen reflects. "How much did I understand? Not everything, but a great deal. Even we children could sense that something ominous hung over us. Nevertheless, there were moments of wild euphoria. One was when there was a rumour that Hitler was dead. Another was when the people held captive in Fort IV and Fort VII returned home. My friend Soreleh was among them but she couldn't stop crying—her father had been shot before her eyes at Fort VII."

Life in the ghetto was perilous, but luck seemed to be on the Werblunskys' side. Helen had arranged to visit her friend Sarah Bernstein on Veliuona Street on the same morning that the Gestapo conducted Operation Kozlowski: "When I went to Sarah's house, the whole family was gone. The whole *street* was gone. If I had arrived an hour earlier, I might also have been taken away."

Helen's mother was courageous—a *rizikantkeh*, a risk-taker. She frequently slipped away from her work party to buy food to smuggle into the ghetto. When the Gestapo decreed that all valuables must be handed over, on pain of death, she concealed her treasured Persian-lamb coat between the spare leaves of her dining-room table.

The family's luck also held on the day of the *Grosse Aktion*. As a member of Beno Liptzer's Gestapo brigade, Helen's father was privileged. "He had *Lebenscheine*, or special passes. Everyone with those passes was safe. Not that the Gestapo couldn't shoot you on a whim despite the pass, but they offered some protection."

When they returned from Democracy Square that evening they found most of the houses on their street empty. Helen's aunt and cousin, who shared their house on Kriksciukaitis Street, had been sent to the Small Ghetto; all their neighbours, all Helen's friends, all the younger children and their grandparents, were gone. "I can remember letting out a sigh of relief that I wasn't among the missing."

The houses on Kriksciukaitis Street did not stay empty for long. Soon after the *Grosse Aktion* the Gestapo announced a reduction in the size of the ghetto. Several streets were cleared of Jews, and the barbed-wire noose around the ghetto drew tighter than ever.

George Kadish did not throw bombs, shoot from ambush, or smuggle weapons. He fought the Nazis with the weapons he knew best; a camera, a radio, and a primitive printing press. Yet he was so effective that the Gestapo put a price of ten thousand marks on his head.

Something of a genius in the design and construction of photographic equipment, he had built a number of secret miniature cameras for the Lithuanian police before the war. When the Germans invaded, he hastily adapted a Leica by mounting a small lens that could shoot pictures through a buttonhole in his shirt; he triggered the shutter with a wire leading from the camera to his pocket. With his equipment Kadish took more than five thousand pictures of Jewish life in the Kaunas ghetto—pictures of old people being pitilessly murdered, mothers being torn from their children, wistful, wide-eyed children who knew no other world than that of hunger, cold, and brutality. His camera followed the Jews as they carried, dragged, and wrestled their possessions from their homes in the *Altstadt* over the bridge into Slobodka, caught the smirk on the faces of guards as they conducted body searches on women returning to the ghetto, captured the resignation and the despair of the residents as they gazed out, through multiple strands of barbed wire, at life on the other side.

Kadish had blond hair and blue eyes that made it easy for him to pass as a Gentile, and had a number of close friends among enlightened students who were willing to hide him, supply him with film, develop his pictures, and provide him with spare radio parts. His parents were not so fortunate—they had been ordered to the ghetto early in August 1941. George would frequently visit them during the day, but took care to leave the ghetto before nightfall. Once he learned of the *Befehl* ordering the total Jewish population of Kaunas to appear in Democracy Square, though, he avoided the ghetto. For several days he remained hidden in a friend's apartment in Kaunas, fearing to come out while the Gestapo were scouring the town for Jews.

Once the Big Operation was over there was a curious sense of relaxation in the ghetto. Jäger made a special journey to Ältesten-rat headquarters to announce that there would be no more selections, no more killings. Kadish came out of hiding and stationed himself once more on the Slobodka bridge, snapping pictures of work brigades marching under guard to field and factory, of young women working on manure piles and airport workers hauling heavy rocks. He tuned in the BBC on the forbidden radio he kept hidden in the basement of his parents' home and printed the news on a homemade printing press; as he walked through the ghetto he would slip copies of this clandestine journal into the pockets of acquaintances.

For close to two years Kadish led a dual life, sometimes living in the ghetto, sometimes staying with Christian friends in Kaunas. But eventually the Gestapo got wind of his work. Someone, somewhere, talked of the young man who was documenting Einsatzgruppe atrocities. Such a person, such a record, was dangerous; the Gestapo permitted no witnesses. In March 1943 they raided his parents' ghetto home. Kadish, who had spent the previous night in the ghetto, said he had a premonition, an acute sense of discomfort, that drove him to hide in the bunker he had built beneath the kitchen oven. Half an hour before the SS arrived he crawled under the wood-burner, lowered himself into a small, windowless room, and pulled a narrow, stone-covered panel over his head. For more than an hour the Gestapo searched the house, but they were unable to discover his hiding-place. Satisfied that

Kadish was not at home, they left the building, but stationed a guard at the door. Kadish was unwilling to stay underground for long—he knew they would be back, and next time they might be more thorough. He must get out of the ghetto.

He evaded the guard at the door by climbing through a window to the roof and sliding to the ground on a rope. A neighbour gave him a white sheet to make him less visible against the March snow. Crawling on his belly, he approached a dark corner of the ghetto fence, hoping to cut a few strands of wire and escape into the city. But the guards seemed to be everywhere, and although he waited in the snow most of the night he saw no chance to escape. In desperation he crawled back from the fence to the shelter of a nearby house, and threw chunks of ice at the barbed wire. Drawn tight by the cold, the wire sang. The guards, believing that someone was making a break, rushed to that part of the fence, and in the confusion Kadish snipped the wire farther along and slipped back into town.

Journalist Yaacov Rabinovitch played a waiting game. As brigade after brigade marched before Rauca and was waved left or right, he hung back, waiting to see which was the good side and which was the bad. Half a dozen times he sidled close to the man on the mound, trying to discern the pattern of his decisions. What prompted the Hauptscharführer to send some left and others right? Was it better to stride by with head held high and make eye contact with Rauca, or was it better to shuffle by humbly with eyes lowered? Should one be neat and cleanshaven, or unkempt and bearded? Were the odds better in a large group, or a small one? A half-dozen times he drifted back to the edge of the crowd where he had stationed his wife Dora and their eighteen-month-old daughter. "Let's wait some more," he said. "I'm not sure yet."

Rabinovitch feared Helmut Rauca, feared his rage and his unbridled power. He had watched at a distance as the Gestapo gave short shrift to the ghetto's intellectuals. Every day they carted off several of the community's lawyers, teachers, and rabbis to the ring of old forts in the hills beyond Kaunas. None of them was ever heard from again. Trapped in the ghetto, responsible for his young wife and daughter, Rabinovitch decided it was safer to dig peat, mend roads, and shovel manure than to confess to being a writer. From time to time he was assigned to the work crew engaged in building the military airdrome several kilometres from the city. The work was hard and the guards were brutal, but sometimes it gave him a chance to trade some piece of clothing or household item for a cabbage, a loaf of bread, or some potatoes.

Smuggling things into the ghetto was risky, but without the extra food there was little hope of survival. The rations issued to Jews in the ghetto were not calculated to nourish but to starve and weaken them, and the purchase of additional rations was *verboten* and strictly punished by the Nazis. The time of greatest danger was when the work party returned to the ghetto, with the forbidden food hidden under jackets and stuffed down pant legs.

Normally the ghetto's main gate, just beyond the bridge over the Vilija river, was manned by Jewish ghetto policemen. Their search was cursory. If they came across anything concealed under your clothing, they winked and let you through. It was not so easy when the Lithuanian auxiliary police hovered at the gate. They enjoyed humiliating Jews, and their searches were more thorough. If they caught you they might arrest you, in which case you would be shot. But just as often they would confiscate the food, beat you, and demand a bribe to let you go.

One day Rabinovitch was part of a small work party sent to the airdrome to clear a clogged ditch at the far end of the runway. Nearby was a peasant farm and a farmer willing to do some illicit trading. When the work party returned to the ghetto that evening there were several Gestapo officers in grey-green uniforms standing at the gate, the dreaded runic SS insignia on their collars and the *Totenkopf* (death's head) symbol on their caps. One was a heavy-set, military-looking man in his mid-thirties whom Rabinovitch recognized immediately as SS Hauptscharführer Albert Helmut Rauca, the Gestapo Jewish Affairs Specialist in Kaunas and commander of the Kaunas ghetto. The young writer felt his knees go weak.

"The man was a devil," Rabinovitch says. "Whenever he appeared in the ghetto there was trouble. People were taken away. People died. We had our own Yiddish name for him, a pun on the name Rauca. We called him 'Ruakh'. It means demon or devil."

The work party had almost passed through the barbed-wire gate when there was an abrupt command in German: "Halt. Search that bunch there."

The work party was ordered to stand in a small circle, hands over their heads, legs apart. Rauca looked on, hands on hips, while Lithuanian auxiliaries in German uniforms searched them. Rough hands pulled at their clothing, hauling food out of linings, pockets, and pant legs, and placing it at the feet of each man.

Whip in hand, Rauca inspected the contraband.

"Ha, potatoes," he said "Rations stolen from the mouths of German fighting men."

He stopped before Rabinovitch's neighbour to examine a small package wrapped in newspaper. "What's this?" he whooped. "Ham! A Jew who eats ham! Damn vermin, you Jews will devour anything!"

There was a sudden loud report and Rabinovitch saw part of his neighbour's head fly off. He stiffened, expecting to be next. Instead, he saw Rauca return his smoking pistol to its holster and walk off.

Rabinovitch stood there trembling for a moment. Then, stepping carefully over the food at his feet, he walked slowly through the ghetto gate. Once he was around the corner he ran until he reached home.

Now he was under Rauca's eye again, as the day in Democracy Square wore on. The cold became more intense. The child cried and could not be comforted. Yaacov and his wife were young and healthy and would probably be waved left, but families with young children, he observed, were often sent right. The last time he approached the mound, Rabinovitch noticed that Rauca was tiring. He was no longer evaluating the "human material", but was dispatching whole groups right and left without much consideration, his decisions growing more and more unpredictable. From time to time Jordan joined Rauca in making the selection, but he soon lost interest and turned to other matters.

Dusk was approaching. A Jewish ghetto policeman spotted Rabinovitch and his family hanging about the edge of the square. "What are you doing here, Yaacov?" the policeman asked. "You'd better come with me." Grabbing him by the arm as if he were taking him into custody, the policeman conducted him to the "good side". "I never passed Rauca," Rabinovitch says, "but I had plenty of opportunity to watch him at close hand that day. How can I ever forget him?"

"Rauca is not a lowbrow like most Nazis," Edwin Geist wrote in his diary. "He is interested in the arts. He seeks to preserve German culture. He wants to save me and my music for the Third Reich. In particular he wants me to write some hearty songs using the poems of local poets for my text. He says the soldiers need uplifting music to sustain their spirits in the struggle with the enemy."

Geist was recognized as a gifted composer, perhaps one of the best in Germany. Before the war he was a much-sought-after instructor at the Berlin conservatory. One of his students was a beautiful young woman with waist-long blonde hair named Lida Bagriansky, who came from the village of Priennai, some thirty kilometres from Kaunas. The statuesque pupil and her thin, bespectacled teacher were soon deeply in love. Geist, a totally non-political person in a country where politics had become everything, cared little who ruled Germany so long as they didn't interfere with his music. He was barely aware that life in Berlin was becoming increasingly uncomfortable for Lida—that, being Jewish, she feared Hitler's rise to power.

When the Law for the Protection of German Blood and Honour* went into effect in September 1935, forbidding marriage, sexual intercourse, and even friendship between Jews and Germans, the pair continued their relationship in secret. But every footstep in the corridor, every knock on the door, became ominous. Finally Lida decided that life in Germany had become too dangerous, and returned to Lithuania. Geist soon followed her and the two spent a few blissful years together in Kaunas. Geist cared little for money. Unable to obtain a position in the local conservatory, he gave music lessons and served as an accompanist in cafés. When the

*Enacted on September 15, 1935, the Law for the Protection of German Blood and Honour prohibited marriage and extramarital intercourse between Jews and persons of "German blood", and banned the employment of German women under the age of forty-five in Jewish households.

war came and the Germans occupied Kaunas, he didn't hesitate to accompany Lida into the Vilijampole ghetto. It did not take him long, however, to realize that Lida was in constant jeopardy and that he could be of no help to her as a ghetto resident. As a German national of impeccable Aryan background, he had no difficulty leaving the ghetto again and mingling freely with the soldiers, policemen, administrators, and carpetbaggers who gathered nightly at the German club. Here he met Helmut Rauca.

As the situation in the ghetto worsened, Geist became desperate to get Lida out. He asked Rauca to free her, insisting that she was only half Jewish and therefore might be eligible to live beyond the ghetto's boundaries. Rauca was sympathetic, but said he would have to see documentary proof of Lida's ancestry. Geist concocted an elaborate scheme to prove that the blonde, blue-eyed Lida was not a full Jew but a *Mischlinge*, a half-Jew.* He persuaded Dr. Brundza, the most popular non-Jewish physician in Kaunas, to supply him with a false document stating that Lida was only half Jewish. A few days before she was born, the document read, while Lida's mother was undergoing examination, she had confessed that the child was not her husband's but the product of a love affair with a Christian Lithuanian. Rauca smiled broadly as he examined the document; to his practised policeman's eye it was a transparent fabrication. "Do you have any other proof?" he asked Geist. "Are there baptismal certificates? Any document to show that the alleged father was a Christian?" The frail musician's voice shook as he told Rauca, "Destroyed. All the records were lost when the city hall in Priennai was blown up by the retreating Red Army. Nothing left."

Rauca didn't challenge Geist. It didn't matter a damn to the

*The First Regulation to the Reich Citizenship Law, enacted November 14, 1935, decreed that only persons of "German and related blood" could be German citizens. But because of the widespread intermarriage between Jews and non-Jews which had taken place over the centuries, the law's drafters felt compelled to distinguish degrees of Jewishness. Three Jewish grandparents made you a Jew. If you had two Jewish grandparents, you were a Jew if you adhered to the Jewish religion or were married to a Jew; however, if you had abandoned the religion and were married to a non-Jew you were a "person of mixed blood" or *Mischling*. The *Mischlinge* might not be "true Germans" but they were generally exempt from resettlement and annihilation.

95

Gestapo Jewish Affairs Specialist whether the cursed Jewess remained in the ghetto or lived outside its gates. She was too pretty, too recognizable, to disappear; they could pull her in whenever they wanted to. His concern was Geist. The musician was a creative man and Germany needed all her creative energies.* At a time when thousands of good German boys were dying, the Reich must conserve all her forces. He wanted to wean Geist from his obsession with Lida, to get him started on a more positive, responsible course.

"Let me think about the matter," Rauca said. "Meanwhile, why don't you return to composing? Why don't you write some songs that will lift the hearts of our weary soldiers?" Geist returned to his room thinking that Rauca was really quite a decent fellow. He sent an optimistic letter to Lida and sat down at the piano to toss off several upbeat songs and one of those sentimental "heart-string-pullers" so popular with the soldiers. Several days later he was back on Rauca's doorstep, pleading to have Lida released from the ghetto. Rauca agreed—but forbade the two to live together. Geist, unable to set his own conditions, consented.

And so in August 1942, after more than a year in the ghetto, Lida moved out again. She took up work as a translator for the German civil administration. At first she and Geist lived separately, but the pull between them was too strong. Geist soon defied Rauca and moved into Lida's apartment. But the simple happiness they had known before the German occupation was no longer possible. The politically naive musician had become aware of the sordid cruelties the Nazis were practising on the people of Lithuania, and he was determined to use the only weapon available to him—music—to expose them. He set to work on an opera about the Incas of Peru. It was easy to understand who were represented by the noble Incas, and who were the heartless conquistadores. Lida pleaded with him to abandon the opera, to avoid such a politically-charged libretto, but Geist would not be deterred.

Rauca soon learned that Geist was again living with Lida. Several times he sought to persuade him to abandon her, express-

*Music had great ideological value in the eyes of the Nazis, as they felt it demonstrated the superior culture of the Aryan race.

ing sympathy for Geist's feelings but warning him to bear his own future in mind. Rauca would alternately flatter the defiant musician, and threaten him and shame him, but Geist would not yield. Despite Geist's obduracy, Rauca was still reluctant to abandon this German genius; since it was impossible to persuade the man, he must deal with the woman. Rauca visited Lida one evening when Geist was at work, and told her bluntly, "You must either be sterilized or go back to the ghetto."

When Geist returned home Lida was in tears. Rather than be separated from Geist, she would agree to sterilization, she said. Geist was beside himself. He rushed out of the apartment to confront Rauca. "Stay out of our lives!" Geist shouted. "By what right do you impose such hard-hearted punishment?" Rauca replied that, given Germany's racial laws, he was being kind. If he chose, he could deal with them much more severely. If Geist couldn't cure himself of his obsession with the Jewess, it was Rauca's responsibility to make certain that no Jews resulted from their union. Geist, losing all self-control, argued that every man and woman who loved each other had a right to bear children and that no government, no band of perverts, could prevent them. Rauca grew angry, drove Geist from his office, and ordered a police raid on Geist's apartment. The raiders found the libretto of the new opera. As he read the text, Rauca realized that Geist was beyond salvation. He had Geist removed to Fort IX, where he was confined in a dank cell for about a month. Each day scores of prisoners were taken from their cells, lined up against the prison wall, and shot—the death volley could be heard throughout the prison. Rauca did not relish shooting a German national, and he visited Geist several times that month in the hope that the horrors of prison life would bring the composer to his senses. But Geist rejected all of Rauca's overtures. Finally Rauca lost all patience and ordered him shot. Lida, learning that Geist had been murdered, committed suicide.

The December cold penetrated his bones. The flames singed his eyebrows. The manacles on his wrists made it agony to wield the shovel and the leg-irons around his ankles caused him to trip repeatedly as he carried the decomposing corpses from the pit to the fire. "Only the Nazis could invent such a hell," Alex Feitelson muttered to himself. Arrested in 1943 by Rauca's men for being a member of an underground organization, the young electrician was tortured for six weeks but divulged nothing. He was then dispatched to Fort IX, where he expected to meet the same fate as all the others. To his surprise, he was clapped into chains and put to work exhuming corpses from the pits and stacking them on huge log and kerosene pyres. At about the same time Michael Itzchaki joined with five others in a desperate attempt to escape the Kaunas ghetto, only to be captured by Lithuanian policemen; two of his comrades were shot and the rest were turned over to the Gestapo. After being tortured unspeakably for several days, Itzchaki was also sent to Fort IX and assigned to the same nightmarish task as Alex.

"We were sixty-four prisoners shackled in chains and guarded by thirty-five Gestapo personnel," Feitelson says. "They were afraid one of us might escape. We were divided into groups: one group had to dig out the bodies; another had to lift them from the pit, remove the gold teeth, and place the bodies on stretchers to be carried to the fire. Initially they were stacked in layers, one layer of wood and one layer of bodies, three hundred bodies a day. Later this was increased to six hundred. . . . There were fourteen mass pits, a hundred metres long, two metres wide and three metres deep."

By the winter of 1942, following the German defeat at Stalingrad, Himmler began to fear the dead as much as the living. The spectre of ultimate retribution at the hands of the allies was growing. On December 17, 1942, British Foreign Secretary Anthony Eden told the House of Commons that Germany was "now carrying into effect Hitler's oft-repeated intention to exterminate the Jewish people of Europe." In the first public statement by any Allied official on the subject, he revealed that Jews from the occupied nations were being sent to Eastern Europe where they "were worked to death in labour camps" or "deliberately slaughtered in mass executions." On that same day the fledgeling United Nations announced that crimes against the Jews would be avenged by the international community.

With the Russian armies surging westward Himmler decided

that all traces of the mass killings in the East must be eliminated. He ordered Paul Blobel, commander of Einsatzkommando 4A, to destroy all evidence of the Einsatzgruppen massacres. Blobel formed a special Kommando with the code designation "1005" to locate the grave sites throughout the occupied territories, dig up the bodies, burn them, and scatter the ashes.

So secret was this gruesome project that the Gestapo never dared refer to its real purpose. The men in the work gang were forbidden to say that they were exhuming bodies; instead, they were instructed to say they were going to the "battlefield". The bodies could not be called corpses, but "dolls". The men who stoked the fires were known as the "fire brigade" and their foreman as the "fire chief". No mention could be made of Fort IX; it was referred to only as "Site 1005B". Berel Gempel was a member of the work gang. One day he recognized his uncle, who had been carried off in Operation Kozlowski, among the "dolls". Another member of the work gang came across the bodies of his mother and two young sisters.

It was the duty of the "fire chief" to keep a count of the bodies as they were added to the stack, and enter the figure in a ledger. Helmut Rauca would show up at the site periodically to ask how many "dolls" had been removed from each pit. He compared the count with the figures written on a slip of paper he carried in his pocket. Sometimes he would say, "Keep digging. There are more dolls in this trench." From this Feitelson concluded that Rauca had kept a careful body count of each *Aktion* and knew exactly how many people had been buried in each pit.

"While exhuming the bodies," Feitelson says, "it could be determined precisely what kind of victims were contained inside the pits. The two pits located next to the cement wall [that surrounded Fort IX] contained the bodies of foreign Jews.* They were recognizable because they lay in the pits fully clothed, dressed just as they had been when they arrived, and identity cards marked Vienna, Frankfurt, and Breslau were found in their clothing. Another pit

*These were German Jews who had been transported to Kaunas for liquidation. Because they regarded themselves as German citizens they refused to submit to the indignity of removing their clothes; some even attacked their guards. As a result they were shot and buried fully dressed.

contained the bodies of the Kozlowski operation. In contrast to the Jews transported from abroad, those were naked. . . . In one pit we were able to identify the victims of the Small Ghetto, since there were so many children's bodies."

On or about December 6, 1943, a lorry drew up to Site 1005B and Rauca and two subordinates dismounted, pushing four people ahead of them—a bespectacled older man, a woman, an old lady, and a boy of twelve. Rauca's crew ordered the work gang to stand away. From where they stood on a small knoll, Feitelson and Itzchaki could clearly see the four being ordered to undress and face the pyre. Once their backs were turned, Rauca and his companions drew their pistols and shot all four in the back of the head. Their bodies were thrown on the pyre by Gestapo personnel. Feitelson and Itzchaki were told to remove the victims' clothing to the guardroom, where they examined the man's overcoat and found a letter indicating that the four were Dr. Nachman Shapiro (son of the Chief Rabbi), his wife, his mother, and his son. Because of his father's fame, international efforts had been made to rescue Nachman Shapiro, a professor of Semitic languages at Kaunas University, and his family. The International Red Cross had requested that they be allowed to leave Lithuania and travel to a neutral country. Such requests were generally honoured by the Gestapo by killing the person and advising the Red Cross that his address was unknown.

Aware that as witnesses to the exhumations they didn't have long to live—that the Gestapo would kill them as soon as the last body in the pits had been burned—the sixty-four members of the work gang plotted to escape. On Christmas Eve, 1943, when the guards were drunk, they fled in a heavy snowstorm, wrapped in white sheets they had found in a store room.

12
The Last *Aktion*

Under Elkes' leadership, the Slobodka ghetto survived long after most ghettos in Eastern Europe had been liquidated. There were few weapons available to the slim, pale physician, yet by one stratagem or another he managed to hold the community together and husband the survivors until July, 1944—just a day or two before the Russians fought their way back into Kaunas.

Elkes' pride and dignity shamed the enemy. He never ceased reminding Jäger and Rauca that what they were doing was wrong and that one day they would have to answer for their crimes. "I did not ask for mercy but always demanded satisfaction for the insults to our faith, for the righteousness and justice of our demands," Elkes wrote. Such was the doctor's presence that the Gestapo leaders smiled bleakly at his warnings but took no action against him.

His most effective weapon was delay. He bargained constantly for more time—time for the council to discuss the issue, time to assemble the necessary people, time to do the job right. He sought to give the impression that he and his people were eager to oblige the German conquerors. He regularly reminded the German administrators that Jewish labour was indispensable to the occupation economy, that without Jewish craftsmen their own efforts would falter.

He was forever playing the German civil administration against the Gestapo. The former was interested in keeping production up, turning out more uniforms, digging more peat, and manufacturing

101

DOUGLAS COLLEGE LIBRARY

more munitions; the latter was primarily interested in killing more Jews. The civil administrators sometimes succeeded in delaying an *Aktion* by arguing that the Jewish workers were needed to finish a contract, to guarantee delivery of the shipment, or to provide warm underclothing for freezing German soldiers. In the long run, however, the killers had the "higher claim", so day by day the number of ghetto-dwellers dwindled.

Elkes fought back by opening covert schools for the ghetto children, although education for Jewish children had been expressly forbidden by the Gestapo. A symphony orchestra and a string quartet continued to perform for ghetto audiences, theatre groups staged plays, and in summer the children were taken on outings to the riverbank. When the SS decreed that all books in the ghetto must be destroyed, he arranged to have whole libraries of scientific and rabbinic literature hidden in specially prepared bunkers.

Elkes had available to him a unique intelligence network. Beno Liptzer's Gestapo brigade kept their ears open as they shaved SS faces, mended SS clothes, and painted SS office walls. Lipman promptly reported any information gleaned by his men at Tornbaum's headquarters. But knowledge of impending disaster seldom prevented it.

For a brief time after the Big Operation there was little German interference with life in the ghetto. Food was somewhat more plentiful and the emptied houses provided additional living space. The Ältestenrat organized its own labour exchange to discourage the Gestapo from assembling work crews by randomly seizing people in the streets. For the community's sake, all Jews were required to register with the exchange, and were required to work. The work was brutally hard. Men and women unaccustomed to severe physical labour dug peat, cut timber, hauled rocks, and quarried minerals. Many died of near-starvation and exposure. Rather than trust to Nazi justice, the council established Jewish courts to mete out punishment to those who disobeyed council rules, and to settle quarrels between neighbours and relatives.

But before long the Jewish courts were abolished by decree of the Gebietskommissar, the labour exchange was taken over by the Stadtkommissar, and the killings started again. Men, women, and

DOUGLAS COLLEGE LIBRARY

children were shot on whim. Jews who concealed their yellow patches, failed to doff their hats to SS officials, or dared to walk on the sidewalk were summarily shot.

In March 1942, SS Brigadeführer Dr. Franz Stahlecker was killed by Red Army partisans in an ambush on the outskirts of Riga. He was succeeded by SS Brigadier General Heinz Jost, but after three months Jost decided he had no stomach for the job and returned to his desk in Berlin. Stadtkommissar Cramer went on to other duties sometime in 1943 and was succeeded by the equally bureaucratic and bloodthirsty SS Obersturmführer Wilhelm Goecke.

Though Elkes played his slim hand with courage and skill through all these changing circumstances, he was helpless to prevent the *Kinder Aktion*—Operation Children.

Early in March 1944, the Gestapo ordered the Jewish ghetto police to assemble for inspection at 8:00 a.m. in a small square not far from Ältestenrat headquarters. Over 150 of the 175 men on the force turned out, their boots carefully polished, their jackets brushed, and their faces closely shaven. The rest, sensing that something was up, called in sick. For an hour the men stood about joking and laughing, waiting for the German police officials to arrive: "So much for German punctuality." Suddenly a line of canvas-covered trucks approached. Police auxiliaries and Gestapo agents jumped down and surrounded the waiting men. At gun-point they ordered the Jewish policemen onto the trucks, and drove them to Fort IX where they were interrogated. "Tell us everything about the ghetto underground," Rauca's men demanded. "Give us the location of all the hiding-places." Most told the Gestapo nothing; some may have given away the locations of Lipman's bunkers. Whether they broke or held out, all of them were shot the following morning. The Gestapo feared these unarmed policemen: they recognized that they were well trained and highly disciplined and that many of them had previous military training. They knew that beneath a show of compliance the ghetto *Polizei* were doing their best to save lives and sabotage German orders. They even suspected that they might be the true leaders of the underground. In any case there was a danger that, pressed too hard, faced with a situation they could no longer stomach, they might dig up concealed weapons and start an armed rebellion. It would be wise, the Gestapo leaders decided, to dispose of them in advance of the *Kinder Aktion*.

With the Jewish police force out of the way, Gestapo and auxiliary police units descended on the ghetto. While loudspeakers blared military music they moved from house to house, seizing every child they could find. Since it was *verboten* to bear children in the ghetto, many of the younger children were hidden in closets, bureau drawers, attics, and basements while their parents were at work. If their cries didn't betray them, Dobermanns and Alsatians smelled out their hiding-places. The terrified children were thrown onto trucks and driven off to Fort IX. As the trucks moved down the streets, parents who worked in nearby ghetto factories came rushing from their workplaces to plead for the lives of their children. Women chased down the street after the departing trucks, weeping and tearing their hair. One young mother pleaded with the Gestapo man riding shotgun on his lorry to give back her babies. "Which are yours?" he asked. "Those two," she pointed. "I can't give you both, choose which one you want." Unable to choose, the woman climbed onto the truck and rode to her death with her children.

The Gestapo came back the following day, and the day after that—they knew that children wanted to play and couldn't remain hidden long. From that time on, no child was seen on the ghetto streets.

No more than a few thousand Jews remained in Kaunas by the time the ghetto was finally liquidated. Elkes pleaded with Goecke to allow the survivors to remain in Kaunas rather than transport them to the death camps. "You have your wireless and we have ours," Elkes said to him. "No matter what the radio broadcasts from Berlin say, you know you Germans are losing the war. In a few days, at most, the Russians will occupy Kaunas. If you let us stay, the Jewish people will reward your generosity. If you transport us to those death camps of yours, be advised that we Jews have long memories."

Goecke's reply was an order for the Jews of Kaunas to assemble at the ghetto gate, ready for travel, within a few hours. Two thousand reported as ordered and were put on trains to Stutthof and Dachau concentration camps. The rest remained hidden within their houses, in attics and chimneys. Although many were driven from their hiding-places by German and Lithuanian police units equipped with dogs, crowbars, axes, and dynamite, most died in the smoke and flames that enveloped Slobodka when the Gestapo, having run out of time, set fire to the ghetto.

Leah Elstein remembers 1942 as a relatively quiet but difficult year. Living conditions in the ghetto worsened, and people were compelled to trade food for clothing and to burn their furniture to keep warm. "It was a cold winter," she recalls. "In our house we began by burning our bedroom set, then the furniture in our salon, and finally our dining-room chairs and table." The Gestapo still swooped without warning, seizing a young man here and a family there, but there were none of the large-scale *Aktionen* that had characterized the previous year. But the next year, 1943—after the German defeat at Stalingrad—was bad. "Whenever something went wrong at the front we became the scapegoats. They would find an excuse—any excuse—to punish us. One time Rauca accused us of lighting flares to guide the Russian aircraft; another time he accused us of harbouring escaped prisoners of war. None of it was true."

By 1944, SS Standartenführer Kittel had replaced Jäger as head of the Gestapo for the Kaunas area. Leah describes Kittel, a former actor with the Viennese State Theatre, as "extremely handsome and devilishly cruel." "Kittel was the one responsible for the *Kinder Aktion* in Kaunas," she claims.

As the youngest member of the Ältestenrat staff, Leah was called on frequently to deliver messages and documents to the headquarters of ghetto commander SS Obersturmbannführer Goecke. There she caught the eye of debonair SS Unterscharführer Pilgram. "He saw me working at the Ältestenrat and admired the way I could type without looking at my hands," she explains. "Every once in a while he would 'borrow' me from Elkes and have me work for him at his office. I was terrified, because I was the only Jew in the place and none of the faces looked friendly."

On March 24, 1944, Pilgram phoned and ordered Leah to report immediately to the Gestapo's ghetto headquarters. "I need you here at once," he said curtly. When she arrived, he gave her some

105

pointless task that hardly merited his urgent tone. Moments later, Leah was drawn to the office window by the blare of a loudspeaker playing brisk martial music. Looking out, she saw a fleet of canvas-covered lorries approach. German, Lithuanian, Latvian, and White Russian police units dismounted and quickly surrounded the ghetto.

"From where I stood I could see them going from house to house, yanking out the children and throwing them on the trucks. Their screams were only partly muffled by the marching music coming from the loudspeaker." When she confronted Pilgram, asking what was going on, he told her sharply that it was no concern of hers. Furthermore, he ordered, she must report again to Gestapo headquarters the following morning.

On the second day of the *Kinder Aktion* the mothers refused to go to work, and stayed home with their children. Few families had followed Lipman's advice and prepared bunkers; the others hid the children under blankets, behind couches, under beds, in attics and cellars. The SS combed through the ghetto again, house by house. In a brutal game of hide-and-seek they routed the children out and promised them candy if they would tell where other children were hidden. They warned parents they would shoot their children right in front of their eyes if they didn't reveal where their neighbours had hidden their children; they tore infants from their mothers' arms and threw them like pieces of baggage onto the waiting trucks. Those mothers who insisted on accompanying their children were invited to mount the trucks for the short one-way ride to Fort IX.

It dawned on Leah that Pilgram had ordered her to report to the Gestapo office to keep her out of harm's way. From then on, he told her, she would work for him. She pleaded with Elkes to extricate her from the situation, but instead he urged her to take the job: it would be extremely valuable, he said, to have someone working inside Gestapo headquarters. Armed with a pass issued by Pilgram, Leah reported to the dingy headquarters building. She typed Pilgram's letters to his wife, corrected his spelling, served as his translator, and delivered messages to his Lithuanian girlfriend. While the Gestapo man dallied, Leah was required to answer the telephone and greet callers with *"Heil Hitler."*

Although Leah was permitted to type ghetto lists and routine memoranda, she was not allowed to see classified documents; these Pilgram typed himself. But he was lazy and would insist that she insert the paper and carbons for him. "I always put in fresh sheets of carbon paper," she says, "so I had no trouble reading them later in a mirror. It was risky but I learned a great deal of what was going on, and passed it on to the Ältestenrat." Pilgram sometimes made suggestive remarks to his Jewish secretary, but Leah would have none of it: she reminded him that severe punishment awaited both of them if they contravened Hitler's *Rassenschande* (race defilement) laws.

Early in June 1944, Pilgram announced the imminent close of the ghetto. All of the survivors were to be sent to German labour camps. The first contingent was sent out by river freighter early in July. The members of the Ältestenrat, their families and associates, were shipped out by train on July 13. Leah's mother and brother accompanied them. Pilgram refused to let Leah say goodbye to them—"You'll see them later," he assured her. "You'll get together again in Stutthof."

Meanwhile, Leah typed the lists of those scheduled for transportation. "Towards the end, Pilgram saw that at least a thousand people were missing from the lists," she recounts. "Either they had escaped or they were hiding. He grew very angry and ordered his men to search the ghetto. They went from house to house shouting, 'We know you're hiding in there. Come out!' If no one came out, they dynamited the house. Pilgram would return to the office every evening excited and happy, exclaiming that they had found this one in the cellar, that one under the latrine. One by one, they uncovered all the hiding-places except one—they never found the bunker we built under the bathhouse."

One group of Jews, Leah says, met secretly with Pilgram and paid him a sum of money to allow them to leave the ghetto unmolested. But as they passed through the gate he was waiting for them and had them all shot.

Leah and Pilgram's Jewish housekeeper were the last Jews to be evacuated from the ghetto. They left on July 17, just a few days before the Russians broke through. On the final day Leah washed her hair, mended her clothing, and packed a few belongings in a battered suitcase. For a time she stood alone at the wire, looking longingly into the houses on the other side and wondering if now, when the guards had been withdrawn, she might not squirm through a break in the wire and lose herself in the city. All thought of escape left her, however, when some Lithuanians, who had gathered to celebrate the liquidation of the ghetto, caught sight of her and shouted, "Hey, there's one! There's a Jewess still alive. Over there, by the fence!" She turned away from the fence saying to herself, "Bloody anti-Semites. There's no place in Lithuania for a Jew to hide!"

When she returned to the office, Pilgram was waiting. "What would you do if I escaped?" she asked. "Do?" he replied. "I would hunt you down. I would shoot you in the blink of an eye."

"Today Motel, tomorrow Berel, and the next day they'll come for me." This frequently repeated Jewish saying typified the ghetto's general mood of resignation and acceptance of its fate. "There was considerable bitterness and irony too," Helen Werblunsky recalls, "but few outbursts of anger and almost no overt protest. There was an organized underground but its work was not particularly visible. The Lithuanian native population did very little to fight the Germans, and it was hard to do much without help from the outside."

The ghetto dwellers' chief form of protest was to continue with their lives. "We went to school, studied hard, attended concerts, and held meetings." Books were forbidden in the ghetto, but Helen always managed to find one. Covertly she read the works of Sholom Aleichem, and other masterworks of contemporary Yiddish literature.

Officially everyone in the ghetto was required to work, but those too old, too feeble, or too rich to do heavy work could hire a *malach* ("angel") to substitute for them. By the age of ten, Helen hired out regularly, trading her labour for food and money. "I shovelled and dug and did the most menial labour," she says. "It meant being outdoors all the time, whatever the weather. We were constantly watched, constantly under the gun. The hardest, most degrading place to work was at the airdrome."

Marching to and from work, the Jews sang songs. Some were

klopfers, ghetto hits, that youngsters like Helen hastened to memorize. One went:

> *Jewish work brigades*
> *Decked out in rags*
> *Containing our sorrows*
> *Lest our spirit sags.*
> *Marching, marching.*

As a member of Liptzer's Gestapo work brigade, Helen's father had influence, and he arranged to have her assigned to the ghetto vegetable gardens. "It was extremely hard work but at least I didn't have to leave the ghetto, and I didn't have to work with a gun pointed at me."

On the first day of the *Kinder Aktion*, Helen's mother was ill and stayed home from work. The family was now living in half a room in an unfinished apartment block; the other half was occupied by two families. Beds and couches filled the narrow space so that it was almost impossible to make one's way through the room. When the Gestapo came, Helen's mother shoved her brother behind a couch and piled pillows over him. Helen hid behind a door in the passageway. They stayed hidden all day, hardly daring to breathe. Miraculously, the searchers missed both children. But the SS were sure to return, and they would look harder next time. A safer hiding-place must be found. That night the Werblunskys put their children in a *malineh*, a hideout hastily created in a nearby room by the erection of a false wall. The next morning the children were wakened by snarling dogs.

"It's wrong to say we were discovered," says Helen. "We were betrayed. We found out later that one of the ghetto policemen gave away our hiding-place when he was threatened with death at Fort IX."

Armed SS troops ordered the two children out of their hiding-place. Helen clung tightly to her little brother, refusing to let him go when rough hands reached out for him. On command, an Alsatian leaped at her and buried its fangs in her arm. She released her grip and her brother was taken away.

"For a long time afterwards I was unable to cope with the guilt I felt for letting go of my brother. He had been put in my care and I had failed him. To this day I don't understand what happened. I don't know why they took him and didn't take me."

Yaacov Rabinovitch was determined not leave Kaunas until the Russians came. His journalistic instincts told him the Red Army could not be far away. And he knew what awaited him and his family if they were transported to labour camps; he couldn't abide the naiveté and self-delusion of those who believed Goecke's promise that there would be no more killings, that at Stutthof and Dachau they would be housed in comfortable barracks, given good clothing, and fed nourishing food.

According to Rabinovitch, about 7,500 people were still in the ghetto when Goecke ordered it evacuated in July 1944. About 3,500 of these quietly assembled at the ghetto gate for resettlement, as they were directed, but the other 4,000 refused to trust Goecke and took to hastily constructed hiding-places. Rabinovitch and his wife and daughter hid in a subterranean bunker, but a unit of the *Deutsche Grenze Polizei* (German Border Police) discovered its crudely engineered air vent. "The Gestapo and Border Police were always the last to leave," says Rabinovitch. "After the army retreated, they stayed on to supervise the final roundup. If we hadn't come out when they called us they would have dynamited our bunker." The Rabinovitchs were escorted to the gate, where they joined the crowd standing by the wire, but in the confusion they slipped away again and took shelter in an old shipping shed. "It was littered with rotted potatoes and cabbages but I knew that around the back there was a double wall. I knew because I had helped build it while working in the ghetto food depot." He and his family shared the narrow space between the real and false wall with two adult women, a teen-age girl and two children.

"There was no food. The space between the two walls was only 90 centimetres wide, leaving little room to turn around, sit, or lie down." Keeping watch through the cracks, he saw that the ghetto was in flames. As the smoke drifted into their hiding-place one of the women and her teen-age daughter panicked and ran from the shed, only to be shot down by police auxiliaries.

The flames crept closer. The smoke became unbearable. Rabinovitch shepherded the remaining women and children out of the highly combustible structure and led them to a concrete root cellar half a block away. Again the fire quickly surrounded them. The wooden door started to smoulder, its smoke making them gasp and cough. Rabinovitch kicked it off its hinges. As he looked out, he realized there was nowhere to run except into the flames.

Holding handkerchiefs to their faces, they remained huddled on the cement floor until the fire passed. Their throats were raw from the smoke, and the children pleaded for something to drink. After dark, they crept out of the cellar in search of water. There was none to find. They ate grass and slaked their thirst on the dew. "We found a burned-out house where we could cover ourselves with rubble," he remembers. "We stayed there for five days, remaining hidden during the day and going out at night to look for food and water." On the fifth day, as they were slinking by the communal bathhouse, they heard muffled voices and caught snatches of Yiddish conversation. "We found twelve Jews hidden in a double wall. We joined them for a while, but there wasn't room for all of us. Besides, it occurred to me that if I could find them, the Gestapo could also find them." Next Rabinovitch moved his brood beyond the ghetto fence to a bombed-out, burned-out section of the city. But a Lithuanian police patrol caught sight of them. The other woman and her two children were shot; the Rabinovitchs made it back to the ghetto. For the next day or two they lurked in basements and charred houses. Finally the Russians arrived.

Rabinovitch estimates that only eighty-four of the four thousand people who chose to remain in Kaunas survived the dogs, dynamite, and fire that marked the Slobodka ghetto's final stages.

Norman Salansky spent much of his childhood in hiding. Because his uncle, Chaim Lipman, had hustled his family into one of his many bunkers, Salansky escaped the *Kinder Aktion*. But from that time on the child was not allowed to venture outdoors. Although a quiet, thoughtful child, he found the restrictions on his play galling. From time to time he slipped out of the house, only to be hauled back by anxious parents and relatives.

Meanwhile, Lipman was engaged in his master project, the

construction of a huge bunker beneath the community bathhouse. He employed only six of his most trusted friends on the project, imposing stringent rules of secrecy. They began by excavating a large chamber under the bathhouse basement: they sprinkled water on the earth floor, tamped it down, installed toilets and washbasins, and furnished the room with beds, mattresses, and chairs.

This elaborate bunker was, however, only a decoy. Ten feet beneath it they dug a smaller chamber, reached by an elaborate tunnel whose entrance was concealed behind a bathhouse stove. The tunnel made its way past a series of blind alleys to a sewer pipe, and that in turn led to the ultimate hiding-place. Lipman even diverted a small underground stream to assure a convenient supply of water, and he devised an ingenious ventilation system to provide a steady supply of fresh air. But food was a problem: without refrigeration, there were few foods that could be stored for long. His solution was to stock the bunker with bag after bag of hard-dried bread. Soaked in water, it was edible; kept dry, it would last for a year. Once they entered the chamber they would have to stay until the Russians arrived—to come and go, even at night, would inevitably give away their hiding-place. The big question was when to begin their mole-like existence. The longer they delayed, the shorter their stay underground. But delay was also dangerous; there was no telling when the Nazis would strike again, making escape impossible. Soon after the bunker was completed, however, five-year-old Norman Salansky decided the question for them.

One day in mid-April, 1944, Norman was playing with a neighbour's child in the narrow space between the couches and beds that crowded the family house. Unaware of any immediate danger, Norman's father went to fetch water from a nearby well. Other family members were away at work and Lipman was out back tinkering with some device for his bunker. Suddenly *Wachtman* Kozlowski—the same Kozlowski who had precipitated the incident on Veliuona Street—appeared on the block. On seeing Norman's father leave, he decided to inspect the house. He immediately caught sight of the playing children who, frightened by his sudden appearance, let out a loud wail. Lipman heard their cries and rushed in from the backyard. Kozlowski, recognizing him for a ghetto tough and a possible member of the underground, decided to take no immediate action in case the fellow was armed. "What are those kids doing here?" he said. "Make sure you deliver them to the *Kommandantur* first thing tomorrow morning." With that, Kozlowski sauntered off, whistling as he went down the street. Lipman knew the policeman's casualness was a pose; as soon as Kozlowski was out of sight he would sprint for Gestapo headquarters. Before dawn their house would be surrounded, the children seized, and everyone in the house marched off to Fort IX. They must enter the bunker that night.

Thirty-two adults and two children made their way to the bathhouse under cover of dark, and crawled through the secret passageway into the dank underground room that now became their universe. There was no day and no night: a single electric lightbulb, its meagre power siphoned from the bathhouse circuit, was the only source of light. There were no mealtimes, workdays, or weekends. Uncles, aunts, cousins, in-laws, neighbours, and friends—they created their own society with its own rules. With no room to run and play, the children spent all their time sitting or lying on their bunks. Conversation was restricted lest someone overhear them. Time seemed endless.

From time to time they heard sounds overhead: shouts, air-raid sirens, the poom-poom of anti-aircraft guns, the thunder of exploding aerial bombs. They were proof the Germans were still in command of the terrain over their heads. One day—they later learned that it was July 31, 1944—there was a huge crash. Dust blew into the room and it became hard to breathe; there were shouts above, and a loud whirring sound as if a huge saw were slicing into the bathhouse wall. "I told everyone to remain quiet, that someone was boring their way into the bathhouse above," Lipman says. "I took a friend aside and told him it was time we reconnoitred. We opened up the passageway and made our way to the false bunker. A bomb had struck the building, collapsing its ceiling. Debris blocked our ventilation system and it was impossible to clear it without being detected. Some people were trapped in the bathhouse wreckage and the sawing we heard was part of an effort to rescue them. The question was who the rescuers were."

Slowly, cautiously, Lipman eased his way through the rubble towards the surface. He heard shouts, and listened hard to hear what the language was. It was Russian.

Down below, the bunker inhabitants gasped for breath. One by one they began to feel faint. Norman lost consciousness and his father laid him next to the ventilation pipe, where a thin trickle of fresh air still flowed into the bunker. He still remembers the shouts, the sound of rubble being removed, and the squad of Red Army men who gently hauled him to the surface. Though the light dazzled him, he stared directly into the sun, amazed that such a thing existed. After three months underground on a minimal diet he had lost the ability to walk; for six months afterwards he crawled about on all fours like a baby. He was one of only three children to survive in the ghetto until the end.

13
A New Life

On June 22, 1944, the Red Army launched its summer offensive. By July 17, the Russians had fought their way back to the outskirts of Kaunas. German resistance was fierce and it was not until July 30 that the Russians were able to re-occupy the former Lithuanian capital, forcing the Germans to retreat towards the Gulf of Danzig. Helmut Rauca fled with them.

There is no record of Rauca's activities from the time he fled Kaunas to the time he surrendered to the Americans at the war's close. Rauca is not inclined to talk about it and queries addressed to his lawyers are met by vague smiles. Horkins, who participated in Rauca's defence throughout the extradition process, believes he was sent to the front with a fighting unit, but is not clear on this point. A survivor of Auschwitz, Joseph Fuerst, claims he saw Rauca at Auschwitz, standing next to the notorious Dr. Josef Mengele, but this allegation also remains unconfirmed.

What we do know is that soon after May 7, 1945, when General Jodl signed the unconditional surrender document on behalf of the shattered German armies, Rauca was back in Saxony. For a time he was held in an internment camp for former SS and Gestapo officers at Ziegenhain, Hesse, in the American occupation zone, but on November 11, 1945, he was transferred to the American military hospital in Karlsruhe where he worked as an orderly for approximately eight months. "A hospital is a hell of a good place to make yourself scarce in," says a veteran Canadian immigration officer who was also stationed in Karlsruhe after the war. "No one goes looking for people among the sick and dying." Following his stint as an orderly, Rauca lived for a time in a hostel for homeless men in Duisburg-Hamborn, and for a year and a half he laboured as a coal miner in the Ruhr.

He left Germany from Bremerhaven on December 19, 1950, on board the Canadian Pacific immigrant ship the SS *Beaverbrae*, and arrived in St. John, New Brunswick, on December 30. His passage was aided by the Canadian Christian Council for the Relief of Refugees, which was a joint effort of the Lutheran and Catholic churches in Canada.

Rauca was one of some 38,000 displaced persons and refugees carried across the Atlantic between 1948 and 1955 on the *Beaverbrae*. The ship, a refitted German submarine tender which Canada had received as part of her war reparations, made fifty-one such voyages before being sold to a Genoese shipping company. On many of these crossings the victims of Nazi concentration camps found themselves sharing quarters with their former captors.

Rauca carried a German passport, number 0507199. He described himself as married; intended occupation, farm worker; current occupation, commercial employee. It is unlikely that he made any mention of his previous career as a secret policeman, SS sergeant, and Gestapo agent. Had he done so, there is little likelihood that the immigration authorities would have admitted him to Canada: post-war regulations forbade the entry of known Nazis. He used his own name on his ship's papers, but, curiously, gave his date of birth as November 3, 1908, instead of April 11, 1908.

Rauca worked for a year on the farm of John McElcone outside Otterville, a cosy town with a population of seven hundred and fifty in the midst of southern Ontario's tobacco-growing country. His immigration contract* only required him to spend a year as an

*The Canadian government was reluctant to accept non-British European immigrants in the immediate post-war period, particularly the thousands of refugees and displaced persons in displaced persons' camps. Nevertheless, acute shortages of skilled labour, particularly agricultural workers, caused the government to recruit in the DP camps for specific trades. The immigrant had to sign a contract stating that he would accept the work assigned to him for a minimum period of one year; at the end of the year he was free to seek other employment.

agricultural worker before he was free to seek other employment, and as soon as the 1951 tobacco crop was in he headed for Toronto. "I worked as a helper for bricklayers for several months, carrying bricks up the ladder," Rauca told the court at his initial bail hearing. "And at nights I was washing dishes at Childs [restaurant]. From then I had a job with O'Keefe Brewing Company... [but] the business slacks off and we were fired. I worked for several months in [a] china and glassware warehouse on Front Street and bought a small lunchroom on King Street...[where I] learned Hungarian food and all about paprika."

Shortly after arriving in Toronto Rauca struck up a friendship with restaurant owner William Machdanz and his wife Auguste. The friendship was to endure. Having gained experience in the food business through his lunchroom, Rauca became manager of a small banquet hall owned by Machdanz in Kitchener, Ontario, the Castle Inn at 1508 King Street East. Although it served some of the local service clubs and church groups, the restaurant was not a particularly successful venture, and it remained closed much of the time. Nevertheless, when Rauca applied for Canadian citizenship in 1956 he gave the restaurant as his home address.

On his application for citizenship, filled out in his own large hand, Rauca described himself as "stateless" although he had arrived in Canada on a German passport. He also spelled his name "Rauka" with a "k" rather than "Rauca" with a "c". The political backgrounds of applicants for Canadian citizenship are routinely checked by Canada's federal police, the Royal Canadian Mounted Police; stamped across the face of Rauca's application is an RCMP seal bearing the statement "No Record". This suggests that either the background check was extremely superficial or the seemingly insignificant change in the spelling of his name was sufficient to defeat the RCMP's records search. Six months later, when he took the oath of allegiance, he switched back again, signing his name "Albert Helmut Rauca".

In 1956 the Machdanzs sold their Kitchener restaurant and Rauca returned to Toronto. For a time he operated a dry-cleaning outlet in the midst of a burgeoning ethnic neighbourhood on St. Clair Avenue West. His longest stay, however, was in the picturesque tourist town of Huntsville, one hundred and fifty miles north of Toronto. For fourteen years, from 1959 to 1973, he was part owner and full-time operator of a main street motel.

Despite the town's reputation for neighbourliness, Rauca was scarcely known in Huntsville. Those who do remember him say he was a hard man to talk to. "He was a solitary person, he didn't mix much," says Henry Szawlowski, owner of the Sunset Inn Motel half a mile down the road from the motel Rauca once operated. "You couldn't get him to join with other motel keepers to publicize Huntsville. If I was sold out and phoned to ask if he had any vacancies, he would give me an abrupt 'no' and hang up the phone."

Anne Mill and her husband owned a motel next door to Rauca's. "When I first came to town," she recalls, "I would greet him, try to be friendly. After all, we were in the same business. All I ever got was a curt nod." Although they were neighbours for several years, their conversation seldom went beyond a brief hello.

Steinborn's Delicatessen, located in the heart of town, is an institution in Huntsville. Its counters are filled with fat German sausages, marbled meats, and delicious European breads. Its owner, Jurgen Kuehnen, is president of the area's thriving German-Canadian Club and a regular participant in all its social activities. Yet he can't remember ever meeting Rauca. "He never came to the store and he never came to any community activities," Kuehnen says. "He never joined, he never participated."

The only person in Huntsville who speaks well of Rauca is former motel owner David Dyment. A slight, grey-haired man in his early sixties, he sometimes spent long, idle winter nights having a "snort" with Rauca. In 1982, sitting on the broad porch of his expensive home overlooking the town, Dyment told a CBC documentary crew that he found Rauca "a very nice guy, very co-operative." Warming to his subject, Dyment said, "Just ask yourself who's pointing the finger at him. Rauca was a soldier. He was told what to do same as I was. Rauca was a fine man. He was very kind to my daughters when they were growing up."

Dyment's wife Lynne, who had been listening intently, suddenly exploded. "C'mon Dave, stop playing the fool," she said angrily. "You know he was a crude, chauvinist bastard. He may have been kind to your daughters and given them candies on

118

Hallowe'en, but he sure as hell didn't show any respect for your wife." Dyment began to argue but, thinking better of it, went into the house for another beer. When Lynne Dyment was calm again, she explained, "Our motel was situated almost directly across the road from Rauca's. One morning, shortly after he came to town, he was having car trouble. He knocked on our door to ask if we knew someplace or someone to fix his car in a hurry. We suggested a mechanic and then invited him in to see our place and have a cup of tea. Dave asked him if there was a Mrs. Rauca and he answered that a man was a fool to have a wife—if he wanted to give a woman a push he could always go to Toronto. How do you think that made me feel?"

By the time Rauca arrived in Huntsville, his marriage to the racially unblemished Gertraud was over; she had chosen not to accompany him to Canada but to remain on in Plauen with their two sons.* In 1956 she divorced him, and soon thereafter remarried. Her present whereabouts are unknown.

Rauca's neighbours say he lived alone in his apartment next to the motel office and showed little need for human companionship. Every winter, when business was slack, he would close the motel for a few weeks and leave town. Lynne Dyment says he vacationed in Mexico, while others had the impression he sometimes visited Lake Constance on the Swiss-German border. One year it might have been Spain. Not a man to report on his travels, he shared no slides or snapshots with his neighbours.

In 1973, the man described by his neighbours as a "loner" retired. He sold the motel he had owned jointly with Auguste Machdanz and went to live with the Machdanzs in their tidy bungalow at 96 Otonabee Avenue. After William Machdanz died in October 1980, Rauca continued to live in the house with Auguste, his old business partner.

---

*At his bail hearing Rauca testified that his wife had divorced him in 1955 or 1956, and that he kept in touch with his two sons in East Germany but that his wife had remarried. According to East German officials the former Mrs. Rauca's whereabouts are "unknown". Since the whereabouts of all East German citizens is well known to their police, either she has fled to West Germany or the East German authorities do not want her interviewed.

14
The Chase

How was Rauca found after so many years? Who betrayed him? What Nazi-hunter tracked him down? Like most Nazis who fled abroad after the war, Rauca kept a low profile. He joined no organizations, and stayed away from community celebrations because there was always a chance that someone from "the old days" might turn up and recognize him. He had few friends and confided in those as little as possible. He avoided political discussions, particularly with strangers. If there was talk of Hitler and the Third Reich, he would shift to safer subjects such as the Communist threat and Russian domination of Europe. He drank moderately, was careful not to speed on the highway, and paid parking tickets promptly.

None of the Jewish organizations played any part in his apprehension. The Canadian branch of the Anti-Defamation League of B'nai B'rith, which maintains extensive files on local anti-Semites and Fascists, first heard of Rauca on the day of his arrest. By the time the leadership of the Canadian Jewish Congress—"the parliament of Canada's Jews"—became aware of his presence in Canada, plans for his arrest were well under way.

Nor was Simon Wiesenthal, the most successful Nazi-hunter of them all, responsible for finding him. Wiesenthal admits frankly that, despite a substantial file on Rauca, he did not know that the former SS master sergeant was living in Canada. Wiesenthal was not surprised, however, by Rauca's presence here—he has claimed repeatedly that as many as a thousand alleged war criminals have found ready shelter in Canada. Over the years he has supplied

Canadian authorities with several lists culled from his massive files. In 1971, for example, he forwarded the name of a Ukrainian auxiliary policeman responsible for the murder of 10,000 Jews to the Federal Department of Justice through the Canadian embassy in Vienna. Nothing came of it. And when he visited Toronto in 1973 he told reporters he had supplied the Canadian government with a list of fifteen war criminals then living in Canada; unfortunately, he said, the government had disregarded the list.

Nevertheless, Wiesenthal had set the stage for Rauca's arrest. "I made the bridge between West Germany and Canada for the extradition of war criminals. I had talks with the West German justice minister, who agreed to apply for the extradition of the people on their list. I wrote to the [then] Canadian justice minister, Jean Chrétien, to ask if he would honour the West German extradition requests. He assured me that when a democratic government asked for the extradition of a Nazi criminal [living] in Canada, this [request would be dealt with in a] quick and non-bureaucratic manner." But Chrétien warned Wiesenthal that, although he was prepared to expedite the extradition of war criminals to democratic countries, he would refuse to return them to Communist countries in which he could not assure them a fair trial.

Who then tracked Rauca down? Did a survivor of the Kaunas ghetto recognize him while shopping in a supermarket? Did one of his former comrades betray him? The real story, much less dramatic, takes us first to East Berlin, capital of the German Democratic Republic, and then to Ludwigsburg, just outside Stuttgart, in the Federal Republic of Germany.

The Communist government of East Germany has devoted considerable effort to tracking down and punishing German war criminals. By 1981 it had tried and convicted 12,867 persons on war crimes charges: 127 had received the death penalty, 262 had been given life terms, 3,188 had received jail sentences over ten years, and 9,290 sentences under ten years. Of these, 955 were members of the Gestapo, SD, and various other German police forces. Headquarters for the East German effort is Hermann-Matern-Strasse 33/34, an old, imperial-style building a stone's throw from the Brandenburg Gate that marks the boundary between the two Berlins. On an upper storey the G.D.R.'s Chief Prosecutor of Nazi War Crimes, Gunther Wieland, has his offices. The search for Rauca began in 1948 when his name surfaced repeatedly in the interrogation of fellow officers by Nuremberg Trial prosecutors. Since Plauen, Rauca's hometown, was now part of East German territory, the prosecutor was particularly keen to track him down. He soon learned that Rauca had been interned at Ziegenhain in West Germany, but in the new Cold War atmosphere there was little chance of the American occupation authorities handing him over. It was not until 1959 that the chief prosecutor discovered Rauca had emigrated to Canada and taken up residence in Toronto. How did he learn this? I interviewed him in his office in July 1983.

"We started where Rauca had last been sighted in East Germany, in Plauen," he told me. "We were looking for people who had knowledge of him so we naturally began with his friends and relatives."

"Did that include his former wife, Gertraud?"

"Possibly," answered Wieland with a broad smile.

"His brother in Trieb?"

"Possibly." Wieland continued to smile.

"Then his family did not necessarily admire Rauca."

"Very possible," Wieland said, with a gesture that indicated the subject was closed.

But the Canadian trail led to a dead end—by 1959 the Canadian government had made it abundantly clear that it refused to extradite anyone accused of war crimes to an Iron Curtain country—so, rather than give up the search, the East German prosecutor thought it best to hand his information on to his West German opposite number.

The war was still raging and victory a distant hope when the Allies agreed that the world's future peace required the elimination of National Socialism and the punishment of the Nazi leaders. Great Britain, the Soviet Union, and the United States of America issued a joint declaration in Moscow on November 1, 1943, stating that anyone who committed war crimes was liable to be tried and punished by the states on whose territory the crime had been committed, but that the major Nazi leaders—whose crimes could not be contained within the borders of any one country—would be dealt with by new international courts created by the Allies. This joint decision was given additional legitimacy through the support of twenty-three nations who signed the Agreement on Punishment of Major War Criminals on August 8, 1945. Four categories of crime were spelled out in the agreement: Preparations for a War of Aggression, Crimes Against Peace, War Crimes, and Crimes Against Humanity.

The first two categories dealt with policies and actions that had previously been regarded as "political": seizing territory by conquest, tearing up peace treaties, substituting military force for negotiation, and creating an armaments industry capable of supporting an aggressive military policy. The War Crimes category was intended to protect the civilian population of occupied countries against murder and to prevent ill-treatment of civilians, deportation to slave labour camps, killing of hostages, plunder of public or private property, wanton destruction of cities, and devastation "not justified by military necessity."

The Crimes Against Humanity section banned the murder, extermination, enslavement, and deportation of any civilian population before or during a war. In the past, there were no international laws to prevent a nation from mistreating its own citizens. Sovereign nations were free to pass laws—as Germany did—that entitled them to treat their citizens as they pleased. Now persecution on political, racial, or religious grounds—whether or not in violation of the laws of the country—was forbidden.

Twenty-four leading Nazi figures faced trial before the International Military Tribunal in Nuremberg, the city in which Hitler had forged the Reich's racial laws and held his greatest Nazi Party rallies. After ten months of hearing evidence, the sentences were handed down on October 1, 1946. Twelve of the men in the dock, including Reichsmarschall Hermann Göring, Foreign Minister Joachim von Ribbentrop, Field Marshal Wilhelm Keitel, and the Minister for Occupied Eastern Territories, Alfred Rosenberg, received the death sentence. The rest were given sentences ranging from five years to life.

Other trials followed. Twenty-three doctors were tried for cruel and dangerous experiments on concentration camp inmates; sixteen leading jurists were convicted of perverting the essential principles of German law to suit the Nazis; senior executives of the I.G. Farben industrial empire were tried for economic plundering, exploiting prisoners of war, and employing slave labour. Similar trials were conducted by French military tribunals, and Belgium, Holland, Denmark, Luxemberg, and Norway tried their own traitors and torturers. Poland, one of the most injured countries, conducted long, careful trials of its war criminals. The Soviets, on the other hand, were thorough but brisk—it is said that a Soviet tribunal could try a group of German generals in the morning and hang them by the afternoon.

But prosecutions in the name of international law did not sit well with the German people. They looked on the trials as "victor's justice", the retribution imposed by conquerors on the vanquished: had Germany won, they argued, Roosevelt and Churchill would have stood in the dock in place of Göring, Hess, and Ribbentrop. While much of the rest of the world hailed the Nuremberg Trials as inspiring landmarks in international law, they were dismissed by a majority of the German people as political trials. Efforts at mass de-Nazification imposed by the Allies also proved counter-productive. The chief instrument employed by the de-Nazification courts was a detailed questionnaire of 131 items. Relatively innocent people who had joined the Nazi party only to protect their jobs and their families were punished if they answered the questions honestly, while Nazi leaders who had engaged in abominable crimes but passed over their misdeeds on their questionnaires were given fresh positions of authority. These ironies and contradictions made Germans cynical about Allied efforts to clean house. It was not until the responsibility for prosecuting German war criminals was returned to German authority under German law that the trials took on ethical significance for the German people.

Ludwigsburg is famous chiefly for its machine tools, ducal palaces, extravagant botanical gardens, and Hohenasperg State Prison which housed many famous war criminals while they awaited trial. Tucked away behind the prison walls, in what was once the women's wing of the prison, is the Central Office of State Judicial Authorities for the Investigation of National Socialist War Crimes. Set up in October 1958, and headed by director Adalbert Rückerl, the Office co-ordinates the search for and prosecution of Nazi war criminals. It has been particularly successful in tracking down the members of the various Einsatzgruppen who wrought such havoc in Eastern Europe. Once caught, they are turned over to the appropriate German state prosecutor.

Following Wieland's 1959 tip that Rauca had fled to Canada, West German officials intensified their search for the former master sergeant. That year the Central Office was preparing to try several of the Einsatzgruppe A officers who had so far escaped prosecution; Jäger and Schmitz were already in custody, and they would try Rauca at the same time if they could find him. But knowing that Rauca was in Canada and locating him were two different matters. With the Canadian police showing little enthusiasm for the chase, and Jäger's trial scheduled to start in Frankfurt on November 6, 1959, the Central Office soon saw that there was little hope Rauca would be captured in time. They therefore took his name off the trial list.

On June 21, 1959, discouraged by the mountain of evidence accumulating against him, SS Standartenführer Karl Jäger committed suicide in his cell at the Hohenasperg Detention Centre—about the same time that Rauca was launching himself on a new career as a motel-keeper in a pleasant northern Ontario town. Three years later Jäger's deputy, Hauptsturmführer Heinrich Schmitz, cut short his Wiesbaden trial by committing suicide just two days after Abraham Tory, his priceless diary in his hands, gave evidence against him.

The Central Office's walls are lined with elaborate charts tracing the intricate chain of command from Hitler to Himmler to Order Police, Security Police, SS, and Gestapo. Cabinet after cabinet of files and cross-files contain the names, last known addresses, ranks, and serial numbers of those who committed atrocities within and beyond Germany's borders. A swarm of clerks patiently thumb through stacks of passport applications, exit visas, and emigration documents—they may sift through a thousand before finding one that matches a name in the file.

It was in just such a routine search, conducted in 1960, that the first documentary evidence of Rauca's migration to Canada came to light: the name "Rauka" was spotted on an old passenger list of the Canadian Pacific's SS *Beaverbrae*.

The West German government immediately renewed its request for Canada's assistance in locating him. The warrant for his arrest charged that "he did aid and abet in the commission of a crime... namely the crime of murder, that is mass killings which were carried out with intent and premeditation for base motives and in a cruel manner." The official approach was first made via the German Consulate General in Toronto to the RCMP, but the Mounties turned down the request, recommending that the Frankfurt Public Prosecutor re-channel his request through Interpol. This response puzzled the West Germans—as any knowledgeable policeman knows, Interpol is active in the search for armed robbers, smugglers, forgers, and swindlers, but as a matter of policy it does not take part in the search for war criminals.

Two more years passed before the West German prosecutor wrote again to the RCMP, saying that there was good reason to believe that a Helmut Rauca, wanted for war crimes, had emigrated to Canada. The Mounties took up the chase again, but what followed was sheer bureaucratic black humour: although Rauca was living openly under his own name, drove a car, possessed an Ontario driver's licence, received an old-age pension, paid his taxes, had several bank accounts, owned a cottage, and travelled regularly on a Canadian passport, it took Canada's legendary police force another ten years to find him. Here's how RCMP Corporal Yetter, the man who eventually tracked him down, described the chase to the court at Rauca's second bail hearing on September 1, 1982.

"On the tenth of October 1972, the Department of Manpower and Immigration was requested to check their records of entry into Canada of one Helmut Rauka, R-a-u-k-a, and a reply came back that there was no record.

"On the seventeenth of November 1972, the same request was repeated and a reply came back, no record.

"Again on the twenty-seventh of November 1972, the same request was repeated and a reply came back, no record.

"On the fourth of January, 1973, the German authorities requested us, via External Affairs, to locate Mr. Rauca, and this time they provided two spellings: R-a-u-k-a and R-a-u-c-a. And he was believed to be residing in Toronto and not to have changed his name.

"On the fifteenth of January 1973, again a request for citizenship records was checked, under the name Helmut Rauca, R-a-u-c-a. No record was found.

"Again on the fifteenth of January, 1973, the Department of Manpower and Immigration were requested to search their records for entry into Canada of Helmut Rauca, spelled R-a-u-c-a. This time a reply came back that one Helmut Albert Rauca, age 42, entered Canada at St. John, New Brunswick on the thirtieth of December 1950, aboard the SS *Beaverbrae*, as a landed immigrant. His destination was stated as John McElhone, R.R. #1, Otterville, Ontario and his occupation was given as clerk."

There the trail seemed to end: three RCMP detachments, London, Toronto, and Simcoe, reported that they were unable to locate Rauca, that no one in Otterville could recall anyone by that name, and that families with the surname McElhone were unable to recall a farm worker named Rauca.

The Frankfurt state prosecutor wrote again to the RCMP on July 8, 1977, repeating his request for Rauca's apprehension on a charge of mass murder. This time he appended a note that Rauca was rumoured to be dead. The Mounties replied that they had searched the records and could find no death certificate to confirm his death. On the contrary, the old-age pension division of the Department of Health and Welfare had just confirmed that it had a file on Rauca—he was alive, in Canada, and receiving benefits. But that was all Health and Welfare was prepared to say; by law, pension files are confidential and may not be shown to anyone, not even the police.

In May 1979, the RCMP tried to trace Rauca through the Ontario Ministry of Transport's computer, hoping to find a driver's licence issued in his name. The computer responded, "no record". They tried again for variations of the surname, still without luck. Later it was discovered that the ministry was saddled with a computer program that responded only when the given names on the licence were identical with those on the information request. The police had requested a search for "Helmut Rauca" but Rauca's licence was made out to "Albert Helmut Rauca"—and the program was too "dumb" to make the connection.

On each voyage from Bremerhaven to St. John, in each boatload of Displaced Persons from the European refugee camps, there were Jews, Germans, Poles, Lithuanians, Latvians, Estonians, White Russians, Ukrainians, Romanians, Hungarians, Croatians, and Slovaks who felt that post-war Europe had nothing to offer them. The Jews couldn't bear to return to the Eastern Europe heartland of anti-Semitism; life could never again be whole for them in the towns and villages where their relatives lay in mass graves; they could never again trust their neighbours not to turn on them. The non-Jews in the camps were a mixed bag. Most were helpless, innocent people who had been compelled to work as slave labourers; now that they were free, they had no desire to trade a German mine for a Siberian *gulag*. Others, though, had enthusiastically embraced Nazism—sprinkled among them were collaborators, instigators of pogroms, SS men, Gestapo agents, members of Einsatzgruppen, and concentration camp guards.

Officially, people with Rauca's SS Gestapo background were unwelcome in Canada—the Canadian Immigration Department had laid down stringent rules against the admission of both Nazis and Communists. But once the former ally, the Soviet Union, had been unofficially redefined as our prime post-war enemy, there was considerable winking at the department's rule against Nazis. For example, in December 1947, Joe Salsberg, a member of the Ontario legislature on a fact-finding tour in Europe, wrote from Germany to Saul Hayes, the director of the Canadian Jewish Congress, that RCMP officers screened and approved "about a dozen men who had been stopped by the doctor before boarding ship because the doctor had discovered the SS mark tattooed under their armpits."

"Rauca could never have gotten past Canadian Immigration unless it was a set-up," says a retired immigration officer who served in Germany in the late 1940s. *The Belarus Secret*, a recent book by former U.S. Justice Department investigator John Loftus, reveals that U.S. intelligence agencies aided and abetted the illegal entry of thousands of Eastern European Nazi collaborators. Many of those admitted had massacred Jews and had served in SS units fighting against American troops. Their records were well known to U.S. intelligence authorities—information on them from every conceivable source was stored in central files in Stuttgart. But U.S. intelligence teams, determined to use these collaborators to organize an anti-Soviet underground, helped slip them by U.S. immigration officials by doctoring their files and omitting derogatory information.

"Most of the émigrés did not even bother to change their names, since usually all that was necessary to defeat...the filing system was a minor variation in spelling," writes Loftus. "For example, [one high-ranking] collaborator, Dr. Ivan Ermachenko, emigrated to the U.S. as Dr. John Jermaczenko, a permissible phonetic transliteration from the Byelorussian Cyrillic alphabet...into the Polish Latin alphabet....The name translation ploy was so successful that it enabled the majority of Byelorussians to escape detection by even the more antiquated filing systems of the FBI."

Similarly, the minor change in the spelling of Rauca's name served to put the police off his trail and delay his apprehension.

RCMP Corporal Wayne Frederick Yetter's chief assignment at the Mounties' Ottawa headquarters is policy development. At the specific request of Solicitor-General Robert Kaplan, however, he and other members of his department now devote a portion of their time to the hunt for war criminals. A tall, precise man whose hands reach out automatically to square up the documents on his desk, Yetter inherited the Rauca file in 1980 from a succession of headquarters-staff predecessors, and resolved to tidy it up. With the help of several of the men in his office, he searched through criminal record files, city directories, telephone books, and the licensing bureau records of all the provinces. He could find no trace of Rauca.

Then, on February 18, 1982—after searching for almost two years—Yetter checked with the passport office and the citizenship registration branch of the Department of Manpower and Immigration. Bingo! An Albert Helmut Rauca had been granted Canadian citizenship on June 12, 1956 and had been issued passport number MA 732056. Rauca had recently applied for a new passport, so the passport office had his current address—but confidentiality regulations, they told Yetter, prevented them from sharing the information with the RCMP.

Word of the passport office's obduracy was passed on to Kaplan. Appointed Solicitor-General in 1980, Kaplan is the cabinet minister answerable in Parliament for the operation of the RCMP. Like most elected politicians, the member from York Centre is a variable mixture of idealism and practical self-interest. A religiously observant Jew who conspicuously donned a *yarmulke* (skull cap) when he took his oath of office, Kaplan says he suffers a vague sense of guilt over the Holocaust; like many Jews of his generation, he believes Canadian officials could have done more to save Jewish lives had they not been so concerned with their own political safety. Now that he himself occupies a position of authority, he is determined not to pass over the issue of war crimes.

As the representative of a Toronto riding whose constituency is one-third Jewish and includes many Holocaust survivors, Kaplan found some spiritual ease and considerable political advantage in criticising the government for allowing Canada to be a haven for war criminals. As a back-bencher he made frequent speeches calling on the government to bring these fugitives to justice.

Appointed to the Cabinet, Kaplan expanded on the theme. He announced on *fifth estate*, the CBC's weekly current affairs program, that he intended to use the full authority of his office to search out war criminals. He hastened to Europe to confer with Rückerl and other chief prosecutors of Nazi crimes, and in Vienna he met with Simon Wiesenthal. To Kaplan's surprise, the interview proved stormy: Wiesenthal, never a man to mince words, berated the Solicitor-General for Canada's failure to co-operate.

Kaplan assured Wiesenthal of his determination to do his utmost now that he was Solicitor-General. To test him, Wiesenthal presented him with a fresh list of "sure-fire" names: "Let's see what you do with this," he challenged. Kaplan sought to explain the realities of Canadian law and government: despite his position as a Cabinet minister, he couldn't *order* the RCMP to undertake an investigation without a proper basis in law. The men on Wiesenthal's list had committed no crimes in Canada; as far as he

130

knew, they had not laid themselves open to deportation under Canada's immigration laws. The RCMP was reluctant to undertake investigations unless there was a clear breach of Canadian law and a reasonable chance of conviction. Canada was likely to act only in response to an official request for extradition, preferably by a western, democratic country. But Wiesenthal was too well informed to be put off: if the RCMP could employ illegal means to investigate a legitimate Canadian political party—the Parti Québécois—then surely they could find a legal way to investigate men responsible for mass murder. Seeking to salvage something from the interview, Kaplan invited Wiesenthal to visit Canada again, but the head of the Jewish Document Centre flatly refused. "I will never return to Canada," he said, "so long as it remains a haven for war criminals."

Although he defended them before Wiesenthal, Kaplan too found the legal restrictions galling. Dissatisfied, he called on the Justice Minister, Jean Chrétien, to review the legislation; there must be some way, he insisted, for the government to be more active in the pursuit of war criminals. At his urging the Justice Department assembled a high-level interdepartmental committee to study the matter. The committee concluded that extradition—based on a valid request by a democratic country—offered the only feasible means of dealing with the problem.

Meanwhile the Jewish community was growing impatient with Kaplan, and it was said by some that he just wasn't strong enough to stand up to the indifference of his Cabinet colleagues. Kaplan, troubled by the criticism, made up his mind that Rauca was not going to get away. When he learned of the passport office's refusal to give the RCMP Rauca's address, he contacted Mark MacGuigan, Minister of External Affairs. "You will recall the discussion of the ministers...on the subject of war criminals, in which we agreed and subsequently stated publicly that we would co-operate with friendly countries in extradition matters," Kaplan wrote MacGuigan on May 5, 1982. "Having taken the decision to subject [Rauca]...to surveillance, I would ask you to supply me with his address and photograph...and thus avoid frustrating Canada's ability to comply with its obligations under the Extradition Treaty." Within a few days the passport office forwarded Rauca's address and photograph to the RCMP.

15
Legal Preliminaries

On May 14, 1982, Crown prosecutor Christopher Amerasinghe was summoned to Ottawa by Don Christie, associate deputy minister of Justice. Christie told him that the RCMP had identified an alleged Nazi war criminal living in Canada; the West German government was demanding his extradition, but the case was fraught with legal uncertainties and political overtones. Before Justice gave the green light, it wanted to be absolutely certain of two things, identity and jurisdiction: the RCMP must be sure they had the right man, and Amerasinghe must be certain Canada was legally entitled to extradite him. Amerasinghe returned home, packed his bag, and took the next flight to Germany to assess the evidence accumulated by the Frankfurt State Prosecutor, Peter Bötte. When he examined the file, Amerasinghe was dismayed. Of the thirty-five depositions it contained, many were hearsay, and some of the witnesses were shaky in their identification of Rauca. This kind of evidence would never pass muster in a Canadian court.

There were, however, seven survivors of the Kaunas ghetto now living in Israel who had been eyewitnesses to the Einsatzkommando operations in the ghetto at close hand. Amerasinghe felt they would make excellent witnesses but to be certain he would have to interview them himself. He flew to Israel with an album of photographs obtained from the Berlin Document Centre in his briefcase. In Tel Aviv, police superintendent Menachem Russek, head of Israel's war crimes unit, gathered the witnesses in his office. One at a time, while the others waited in another room, they were shown the album. There were approximately one hundred pictures of the men—and a few women—in Rauca's Einsatzkommando, some in civilian clothes, most in uniforms. Five of the seven witnesses quickly picked out three passport-sized photos of a full-faced, burly young man in SS uniform as Rauca; when shown a picture of a white-haired, gaunt-faced, elderly man taken that week by an RCMP surveillance team on a Toronto street, they were less certain it was the same man. The remaining two witnesses identified one or two, but not all three, of the pictures of Rauca. The clear memory of the witnesses after forty years, the certainty with which they pounced on Rauca's pictures, is not surprising—among those gathered in Russek's office were Abraham Tory, Leon Bauminger, Alex Feitelson, Baruch Direktor, and Michael Itzchaki.

With the accounts of the eyewitnesses in hand, Amerasinghe returned to Canada confident he could make an effective case for extradition. But he was immediately faced with several unexpected problems. The first was a series of persistent telephone calls to Solicitor-General Kaplan from a Toronto radio station reporter named Jeff Ansell. The reporter had somehow learned that the West German government was requesting the extradition of a prominent Nazi war criminal; why, Ansell demanded, had no arrest been made? Who was protecting the wanted man? Ansell threatened to broadcast the story unless the war criminal was promptly taken into custody. Amerasinghe feared Rauca might run if the station aired the story. It would take only a few hours for a German-born Canadian citizen holding a valid passport to join his former comrades in Argentina, Colombia, or Paraguay.

Also, a Jewish newspaper in New York, *Vorwarts*, had learned of the story and had published a brief item reporting that Helmut Rauca had been traced to Canada. Although Amerasinghe doubted that Rauca read the New York Yiddish press, Rauca might hear of the story nevertheless, and realize the hunters were closing in.

Finally, the RCMP surveillance team, charged with keeping Rauca in sight at all times, lost track of him—the old man just disappeared. Two weeks later he reappeared, and the Mounties later learned that he had taken a brief vacation in Europe, but it was unnerving that he could leave and return without their seeing him come and go. Furthermore, the team reported, Rauca was withdrawing money from the bank and engaging in other activities that suggested he was getting ready to travel. Amerasinghe concluded that there was no time to waste; the former commander of the Kaunas ghetto must be placed under immediate arrest. Kaplan, who had been deeply concerned that the RCMP might inadvertently let Rauca get away, applauded the decision.

The decision launched Amerasinghe in a race against time. Canada's extradition act protects fugitives from being held in jail for months or years while the requesting country pokes about gathering evidence to support its charges; once the arrest is made, the Crown must proceed rapidly or risk having the case thrown out of court on grounds of unreasonable delay. "It wasn't my intention to arrest Rauca at that time," Amerasinghe says. "Under Canadian extradition law you have only forty-five days from the time you put a man under arrest to the time you must present your case in court. That didn't give us much time to gather up the evidence and review the law." Once Rauca had been arrested, a series of brief but crucial court appearances followed swiftly.

The Crown was anything but happy with the results of the first bail hearing before Justice Griffiths. No matter how high the bail, no matter how stringent the conditions, a man who had successfully evaded capture for forty years was clearly capable of giving the RCMP the slip and disappearing somewhere in South America. Amerasinghe wanted him safely in jail. On July 3, 1982, the Crown appealed before a three-judge panel of the Federal Court of Canada to quash Griffiths' bail order. The appeal was dismissed. Griffiths had made no error in granting Rauca bail, said the federal judges.

Ironically, although Rauca was free to leave prison on bail, he chose to remain behind bars. "Raising the money was not the problem," said William Parker, an experienced criminal lawyer who had joined Horkins in Rauca's defence. "But reporting daily to the RCMP makes it all too easy for the Jewish Defence League to pick up his trail. Not that my client fears for himself, but he does not wish to create difficulties for his friends and neighbours." So Rauca stayed in Toronto's dingy lockup for over a year, assigned to the hospital ward because of his age and a minor heart condition. He spent his time reading and rereading a stack of paperbacks borrowed from the prison library, and left only for brief, heavily guarded court appearances.

Meanwhile, Amerasinghe was pursuing his evidence around the world. In Israel he arranged to have all seven witnesses make depositions before magistrates in Tel Aviv and Jerusalem courts.

In Moscow, he found himself engaged in his own small-scale version of the Cold War with the Soviet Union's Procurator General. Amerasinghe was determined to bring back to Canada an original copy of the infamous Jäger Report. Written December 1, 1941 by Rauca's superior officer, Colonel Karl Jäger, the report is a cold-blooded catalogue of the killing operations conducted by Einsatzkommando 3, Einsatzgruppe A, throughout Lithuania.

Photocopies of the Jäger report are in every war crimes archive in the world, but Amerasinghe was concerned that, without reference to the *original*, the authenticity of photocopies could be challenged in court. The Russians, though, were not in a mood to co-operate. Their Procurator General pointed out that Canada had six times refused to extradite Soviet citizens convicted *in absentia* by Soviet courts for war crimes. The Soviets were particularly peeved that Canada had not extradited Haralds Puntulis, convicted of war crimes by the Latvian Socialist Soviet Republic in 1965.*

"I told them the Soviet Union did not have an extradition treaty with Canada and that was something they had to sort out at the political level," Amerasinghe says. "I was interested only in the Rauca case." As one prosecutor to another, the Procurator General understood Amerasinghe's point of view, but the Jäger Report was too valuable to be turned over to a foreign country. The copy in the Vilnius vault—the fourth of the five copies forwarded by Jäger to his superiors—is the only one to have survived the war and its aftermath. It could be made available to Canada only if it remained in the custody of the Soviet ambassador in Ottawa. Amerasinghe readily agreed.

In Germany, Amerasinghe encouraged Peter Bötte to revise the

*Puntulis was convicted of treason *in absentia*; for details see Appendix.

charges against Rauca from the relatively ambiguous "aiding and abetting in the murder of 10,500 Jews" to five indictments charging Rauca directly with the murder of 11,584 Lithuanian Jews—a charge more consonant with Canadian law.

One last piece of evidence still needed to be put in place. At the original bail hearing, Rauca had testified that he'd been in Prague on a counter-espionage course during the fall and winter of 1941, that he hadn't reached Kaunas until February, 1942—well after Operation Intellectuals, Operation Kozlowski, and the Big Operation. In case the eyewitness identification faltered, Amerasinghe needed concrete proof that Rauca had in fact been in Kaunas on the dates described in the charges. He also wanted irrefutable proof that the Plauen policeman who filled out the Race and Settlement form, the SS master sergeant who stood on the mound in Vilijampole, and the man who lived on Otonabee Street were indeed one and the same.

Amerasinghe found his evidence in several yellowed pieces of paper stored in the archives of Yad Vashem, the Holocaust museum in Jerusalem. One, addressed to the Gestapo by the Kaunas Ältestenrat, was a request for the delivery of a load of firewood; the recipient had written "Request granted" and countersigned the document. The other was a letter from the Gestapo to the Lithuanian police commander warning him that his men were exacting bribes from Jews before killing them; the money, the writer complained, was being pocketed instead of being put into Gestapo coffers. Both pieces of paper bore Rauca's signature, and both were dated during the time Rauca claimed to have been in Prague.

To nail down the identification, Yetter presented the RCMP's top handwriting expert, Sergeant Bob Fawcett, with the cancelled cheques and driver's licence seized in Rauca's home and asked him to compare them with the handwriting on Rauca's Race and Settlement form. He also asked for a comparison with the Yad Vashem documents. Fawcett reported that the writing on all three sets of documents *seemed* to be by the same person, but to be certain he needed to see the originals. There was no time for further correspondence; Fawcett packed a bag, flew to Berlin and Jerusalem, and returned to Canada the night before he was scheduled to give evidence at the extradition hearing. His conclusion: the handwriting on all three sets of documents was by the same person.

Armed with a new set of charges and a fresh batch of depositions, Amerasinghe was determined to keep Rauca under lock and key. He directed Corporal Yetter to swear out a new set of complaints, before Chief Justice Gregory T. Evans, charging Rauca with five separate counts of murder. The original charge of "aiding and abetting in the murder of 10,500 persons on or about the 28th day of October, 1941 at Kaunas, Lithuania" was revised to read, "On or about the 28th and 29th days of October, 1941 the said Helmut Rauca did commit the murder of approximately 9,200 persons by selecting the said persons on the 28th day of October in the Square of the Democrats in the ghetto of Kaunas and having them conveyed to a place called the 'Small Ghetto'. . . from whence they were conveyed the following day to Fort IX where they were shot in rows on the edge of prepared mass graves."

In addition, Rauca was charged with the murder of the 534 persons removed from the ghetto on August 18, 1941 in Operation Intellectuals; the murder in early September, 1941, of an unknown person in the incident over the silver fork (Operation Valuables); the murder of 1,845 people arrested on Veliuona Street and removed to Fort IX where they were "fusilladed" (Operation Kozlowski); and charged finally, "that between the 18th day of November, 1943 and the 25th day of December, 1943. . . the said Helmut Rauca. . . jointly with two other SS personnel shot and killed the son of the Jewish Chief Rabbi, Doctor Nachman Shapiro, his wife, his twelve-year-old son, and his mother, personally killing at least one of them by firing his pistol into the back of the head of one of the said victims, thereby committing the murder of the aforesaid four persons."

The new charges required that Rauca—despite the fact that he had chosen to remain in custody—be re-arrested and produced before the court. Since the charges were new, Rauca's lawyer, William Parker, had to make a fresh application for bail.

The new bail application was heard before Associate Chief Justice William D. Parker of the Ontario Supreme Court (no relation to William Parker, Rauca's lawyer) on September 1, 1982. Step by step, Amerasinghe recounted the horrors inflicted on the Jewish community of Kaunas during the German occupation, reviewed the deposition of witnesses, and gave a detailed account of the long chase that had led to the accused's eventual arrest. He argued that bail is rarely granted in extradition cases and that Canada had a special obligation under the terms of its 1979 extradition treaty with West Germany to deliver the accused. Canada, he said, could not risk losing him again.

Horkins, in turn, argued that the same principle that applied in common criminal cases held true for his client. "A Canadian citizen's right to bail is enshrined not only in the Bill of Rights but in our Charter of Rights," he said. "It is not diminished by the treaty obligations that Canada has entered into." His client, he insisted, was subject only to the usual conditions for bail.

After hearing the arguments, Justice Parker denied the application for bail, ruling that "Not only is a great deal more evidence relied on [than at the earlier bail hearing], but the evidence is much stronger.... In addition the applicant is now charged with five counts of murder instead of one count of aiding and abetting.

"Considering the enormity of the crimes with which the respondent is accused, I am not satisfied that this is a proper case for granting bail. The temptation to flee is much greater now that the applicant has learned of the new charges and heard the evidence against him." The choice of whether he would remain in prison or leave it was no longer Rauca's. He would remain behind bars until the extradition issue was decided.

Also in the courtroom that day was Bert Raphael, a Toronto lawyer active on several Canadian Jewish Congress committees. Raphael had been retained by the Congress to request the court's permission to intervene in the Rauca case: as the acknowledged representative of Canada's Jews, Raphael argued, Congress leaders had a special interest in the case and a special understanding of its background and meaning; moreover, a CJC legal committee had made a study of Canadian legislation concerning war crimes, so Congress lawyers possessed special legal expertise that would benefit the Crown. But permission to intervene—granted frequently in the United States—is rarely allowed in Canada, and almost never unless the Crown prosecutor agrees.

In this case the Crown prosecutor, Amerasinghe, was bitterly opposed to Congress intervening. His objections were twofold: first, he was concerned that he might lose control of the case—he trusted his own performance but feared that a chance comment, an unfortunate word by Congress lawyers, might turn a sympathetic judge hostile; secondly, he was concerned that it would create a bad precedent—if partisan groups were allowed to intervene in extradition cases, on either side, the courts might be turned into a political arena.

When Raphael sensed the depth of Amerasinghe's opposition he decided to withdraw his petition. He was to renew it another day, in another court.

The eagerness of the Canadian Jewish Congress to intervene in the Rauca case was not based on any lack of confidence in Amerasinghe, but on the conviction that no non-Jew could fully comprehend how deeply Jews felt about the Holocaust, or could be as zealous in the pursuit of the perpetrators. They were also spurred by their need to silence critics within their own ranks who accused them of being a do-nothing organization—a charge that had rankled for years.

Despite strenuous efforts, the Canadian Jewish Congress had been unable to persuade the Canadian government to admit more than a handful of the Jews seeking refuge from Nazi persecution between 1933 and 1945. In this they were no more successful than the Jewish communities of the United States, England, and most Latin American countries: anti-Jewish sentiment ran high in those years, and few people in the government and civil service were willing to risk helping Jews. The Congress, committed to "quiet diplomacy" as the only effective means of dealing with government, was sharply criticized by those Jews who saw mass demonstrations and political action as more effective ways to change government policies.

In the post-war period the Congress did battle with those who sought to limit the immigration of the Holocaust's survivors. In concert with Protestant and Catholic church groups, they pressured the Canadian government to receive the unfortunate victims of the war in Europe. In 1947 the doors opened a crack and the first trickle of refugees arrived from the displaced persons camps. The CJC knew some ex-Nazis and war criminals were slipping into the country along with the innocent refugees, but in their view this was no time to ask the government to pick and choose; the emphasis must be on keeping the immigration doors open and rescuing the living, rather than on avenging the dead. There would be time to deal with the war criminals later.

"Later" proved to be a long time.

For more than thirty years the CJC politely but firmly prodded successive ministers of justice to take legal action against those deemed guilty of war crimes. From time to time delegations visited Ottawa with lists of names and addresses forwarded by Jewish organizations in Europe and Israel. But Canadian officials were cool: experience, they contended, had shown such lists to be useless; the names and addresses would be hopelessly inaccurate; by now memories must be fading, and witnesses dying; much of the so-called evidence would be hearsay and inadmissable in a Canadian court. Moreover, most of the requests for extradition came from Soviet-bloc countries, and many Canadians would find it distasteful to hand people over to the Communists. Congress leaders understood all these difficulties—but they believed they could have been overcome if only government officials had cared more, if only they had felt as Jews did about the Holocaust. But they sensed that the Holocaust was regarded as an exclusively Jewish obsession—and not a particularly attractive obsession, at that. Canadian political leadership was largely apathetic; unless politicians represented ridings with a significant body of Jewish voters, they had little to gain by pursuing the issue. And Canada's half-million Jews are vastly outnumbered by several million non-Jewish post-war immigrants—from the Baltic countries, Yugoslavia, Hungary, Romania, and the Ukraine—who would bitterly oppose any effort to identify their comrades as war criminals.

Outnumbered and outgunned, Congress formed a Holocaust Remembrance Committee which sponsored annual Holocaust memorial services. It called on its legal committee to study ways in which the Canadian government could be prompted to action, and to enquire whether, if, and how charges could be laid against alleged war criminals under existing Canadian laws, or what amendments would be required under the criminal code. Year after year, the committee reported that the problem was difficult and that, on the whole, Canada's criminal code was not suited to the prosecution of crimes committed by foreign nationals in foreign countries.

This wasn't good enough for the most militant of the survivors— those who still bore a concentration camp number tattooed on their forearms, those who had survived the Nazi occupation of Lodz, Warsaw, Kaunas, or Vilnius, those whose wives, children, mothers and fathers had been buried in the pits at Fort IX or cremated in the ovens of Auschwitz. They wanted to do more than build memorials to the dead. They wanted the guilty punished. In their bitterest moments they accused the Congress of being a Canadian version of a collaborationist *Judenrat*.

The Congress could not ignore such criticism; it might be unfair, but it rankled nevertheless. Its leaders, and particularly its then-president, McGill University law professor Irwin Cotler, ached to enter the Rauca case—to represent an aggrieved Jewish people in the courts of the nation, and to claim a share of the credit for the extradition of the first Canadian citizen to be charged with war crimes.

16
Extradition

Extradition is a time-honoured, well-recognized procedure adopted by most countries to facilitate the surrender by one state of a person accused or convicted of a serious crime within the jurisdiction of another state. The procedure is initiated by the requesting state and may be agreed to or denied by the state to which the fugitive has fled.

Each nation may choose or refuse to sign a formal extradition treaty with any other nation. In Canada that choice is made by the Cabinet as part of its treaty-making powers, without the need to consult Parliament. The government has chosen, for example, not to negotiate treaties with Soviet-bloc countries on the grounds that returned fugitives might not be given a fair trial.

Canada's Extradition Act, which has been in place for more than a hundred years, sets out the procedure by which fugitives may be extradited. If the executive—normally the Minister of Justice—looks favourably on the extradition request, the fugitive must first be heard in Canadian courts to determine that the request is not frivolous, that the evidence is strong enough to merit a trial under our rules of evidence, and that the crime in question would be deemed a crime in Canada: for example, certain economic activities which are serious crimes in the Soviet Union are regarded as commendable forms of private enterprise in Canada. The act specifically rules out extradition for political activities or membership, unless the political act takes the form of violence against a state we support and with which we have signed an extradition treaty.

The final decision, however, rests with the Cabinet. Even if the court rules against a fugitive and orders him extradited, the Minister of Justice may set the decision aside. The minister's decision cannot be appealed, nor is he obligated to explain it.

The extradition hearing for Albert Helmut Rauca, postponed several times, finally got under way on October 12, 1982 before Chief Justice Gregory Evans of the Supreme Court of Ontario, in the white marble and fumed-oak courthouse on Toronto's University Avenue that has seen so many dramatic trials. The large number of Holocaust survivors who swarmed the corridors and crowded the gallery amplified the tension, and security was extremely tight. Uniformed police officers electronically frisked everyone entering the court, and searched briefcases and handbags. Reporters, usually admitted with a nod, were required to produce their press credentials. In the courtroom, a row of RCMP officers in plainclothes formed a human barrier directly behind the prisoner's box, while uniformed provincial policemen stood at the rear, carefully eyeing the audience.

On the street outside the courthouse, the Jewish Defence League paraded. As they marched, they chanted in cadence, "Who do we want? Rauca! How do we want him? Dead!" Their local spokesman, Meir Halevi, told reporters that if the courts didn't take care of Rauca, the JDL would. An older, more sedate group of Jewish citizens, representing the Holocaust Remembrance Committee, marched separately, carrying placards calling on the Canadian government for action on war criminals.

When Rauca, handcuffed to a police officer, was first led into court, a wave of anger swept through the courtroom. There were strangled cries of "Butcher!" "Murderer!" Chief Justice Evans would have none of it; he warned the court sternly, though not unsympathetically, that he would deal quickly and severely with any disturbance. "This is a hearing; it is not a picnic," he said. "I expect you to behave properly."

The Crown's task was to prove Rauca's identity, persuade the judge that the court had jurisdiction, and demonstrate to the court that the crimes with which Rauca was charged by the West Germans were also crimes in Canada. Finally, the Crown needed to convince the Bench that there was sufficient evidence, not to prove guilt beyond a reasonable doubt, but to establish a *prima facie* case against the accused.

Amerasinghe came well prepared. He presented three affidavits collected in Germany from former Gestapo officers who had served with Rauca in Kaunas and remembered him as the big, beefy fellow who had commanded the Gestapo operations in the ghetto. The depositions from the seven Israeli witnesses read like a chronicle of the Holocaust: Tory, Bauminger, and Direktor detailed Rauca's role in Operation Intellectuals; Direktor related the incident of the silver fork; Feitelson and Tory described the punitive operation on Veliuona Street. Feitelson and Itzchaki testified that they had seen Rauca participate in the murder of Dr. Shapiro and his family. As for the Big Operation in Democracy Square, Rauca was identified by Tory, Feitelson, Itzchaki, Direktor, and others as the man on the mound who had directed people to the right or to the left.

While all these statements were being read, one man sat quietly in the courtroom, waiting to be called to the witness stand. He was Abraham Ric, the only Kaunas ghetto survivor living in Canada whose evidence was presented to the court. Ric, who prefers not to talk about the years of horror during the Nazi occupation of Kaunas, was persuaded by friends to testify at the Rauca hearing. He owed it to the dead, they told him. Ric, his wife, his two sisters, his mother, and his mother-in-law were among those waved to the right by Rauca in Democracy Square. After spending the night in the Small Ghetto, they were marched the six kilometres to Fort IX. On reaching the mass extermination site, Ric testified, he saw people "running naked and half-naked, including children, who were thrown into ditches filled with lime. . . . Lots of German soldiers were standing around and they were shooting people there." While the guards were busy elsewhere Ric, followed by his older sister, broke free from the crowd and ran for a nearby sewer-pipe. Before they could reach it, a bullet hit Ric in the back, but he managed to keep running. Scrambling on all fours, the pair escaped into the dark tunnel. They could hear the voices of the patrols searching for them, but no one looked into the sewer. They waited until nightfall—huddled together in fear, cold, and pain—and then made their way back to the Large Ghetto.

But the most damaging evidence came from the Nazis themselves, as Amerasinghe placed in evidence a certified copy of the Jäger report. In orderly columns, the report lists the numbers of men, women, and children murdered in each of the Einsatzkommando's operations in Lithuania. It begins in late June 1941 with the "executions carried out by Lithuanian partisans, under my directive and by my orders," and continues, community by community, *Aktion* by *Aktion*, to the end of November, by which time Jäger boasts that his men have rid Lithuania of 137,346 Jews. The report lists the massacre of thousands in Marijampole, Panevezys, and Rokiskis; it details the "mercy killing" of 544 mental patients in Aglona; there are entries for Operation Intellectuals and Operation Kozlowski. Most important for Amerasinghe's case, it lists the 9,200 victims of the *Grosse Aktion* in Democracy Square on October 29, in what Jäger described as a "purging of the ghetto of redundant Jews." Jäger was a meticulous bookkeeper and records-keeper; each date and number in his account tallies with the testimony offered by eyewitnesses.

The efficient execution of such operations, Jäger explained to his superiors, was primarily a matter of organization. The Jews had to be collected in one place. Pits had to be dug in suitable locations not more than four or five kilometres from the collection point, since the Jews had to be marched to the execution site; motor transport was rarely available. He was short of personnel and the job had to be completed within twenty-four hours. There were occasional attempts to escape which had to be met by his men. "What problems and nerve-racking labour this entailed," he complained. In comparison to the "tremendous difficulties" encountered elsewhere, he described the operation in Kaunas as a "salute-firing", the equivalent of shooting fish in a barrel. He reported proudly to his superiors in Riga and Berlin, "Today I am able to state that the objective of solving the Jewish problem for Lithuania has been achieved. . . . There are no further Jews in Lithuania excepting the Jewish labourers and their families. . .in Kaunas *circa* 15,000, in Vilnius *circa* 15,000." Much as he regretted the continued survival of these Jews, they were engaged in ghetto industries, Jäger wrote, and his wish to eliminate them was strongly opposed by the military and civil administration. As an

145

interim measure he recommended the immediate sterilization of Jewish male labourers to prevent procreation. "In case a female Jew becomes pregnant nevertheless, she will be liquidated."*

Early on, Parker and Horkins let it be known that they would not contest the facts—and they readily admitted that the man in the dock was the Helmut Rauca named in the West German warrant. But they insisted that he was protected by Canada's new Charter of Rights and Freedoms: "Every citizen of Canada has the right to enter, remain in, and leave Canada." As Parker said to the court, "My Lord... we don't propose to argue on [Rauca's] behalf that there is not sufficient material in front of you to order extradition on the factual ground. Our only position is that there are certain citizen rights now that arise out of the Constitution of Canada, and we propose to deal with those."

The hearing, which had been expected to last a week, took only two days because of the defence's strategy. Parker and Horkins chose not to challenge any of the Crown's depositions or produce any witnesses of their own. They presented no character witnesses, no one who might substantiate Rauca's claim that he had not arrived in Kaunas until February 1942; they called no one to challenge the Crown's authorities on German law; they barely cross-examined the Crown's handwriting expert. But, as Parker was careful to point out, this didn't mean Rauca was admitting guilt: "My client instructs me to say that we are not the person guilty of these crimes. If these crimes occurred, they were not committed by us."

The entire case, then, turned on Section 6 of the 1982 Constitution Act, and on an interpretation that many lawyers found "clever" and "appealing" but not likely to impress the Court: that Rauca, as a Canadian citizen, was entitled to enter, remain, or leave Canada as he chose. While other rights specified in the constitution—assembly, speech, privacy—are relative and may be limited by legislation, Parker argued, mobility rights are enshrined

*The first page of the Jäger report indicates that five copies were circulated. One was undoubtedly sent to Jäger's superior officer, SS Brigadeführer Dr. Stahlecker in Riga, who incorporated much of the material into his second summary report forwarded to Berlin on October 15, 1941. The Stahlecker report, known to students of the Holocaust as International Military Tribunal Document No. L-180, was a damning piece of evidence at the Nuremberg trials.

in the supreme law of the land and can be modified only by formal constitutional amendment. Furthermore, the new Constitution overrides Canada's extradition treaties. In any event, he added, the 1979 treaty with West Germany was a poor one because it lacked what all good extradition treaties should have, reciprocity. West German law forbids the extradition of German nationals; if a German citizen commits a crime in Canada and makes it back to his homeland, he won't be returned to Canada, but will be tried in Germany before a German court on evidence supplied by Canada.

The defence further argued that the mass murders of which Rauca was accused had been committed in Lithuania, well beyond the territorial limits of pre-war Germany: Lithuania was not Germany, nor did German law extend to the conquered territories. "It's fair to say to Your Lordship...that there was no system of laws in Lithuania at the time we're talking about. . . . And it cannot be said. . . that German law applied there." While the Federal Republic may claim jurisdiction over German nationals who saw wartime service in Lithuania, Canada is under no obligation to recognize that claim. Indeed, Canada, like all Common Law countries, takes a strongly territorial view of crime—those accused of criminal acts must be tried in the same jurisdiction in which the crime was committed—and Canada itself claims no jurisdiction over crimes committed by Canadians beyond its borders except in a few special "international" cases such as hijacking, piracy, and mutiny.

The defence did concede "that if the depositions...are true, then [Rauca] must be punished"; his trial, however, should be that of a Canadian citizen, and held in Canada. To those who asked, "Under what law should he be tried?" Parker suggested that the 1946 War Crimes Act or the Geneva Convention Act of 1949 would do nicely. If neither of these acts was appropriate, then Parliament would be obliged to pass new legislation. Such a new act, Parker suggested, could be named after Rauca.

Then it was Amerasinghe's turn.

Disarmingly quiet, and painfully polite, Amerasinghe systematically attacked Parker's arguments and called for a traditional interpretation of Canada's extradition laws. The Constitution had never been intended to serve as a shield for wrongdoers. The

Charter created no new law and no new rights; Canadian citizens had always enjoyed the right to remain in Canada and extradition laws had always infringed that right. No right is without limit; all rights set out in the Charter were subject to "such reasonable limits prescribed by law as can be demonstrably justified in a free and democratic society." The key issue was whether extradition imposed a reasonable or an unreasonable limit.

On November 4, after considering the issues for three weeks, Chief Justice Evans handed down his judgment. He was not persuaded by the arguments offered by the defence. He was not disturbed, for example, by the lack of reciprocity in Canada's treaty with the Federal Republic of Germany: "Treaties are agreements between sovereign nations which are not subject to review by the courts. One assumes that the Canadian government was aware of the absence of reciprocal arrangements...when the treaty was signed." There was no question that extradition did interfere with a citizen's right to remain in Canada, he ruled, but such a restriction was reasonable and justified in a free and democratic society. He dismissed the argument that Germany had no jurisdiction over crimes committed in wartime Lithuania: at the time the alleged murders were committed, Lithuania was under *de facto* control of Hitler's Germany—"Between 1941 and 1944, while the Germans were in occupation of Lithuania, German law applied to all persons in Lithuania."

Hardly pausing for breath, the Chief Justice dismissed the defence suggestion that Rauca be tried in Canada under the existing legislation. "In my opinion, the Geneva Conventions Act and the War Crimes Act have no application." As for Parker's suggestion that Parliament enact new legislation to cover old war crimes, Evans pointed out that in Canada Parliament is supreme and cannot be commanded by the courts; and that, in any event, the enactment of retroactive legislation is repugnant to our system of law.

As for the crimes in question, Evans was satisfied that there was enough evidence to commit Rauca for trial. "There is the direct evidence from former associates that Rauca was in Kaunas during the relevant period; that he was a member of the Gestapo and the officer in charge of the Jews under the command of Karl Jäger."

148

Evans said he found the evidence of the five Israeli eyewitnesses who had identified Rauca from his photograph as the person involved in the executions highly convincing. An RCMP handwriting expert had also identified the man in court as the SS officer whose file was in the Berlin Document Centre, who must have been in Kaunas in 1941. There was sufficient evidence, he concluded, to make a case on all five counts.

"I accordingly direct . . . the fugitive, Helmut Rauca, to surrender into custody at the nearest convenient prison, there to remain until surrendered to the Federal Republic of Germany or discharged according to law." With that, the Chief Justice swept up his papers and withdrew to his chambers.

Rauca, who stared fixedly ahead while the judge was reading his decision, showed no emotion when the proceedings ended. He stepped quietly from the box, meekly extended his wrist to be handcuffed, and walked out briskly. A buzz of satisfaction could be heard in the courtroom. Spectators rose and congratulated each other as if they had witnessed some great historic event; newsmen rushed off to file their stories or stand before their TV cameras. In the corridor, a cluster of lawyers gathered to discuss Evans' judgment: "Typical Evans." "No surprises, no far-out interpretations." "Right down the middle of the alley where it will be impossible to attack." "Historic. It will probably be the precedent for all future Charter cases."

Under the Extradition Act, Horkins and Parker had fifteen days in which to apply for a writ of *habeas corpus* before their client was surrendered to the requesting state. The writ was denied on November 22, opening the way for an appeal before the five-member Ontario Court of Appeal. That appeal was heard on February 12, 1983.

Both sides reiterated their original arguments—although by now they were considerably polished. The situation was complicated, however, by the presence of three black-robed Canadian Jewish Congress lawyers at the Crown's bench. The Congress had again applied for permission to intervene—this time to the Appeals Court—and had been given leave on condition that it limit itself to two legal issues: whether the extradition order was a violation of

149

Rauca's right to remain in Canada under the Canadian Charter of Rights; and whether the Federal Republic of Germany had jurisdiction over crimes committed in wartime Lithuania.

The CJC lawyers, Bert Raphael of Toronto, Irwin Cotler of Montreal, and David Matas of Winnipeg, found themselves in a legal strait-jacket. They had no wish to argue against the validity of the West German extradition request, yet what if the request were denied?; what if the courts decided that extradition was an infringement on Rauca's rights under the Charter and Rauca went free? Then—under existing interpretations—there would be no legal means by which he could be brought to justice.

In fact, the Congress was far from satisfied with extradition as the sole means of bringing war criminals to trial—if only they could be tried in Canada! But the Congress couldn't urge this without coming dangerously close to the defence position, namely, that Rauca could only be tried in Canada. It compelled them to argue that charges could be laid in Canada under the War Crimes Act or the Geneva Conventions Act, although both acts were passed well after Rauca had allegedly committed his crime. They argued that this did not mean that he would be punished retroactively, i.e. for acts that were not crimes at the time they were committed, for—as they pointed out—the Nazis had never dared revise the criminal code to make the killing of the deformed, the defective, and the insane legal. Although racial laws had been passed barring Jews from participation in government, business, university, and the arts, there were no laws *legalizing* the extermination of Jews. The killing of Jews remained a *de jure* crime in Nazi Germany although it is doubtful if anyone would have been prosecuted for atrocities had Hitler *won* the war. As a result, Congress found itself trying to argue simultaneously for Rauca's extradition and for his trial in Canada.

The court noted the contradiction. "The intervenant...sought to take an inconsistent position...and to argue that the appellant could be prosecuted in this country," said the five justices in their final opinion. "[The Congress's] interest seemed to be in what would happen to the appellant if extradition were denied. That, of course, is not a matter which is before us. This would only become a viable question if extradition is denied."

But the court did not intend to deny extradition. It found that, during the time the German civil administration was in operation, there was no other government in power in Lithuania. Consequently the German criminal code applied to all German nationals in Lithuania between 1941 and 1944. According to experts in German law, the Reich survived the collapse of 1945 and continues to exist in the form of today's Federal Republic of Germany. Thus the requesting state was not just the "legal successor" to the Reich but was identical to it, even though its boundaries had been altered. West Germany did, therefore, have clear jurisdiction in the Rauca case.

As for trying Rauca in Canada, the appeals court agreed with Evans that there was no appropriate law under which to try him. The Geneva Conventions Act of 1949 states that it is the universal duty of all signatories to the Conventions to search for and arrest suspected war criminals and to try them or arrange for their extradition. The judges stated, however, that "not only is the Geneva Conventions Act not a statute of general application, but it is a piece of substantive law which does not have a retroactive effect"; in other words, it could well apply in future wars but it does not apply to past wars. The War Crimes Act of 1946 provides for trial, by a military court, of soldiers or civilians who commit atrocities against Canadian troops: "The War Crimes Act...by its very terms does not cover the [Rauca case] where the crimes were not committed against Canadian citizens," the court concluded.

In support of Evans' judgment, the appeals court found that there was no alternative to extradition and that extradition did not constitute an unreasonable limit on Rauca's rights. His sole remaining recourse, an appeal to the Supreme Court of Canada, was filed on April 22 and a court date was set for June 20.

But on May 12 Rauca abandoned this plan and dismissed his lawyers.

Why did he throw in the sponge?

Horkins admits his client's action took him by surprise, but says he supposes that Rauca "had been leaning that way for some time." The man had been in continuous custody for almost a year and still had a long way to go; perhaps he wanted to move things ahead, to come before a German court where he could deal with the evidence, with the facts, instead of with constitutional issues.

But hadn't the defence deliberately avoided dealing with facts, choosing instead to rely on the constitutional issue?

Horkins says it wasn't a matter of avoiding the facts. The defence hadn't been able to present its own evidence and cross-examine witnesses because, in an extradition proceeding, the Crown was not obligated to produce its witnesses in court; it need only present depositions. "Rauca has a defence to the charges, and witnesses to call on his behalf. It's not a case of: 'I was in the chain of command and did what I was told.' It's a denial as firm and fixed as any I have dealt with as counsel for the defence."

Horkins, who frequently visited his client in jail, says he got to know him fairly well and developed "a fair amount of respect" for him. "Just trying to project myself into his shoes—it was a terribly difficult thing to be confronted with at his stage in life, when he had no family or friends to help him; to be picked out of his backyard one afternoon and held in jail for a year." And Rauca resented the allegations made against him. His attitude, Horkins said, was, "How can they say these terrible things about me, and how could I find myself in this situation?"

Rauca did not deny to Horkins that he was a member of the SS. "It was not a period of his life he was particularly proud of, but he was far from ashamed of it. He was proud of his career, proud of having worked his way up from a cop on the beat to investigative sergeant." In Horkins' view, Rauca's advance to the rank of SS master sergeant in the *Sicherheitsdienst* and membership in an Einsatzgruppe was propelled partly by his own driving ambition and partly by political forces over which he had no control—like Himmler's centralization of the German police forces, and the outbreak of war. "From being a cop in a local police force, all of a sudden he finds himself part of the state police and member of an Einsatzgruppe in Lithuania." But Rauca does claim that he had little contact with the ghetto, and that he wasn't in Kaunas when most of the atrocities happened.

Then how could witness after witness identify him as the man on the mound that day of the *Grosse Aktion*? How could they pick out his picture from an album of a hundred photos?

Horkins had asked the same questions. Rauca's reply, he says, was, "How would these people know me?" He insisted that he had been chiefly involved in counter-espionage, and most of his activity during that stage of war was to flush out Soviet partisans, an activity which kept him away from Kaunas much of the time. He had little contact with the ghetto. He couldn't explain how the ghetto-dwellers could connect him with events in the ghetto.

Then how did his signature come to be on a request for wood submitted during the period he claimed to have been in Prague?

Rauca's explanation was that he might have countersigned the form at some later date in an effort to catch up with paperwork.

What of the depositions by three of his former fellow officers in Kaunas, identifying him as head of the Gestapo for the ghetto?

"They named Rauca during their interrogation because they believed him to be dead, so it wouldn't matter if they blamed him instead of themselves," says Horkins. "That's the only way Rauca can explain it."

Justice Minister Mark MacGuigan signed the extradition papers on May 17, 1983, and shortly thereafter Rauca, in the custody of two German policemen, was flown to Frankfurt to stand trial before a German tribunal. On September 28 he was charged in a Frankfurt court with the murders of more than 11,500 Lithuanian Jews; though he was suspected of many more murders, the public prosecutor explained, the charges involved only the three actions in which the 11,500 were killed.

The trial was likely to be a lengthy one; recent war crimes trials held in Germany have taken from one to three years. If convicted, he would still have numerous avenues of appeal. His trial, however, would never take place: according to Canadian news sources Albert Helmut Rauca died of natural causes on Saturday, October 29, 1983, in the prison hospital at Frankfurt. His death surprised his lawyer, William Parker, who said he was unaware that Rauca suffered from any serious illness.

17
THE ISSUE

Rauca's arrest in Toronto in the summer of 1982, and former Gestapo chief Klaus Barbie's extradition from Bolivia to France early the following year, created considerable anxiety among the more than 1,000 Nazi collaborators living in Canada, who fear they may be next on the list. In a speech delivered in Toronto in March 1983, Solicitor-General Robert Kaplan revealed that since the war there have been 110 requests for extradition of alleged war criminals, from such democratic, western European countries as France, Holland, Belgium, Norway, and Germany. The fugitives are accused—and in some cases have been tried *in absentia*—of crimes ranging from collaboration with the Nazis during the war to informing on the underground, revealing Jewish hiding-places, assisting in the round-up of Jews, and joining in their slaughter. Some were members of the Belgian Rexists, the French *Action Française*, the Flemish National Brotherhood, or the Dutch National Brotherhood; some joined Finnish, French, or Walloon SS units which earned a reputation as the Führer's most stubborn fighters.

But the majority of the collaborators now in Canada came from eastern European countries. On that list are men who were members of the Hungarian Arrow Cross, the Romanian Iron Guard, and the Latvian Thunder Cross—organizations that were viciously anti-Semitic and devotedly pro-Fascist. Radical-nationalist Ukrainians, Byelorussians, Georgians, and Estonians formed their own SS divisions. Their military formations, largely German-led, fought alongside the Germans against the Allies.

Some of those being sought were among the most vicious of the many non-Germans who volunteered to serve as concentration-camp guards. Others were members of auxiliary police brigades, punitive units, and Einsatzkommandos which slaughtered thousands of Jews. Still others were civic and state officials in puppet governments that meekly did the Nazis' bidding and sought to curry favour with their masters through anti-Semitic activities: they launched "spontaneous" pogroms, issued anti-Jewish ordinances, called on the Nazis to establish Jewish ghettos, and turned over Jews who had escaped from ghettos into forests and villages.

Some acted out of hatred for the Russians, some out of hatred for the Poles. Some hated Communism; some had the naive belief that the Germans would help them regain national freedom; some were indulging in crass opportunism. But underlying all their motives was an unquestioning acceptance of the centuries-old anti-Semitism endemic in their countries.

Aware of the fate that awaited them in their homelands, they fled to Canada after the war, where they were welcomed as displaced persons and political refugees. Some managed to slip by on forged identity papers. Many simply relied on subtle name changes sufficient to confuse the immigration department's primitive filing system. There is reason to suspect, though, that some passed through with the tacit connivance of Canadian officials, acting on their own or in tandem with American intelligence units such as the Central Intelligence Agency and the State Department's top-secret Office of Policy Co-ordination. The Nazis might have been beastly, but they were no longer public enemy number one; Communism had been declared the new menace. "If the Canadian immigration authorities had wanted to check out Rauca's background when he applied for admission in 1950, they need only have telephoned the Plauen police department to obtain full information," says Gunther Wieland, the East German Chief Prosecutor.

Only forty-seven extradition requests have been received from Iron Curtain countries. The small number can be readily explained by Canada's consistent refusal to compel anyone to return to a Soviet-bloc nation. However, the unprecedented diligence with which the Solicitor-General pursued the Rauca matter worries the leaders of some Eastern European émigré organizations, who fear that attitudes may be changing.

Adding to their concern is the widespread publicity following the disclosure that, unknown to the U.S. Congress, the Office of Policy Co-ordination had recruited members of pro-Nazi, wartime, puppet governments in the hope of organizing anti-Soviet espionage and guerrilla organizations in Soviet-bloc nations. Between 1948 and 1950, about 5,000 of these collaborators—some of whom had played an active role in the massacre of the Jews—settled in the United States with their families, even though their past activities should have disqualified them for entry under the U.S. Displaced Persons Act. They went to work for Radio Free Europe, Radio Liberty, the Voice of America, the CIA's language school in Williamsburg, Virginia, and the Defense Language School in Monterey, California, where intelligence officers of the armed forces learn the languages of Eastern Europe. In late 1982, the world was further shocked to learn that, at about the same time, U.S. army intelligence units were so intent on developing information on the Communist movement in France and Germany that they hired former Gestapo commander Klaus Barbie, "The Butcher of Lyons", and protected him from arrest by the French government. In September 1983 the U.S. government apologized formally to the French government for what was clearly an illegal act by its officers.

Canadian intelligence agencies worked closely with their British and American counterparts during and after the war. Collaborators whose pro-Nazi profiles were too high to be admitted safely to the United States could count on the Canadians to ask fewer questions. The Canadian Immigration Branch, which had successfully barred the door to Jewish refugees before and during the war and was equally opposed to Jewish immigration after the war, did not hold the same abiding prejudice against non-Jewish Eastern Europeans; General Anders' Polish Division, which had fought alongside the British in North Africa, was welcomed to Canada but was encouraged to exclude its Jewish members. Of all the refugees created by the war, the Estonians and Latvians were the least objectionable to Canadian officials; next came the Lithuanians,

156

Ukrainians, and Poles. Jews rated last. Small wonder, then, that Canadian authorities were not overly concerned if some of those admitted had once been nasty to the Jews. Best to take their statements at face value: if they said they had spent the war farming or in a German labour camp, why challenge it? There was certainly no point in going overboard to verify the information. As for the information freely available from the Soviet zone, it was generally ignored as unreliable and politically motivated.

In theory a person who gains entry by making false statements on an immigration application can later be deported. But unfortunately, as Robert Kaplan explains, "we can't go back now and check the immigrants' original declarations. We didn't keep the documents. In Canada we don't save everything the way they do in the United States; here we throw out the applications after five years. We can't afford the vast public archives you find in the States." As a result, Canada's Justice Department is unlikely to employ the U.S. Justice Department's strategy of initiating denaturalization proceedings followed by deportation hearings; without the original applications we can prove nothing.

In any case, the question remains: how much will is there on the part of the Canadian government to pursue war criminals? The answer is, apparently, not much; the government sees little political profit in pursuing the issue, regardless of its morality. French Canada wasn't keen on the war and isn't keen on the issues that arose in its aftermath. To many post-war Eastern European immigrants and their Canadian-born children, all talk of war criminals is anathema, and there aren't enough Jewish voters, or enough Jewish influence, to make the pursuit of war criminals an election plank for any of the major political parties. Edward Greenspan, a prominent Toronto lawyer, questions the sincerity of the federal government even in the Rauca case. He suggests that Rauca's extradition was a token gesture to the Jewish community, a face-saver by a government that has been dragging its heels for thirty years; a last act rather than a curtain-raiser. Greenspan's skepticism can be answered only by further extraditions.

If the government is wary on political grounds, where do the RCMP stand? How eager are they to track down war criminals? Here again, the answer is, not very. Despite recent proposals for a civilian security service, the Mounties remain Canada's major intelligence arm. To gather information on Soviet-bloc countries, they have cultivated the radical, right-wing nationalists in the Baltic, Ukrainian, Hungarian, Romanian, Croatian, and Polish Canadian communities. It is even possible that some of those sought as war criminals are among the RCMP's chief informants.

All police forces have priorities, and chasing down war criminals has simply never been high on the list for the RCMP. To raise it higher would require a clear-cut political decision by the Prime Minister, the Minister of Justice, and the Solicitor-General; it would also require constant monitoring by deputy ministers to keep the Mounties on the trail. Canada's top federal police officers see little glory in "getting their man" when he is an "old geezer who has kept his nose clean for forty years and hasn't committed any crime in Canada"; otherwise how could it possibly have taken ten years to find a man who was living openly under his own name, enjoying an old-age pension, driving a car, and scrupulously paying his taxes? The RCMP's efforts were token, at best, until Corporal Yetter took over, and if the matter hadn't touched Yetter's professional pride, Rauca would undoubtedly still be free.

Many Canadians feel that, despite the atrocities of the Nazis, it's time to "let bygones be bygones"; they wonder what point there is in bringing people to justice after so many years. Ought we not, as Klaus Barbie has suggested, simply forget about it? "I have forgotten the events of the war years and I think it is time the world also forgot them." In reply, Jews quote the famed eighteenth-century founder of Hasidism, the sage Baal Shem Tov, who said, "Forgetfulness leads to exile, while remembrance is the secret of redemption."

But if we dare not forget, the argument goes on, ought we not to forgive? Shouldn't we show compassion to an old man with only a few years more to live? After all, Rauca was a mere master sergeant. He didn't design the Holocaust; he simply helped carry it out. What choice did he have? Wouldn't he have been shot if he had disobeyed orders?

Rauca did in fact have a choice. A significant number of Nazi Party members—from generals to privates—did refuse assignments to killing units, or demanded transfers as soon as they knew

158

what was being asked of them. There are verified accounts of both officers and enlisted men who refused point blank to carry out the Gestapo's orders to become part of the killing machine. They weren't shot and they weren't disciplined; they may not have been promoted, but that was the end of it. The Nazis knew all too well that, legally and morally, they were on shaky ground. That's why Propaganda Minister Goebbels declared in 1943, "We will go down in history as the greatest statesmen of all times or as [history's] greatest criminals." That is why the Führer-order authorizing Himmler and Heydrich to go ahead with the Final Solution was transmitted verbally and never written down. That is why the Nazis sought—unsuccessfully—to keep the mass murder of Jews secret even from their own people.

If the accounts of the Kaunas survivors are accurate, moreover, Rauca not only fulfilled his orders but exceeded them. In Operation Intellectuals he seized thirty-four more men than originally called for. In Operation Kozlowski he responded to what was probably no more than a loud noise with the murder of 1,800 people. In Democracy Square he so relished the task of deciding who should live and who should die that he didn't even take time for lunch. Nor did he limit himself to decision-making: he personally shot down a man in the silver fork incident, and joined in the shooting of Dr. Shapiro and his family.

Emil Fackenheim is a philosopher and theologian who teaches at the University of Toronto. He was born in Halle, Germany. The son of a lawyer and the grandson of a rabbi, he studied for the rabbinate in Berlin, but three months in Sachsenhausen concentration camp in 1938 persuaded him he had no future in his homeland, and he fled to England. Most members of his family lingered in Germany too long, and died in concentration camps. Bearded, ascetic, Fackenheim inveighs like an Old Testament prophet against those who would hand Hitler a "posthumous victory". To declare a moratorium on discussion of the Holocaust is to risk its repetition, he says; to declare a statute of limitations on Nazi war crimes is to defile the memory of the dead. "It is the first time in history that people were killed and tortured simply because they existed. No one was too young, no one was too old.

No one was too saintly, no one was too weak. Even in the worst of states, people are punished for having done something against the laws of the country—even if the laws are evil—but to put together existence and crime is unheard of. The precedent is that one group—[the Jews]—was considered less worthy of existence. That precedent can be turned against any of us."

Fackenheim bristles when asked why Jews can't forgive and forget what was done to them by the Nazis. "The people who ask that question are indulging in the ancient stereotype of the vengeful Jew and the forgiving Christian. It is not out of revenge that we demand the prosecution of war criminals but out of a sense of universal justice. The Holocaust was a tragedy inflicted on the Jews, but it was also an act of pure evil that affects all mankind."

Sister Mary Jo Leddy, editor of the *Catholic New Times*, agrees with Fackenheim. "It's a standard Christian platitude to say forgive and forget. Forgiveness is a much more profound process than that. It first involves acknowledging publicly what one has done. There can be no forgiveness without confession of guilt.

"People don't understand that the judgement of a person's actions can be the most dignifying of human processes. It is based on the assumption that people are responsible for their behaviour and not just the victims of fate or the blind executioners of some historical law. In any event, I don't see how we can presume to forgive in the name of millions of victims. Only the victims are entitled to forgive."

Contrition, admissions of guilt, are not Nazi traits. There were few guilty pleas by the hundreds of Einsatzkommandos, slave labour bosses, extermination camp commandants, and political Gauleiters tried on similar charges. Some denied that the acts had occurred; most simply denied that they had been wrong. At Nuremberg in 1945, Hitler's deputy, Reichsmarshall Hermann Göring, was asked how he pleaded. "Not guilty in the sense of the indictment," he replied. Of the twenty-two Einsatzgruppen leaders tried at Nuremberg, "All pleaded not guilty. Not one expressed the least regret over what he had done. At most they dwelt on the harsh necessities of war and their obedience to orders. When the president of the tribunal asked [Pastor] Biberstein [one of the leaders] whether, as a former churchman, he did not deem it necessary to speak words of comfort...to the Jews about to be slain, Biberstein replied, 'Mr. President, one does not cast pearls before swine.'" In Jerusalem, sixteen years later, Adolf Eichmann explained at great length that he too had no pricks of conscience about his work; he had done his duty, obeying not only orders, but the laws of the land based on the Führer's wishes. "I was free of all guilt. . . . Who was I to judge? Who was I to have my own thoughts on the matter?" Reichsführer SS Heinrich Himmler, addressing the highest ranking leaders of the SS in Poznan on October 4, 1943, said; "Most of you probably know what it is to see a hundred corpses lying together in one place, or to see five hundred or a thousand. To have gone through that and yet, aside from exceptions due to human weakness, to have preserved our decency—that is what makes us hard."

Whether or not Rauca himself feels a sense of moral guilt may never be determined. There is none expressed in the open letter he issued from his prison cell on November 22, 1982.

> I have read newspaper accounts of the proceedings against me and I see it has never been made clear that I have said and I say now that I am not guilty of murder or murders while I served in the forces of the Third Reich. I am writing this letter so that other Canadians can hear me say that I did nothing before coming to Canada to warrant the charges against me. . . .
>
> I. . . have tried not to dwell on the events of the war in which I was involved, in much the same way, I expect, as others who fought in the war.

Rauca was regarded in the ghetto as an "honest Nazi", that is, ruthlessly dedicated, a true believer in Hitler's dogma, a convinced member of the master race. There is nothing we have learned from fellow motel-keepers, his neighbours, or his lawyers to suggest a subsequent change of heart. There is nothing in the life he has apparently led since coming to Canada that implies an effort to make amends.

Is there any point in tracking down and punishing an ageing generation of war criminals? Are they not incapable of further harm? Fackenheim answers, "It may be said of any crime that it unsettles the world. The Holocaust was conducted on such an enormous scale, it was such a horrendous crime, that unless men like Rauca are punished, humanity is for ever wronged and the world can never be put right again.

"It is the task of all men of good will to set the world right again."

Epilogue

It was December, 1982, and the federal courthouse in Tampa, Florida was small, hot, and crowded. On trial was Kazimieras Palciauskas, wartime mayor of Kaunas. He was charged with having illegally gained entry to the United States by concealing his active collaboration with the Nazis during the German occupation of Lithuania. Among the witnesses waiting to be called were Abraham Tory, Leah Elstein, George Kadish, and Yaacov Rabinovitch.

The complainant before the U.S. District Court of Central Florida was the Department of Justice's Nazi-hunting Office of Special Investigations, then headed by Allan A. Ryan Jr. OSI lawyers charged that Palciauskas, appointed mayor of Kaunas on June 25, 1941, by Lithuania's short-lived provisional government, had signed the order requiring all Jews to surrender their homes and move into the Vilijampole ghetto. The orders compelling Jews to wear the yellow star and banning them from public streets from eight in the evening to six in the morning also bore his signatures. The mayor had been responsible as well for collecting the valuables confiscated from Jews and turning them over to German authorities.

Tory testified that he was one of two Jewish representatives on the Ghetto Transfer Committee charged with organizing an orderly, street-by-street evacuation of Jews from Kaunas and their resettlement in the ghetto. One day—departing entirely from the plan—Palciauskas had ordered all Jews to vacate a given street within twenty-four hours. Tory had visited Palciauskas's office, in the hope of persuading the mayor to postpone the order and avoid unnecessary suffering, but Palciauskas had refused to see him. Instead his secretary brought the message that if Tory ever dared enter the mayor's office again he would be kicked—not down the stairs—but right through the second-storey window. Palciauskas continued to serve as mayor until May 1, 1942, when the Germans abandoned all pretence of local rule and took over the administration directly. When the Germans fled Kaunas in 1944, the former mayor fled with them, and when the war ended he remained in Germany rather than return home.

The 1948 U.S. Displaced Persons Act made thousands of European refugees eligible for immigration to the United States. However, those who had collaborated with the enemy or assisted in the persecution of civilians were specifically barred. If they lied about past activities or concealed relevant facts, their admission was deemed illegal and therefore revocable.

When Palciauskas applied for refugee status so as to be eligible to enter the U.S., the former mayor stated that from 1938 to 1943 he had been employed as a clerk. He swore that he had not voluntarily assisted any country at war with the Allies. He was admitted to the U.S. Five years later, when he applied for citizenship, he again failed to mention his service as mayor of Kaunas and his participation in the persecution of the city's Jews. Thus he was now threatened with revocation of his citizenship, and eventual deportation.

The government had little difficulty proving that Palciauskas had served as mayor of Kaunas, but his defence was that he had been only a token mayor under the Nazis, and that his authority had been so limited that he was little more than a clerk. Moreover, his lawyers insisted their client had always been anti-Nazi and anti-Communist—never anti-Jewish. The allegations against him, they contended, had been trumped up by the Soviets. The repressive orders bearing his signature must be Soviet forgeries. In the courtroom, Palciauskas himself suffered strange losses of memory. He could not recognize his own photograph on his application for a visa; the best he could say was, "I don't know if that is my photograph, but it reminds me of myself."

At twenty-six, Bruce J. Einhorn was the "baby" of the Office of

Special Investigations prosecution team. Rotund, bearded, sweating through his summer suit, he sat no more than a foot away from the row of Palciauskas supporters who crowded the tiny courtroom each day. As he rose to question a witness, an elderly woman in a cotton sundress mumbled just loud enough for him to hear, "You son-of-a-bitch, I hope you die of a heart attack." Startled but unshaken, Einhorn gave her a quick glance and continued with his examination. During a recess, when District Judge Robert Morgan, who was hearing the case, passed her in the corridor, the same woman loudly proclaimed, "That's Jewish money talking. They've gone out and bought themselves a judge."

On March 23, 1983, Judge Morgan stripped Palciauskas of his American citizenship. Once he had been denaturalized, the Office of Special Investigations was free to seek his deportation.

Palciauskas is one of 350 suspected war criminals under active investigation by the OSI. Of these, twenty-eight of the strongest cases have been chosen so far for litigation. In twelve of these cases the Justice Department is asking the courts to strip the defendants of their citizenship; in another twelve the defendants have been denaturalized and the OSI is calling for their deportation. The defendants in the remaining four cases either have died or are too ill to participate in their own defence. "My goal is to bring to trial every war criminal alive in this country," says former OSI chief Allan Ryan. "Every day these people have lived here, they have lived free and in peace, which they are not entitled to do."

Until recent years accused war criminals had every reason to believe they would live out their lives quietly in the United States. The immigration service was not aggressively searching for them, and Federal prosecutors did not have the staff or expertise to follow trails that had turned cold twenty years earlier. Then in the early seventies, the West Germans won the extradition of Hermine Braunsteiner Ryan, a former SS camp guard who had immigrated to the United States from Canada. She was the first naturalized citizen extradited for trial on war crimes charges. With that precedent, Congress, prodded by Representative Elizabeth Holtzman of New York, funded the Justice Department's special squad in 1978.

Despite the unit's dedication, and its staff of twenty lawyers, nine investigators, and five historians, the OSI has so far deported only one war criminal, ex-Nazi Hans Lipschitz. The process is painfully slow. "There are seven legal steps that we have to go through, including appeals, before we reach the stage of deportation," Ryan says. "It can take as long as seven years." U.S. courts regard revocation of citizenship as an extremely serious matter requiring clear, unequivocal, and convincing evidence, he explains, and the evidence is hard to gather—much of it must be obtained through diplomatic channels. The witnesses are scattered throughout the world. "It's an uphill battle persuading the courts that these elderly people in their sixties, seventies, and eighties are mass murderers. They're not the kind of people who posture like storm troopers, fly the Nazi flag, or maintain Nazi museums in their homes. What the judges see are defendants who have lived ordinary, unassuming, middle-class lives since coming to America; people who cut their lawns and are nice to their neighbours."

Few of the people on Ryan's list are German. Most are Latvian, Ukrainian, Lithuanian, Romanian, Hungarian, or Bulgarian. Among them are:

> –Andrija Artukovic, the wartime Interior Minister of the Croatian puppet state, accused of ordering the deaths of 600,000 Jews, Serbs, and gypsies. For twenty-one years Artukovic has been under a deportation order for his alleged wartime activities, but he remains comfortable and secluded in an expensive beachfront apartment compound in Surfside, California.
>
> –Boleslaus Maikovskis, alleged former chief of police in Rezekne, Latvia, sentenced to death *in absentia* in 1965 by a Soviet war crimes tribunal. A series of witnesses testified that he razed the village of Audrini and shot 170 of its Jewish inhabitants. A retired carpenter, Maikovskis lives on a pleasant, tree-shaded avenue in Mineola, New York.*
>
> –Karl Linnas, sentenced to death by the Russians in 1962 on charges of being the head of the concentration camp in Tartu, Estonia, where 12,000 died. Linnas, a factory worker in Greenlawn, New

*For more detail on Maikovskis, see Appendix.

York, is reported to have a sticker pasted on the bumper of his car bearing the legend, "I brake for animals."

–John Demjanjuk, a Ford Motor Company machinist in Cleveland, Ohio, allegedly known in Treblinka and Sobibor concentration camps as "Ivan the Terrible". Born in the Ukraine, Demjanjuk was accused of brutalizing inmates and helping run the camps' gas chambers. Witnesses testified that he wielded an iron pipe to split open the skulls of prisoners trying to escape.

–Valerian Trifa, accused of being president of the highly anti-Semitic National Union of Romanian Christian Students and a member of the Fascist Iron Guard; a speech by the student leader is said to have touched off four days of riots in Bucharest in which 300 Jews were brutally killed. Trifa later became the Romanian Orthodox archbishop, running his episcopate from Grass Lake, Michigan. He was ordered deported in October 1982, but is still in the United States because no country has so far agreed to accept him. Switzerland rejected him in December and "a Swiss official in Bern said the archbishop intended to apply to an easier country— Canada."

Abraham Tory was exuberant after giving evidence in the Tampa courtroom: he and his diary had helped bring another war criminal to justice. The former secretary to the Ältestenrat emigrated to Israel soon after the war, where he is a highly respected member of Israel's bar and Honorary Secretary General of the International Association of Jewish Lawyers and Jurists. Remarkably vigorous at 73, he maintains an active practice, travels widely, and can recall events of forty years ago in overwhelming detail. "The lawyers who defend these bandits may seek to deny the accuracy of my recollections," he said. "But they cannot deny the accuracy of my diary."

Leah Elstein and Abraham Tory remain good friends and live not far from each other in Tel Aviv. When the last of the SS personnel fled Kaunas, they took Leah with them; Unterscharführer Pilgram escorted her to Stutthof concentration camp where he arranged to have her assigned to the *Schreibstube* or secretarial pool. But she didn't choose to stay there long. "The girls were too pretty, too well

167

dressed," she says. "There was something strange going on. I preferred to go to a regular barracks where I had my head shaved and wore a striped uniform." Leah found her mother again at Stutthof. Together, they worked for eight months digging and clearing drainage ditches. Leah became ill from the hunger and cold. Typhoid was rampant in the camp—"You might wake in the morning and find that the girl who shared your bunk was dead," she recalls. British bombers attacked the camp one night, killing many of the prisoners. Towards the end of April, 1945, Leah and other camp inmates were evacuated by ship, but the British bombed the boat. They were rescued by a German battleship, but the battleship was sunk by a British cruiser and most of the passengers and crew were drowned. Leah was among the handful rescued by a German yacht. Eventually she emigrated to Israel and married a famous Israeli cabinet minister, the late Pinchas Lavon. Although she doesn't dwell on the events of her youth, each incident remains etched in her memory. Does she remember Rauca? "What a question!" she replies. "He came frequently to the Ältestenrat. How can I forget him?"

When they met at the trial in Tampa, George Kadish and Leah Elstein had not seen each other since their ghetto days. "I remember you," he said. "You wore a trench coat and that cute little beret." Leah laughed, and her eyes sparkled. They talked of musicales and plays presented by the young people in the ghetto, and recalled picnics held under the very guns of the Gestapo. "It was our form of defiance," said Leah. "It was our assertion of life in the face of death." Kadish nodded his agreement. "Say," he said, "do you remember the time the students held a dance and you and I spent all night doing the tango?"

Kadish spent three months of 1943 living with a non-Jewish friend in Kaunas; on June 17, however, he was seized in a house-to-house search. But the Gestapo never learned that he was the much-wanted ghetto photographer. When arrested, he told them his name was Abramavitz, and produced papers of sorts to prove it. Under that name he survived two years in Dachau and Stutthof, until he was liberated by American troops in April 1945. Kadish was the only member of his family to escape death at the hands of the Nazis. His parents, his brother, and his sister, her husband, and their two children were all slain.

Kadish returned to Kaunas after the war to recover the pictures he had left behind, sealed in metal containers and buried in bunkers. Then he went to work for the American Joint Distribution Committee in Germany as photographer and correspondent covering the work of the United Nations Relief and Rehabilitation Agency. He completed four documentary films dealing with life in the displaced persons' camp. During his travels in the American occupation zone he discovered that many German soldiers had souvenir photographs they had taken of death camps in Poland and massacres in Soviet territory. They were willing to give them up in exchange for a can of Spam or some chewing gum. In one picture, obtained for a few cigarettes, a soldier is about to fire his pistol into the head of a dazed, expressionless Jew who is kneeling at the edge of a pit partially filled with other victims. In a second, Germans are using a pair of ice tongs to drag away a body; in a third, crematory attendants are pushing a body into a furnace.

After settling in the U.S., Kadish became a major inventor and manufacturer of television studio equipment. Many of the booms and spiders used by the CBC and other networks are products of Kadish's New York company. Now retired and living in Florida, he has donated his collection of negatives and photographic prints to Israel's famous museum of the Holocaust, Yad Vashem.

Three months after the *Grosse Aktion* in Democracy Square, Leon Kupferberg's wife gave birth to a girl. They decided the infant had little chance of surviving in the ghetto, and rather than let her die, they gave her to a friendly Lithuanian family for safekeeping. Indomitable, the Kupferbergs survived the ghetto and the death camps; they made their way back to Kaunas after the war and reclaimed their child. In 1950 they emigrated to Canada, settling in Montreal. Their daughter grew up, married, and moved to Toronto. A lovely woman with children of her own, she was shocked to tears to learn that Rauca—the man her parents feared so much that they gave away their own baby to save her life—lived only a block or two away from her North Toronto home.

Yaacov Rabinovitch, one of the handful who survived in the ghetto until the Red Army retook Kaunas, has returned to journalism. He writes regularly for Montreal's Yiddish newspaper, *The Canadian Eagle*, and is Canadian correspondent for several Jewish community newspapers in the United States. He and his family live in Montreal.

In July 1944, the Werblunsky family was loaded on cattle cars and transported to Germany. On a siding near Elbing, the men were separated from the women and children and sent off in a different direction. "That was the last I saw of my father," Helen says. "He was shipped to Dachau, near Munich, while mother and I were taken to Stutthof, not far from Danzig." They were greeted at Stutthof by tall chimneys belching black smoke—"We assumed that cremation would be our fate." To their surprise, Helen and her mother were sent to a barracks rather than to the gas chamber. Several weeks later the camp authorities shipped them to a small work camp where they spent the cold, damp winter months digging ditches and tank traps. "We slept in the tents on dirty straw beds," Helen remembers. "My mother and I had only one pair of oversize wooden clogs between us. Our clothes were in tatters, I was covered from head to toe with scabies. We were so hungry that when we passed a farm one day, we drove off the pigs and ate their swill from the trough." Life had become so meaningless that death was preferable. When camp authorities called for volunteers to return to Stutthof, mother and daughter agreed to answer the call, although they knew full well that the gas chamber awaited them. "We were the first in line to register," she recalls. "We were giving up. There was no reason to prolong the agony." But the guards were up to their usual sadistic tricks. Instead of beginning with those first in line, they reversed the procedure and took those in the back of the line first. By the time the guards worked their way back to Helen and her mother, the Stutthof quota was filled, and Helen and her mother found themselves condemned to continue living. It wasn't until spring that the Russians overran their typhus-ridden camp, deloused them, threw them some bread, and charged off down the road after the enemy. It was weeks before they were well enough to drag their emaciated bodies to a hospital where they were given medical treatment and care. "There were some other Jewish women in the hospital," she says. "We learned from them that it was the first day of Passover."

Today, Helen Werblunsky is a handsome, forceful woman who lives in an impressive house on a winding suburban street in Toronto. Now that her family is grown, she fells obligated to engage in some mission, some humanitarian gesture, that will express her gratitude for having survived the horrors of the ghetto, forced labour, death camps and death marches. By coincidence, she lives only a block away from another childhood survivor of the ghetto, Norman Salansky.

Salansky became a world-famous scientist. One of the first of the widely publicized Jewish *refuseniks* who insisted on being allowed to emigrate from the Soviet Union, he was the object of a world-wide campaign to persuade the Soviet authorities to release him. Freed in 1977, he came to Canada the following year, where he joined the faculty of the University of Toronto's Department of Applied Physics and Engineering. His uncle, Chaim Lipman, lives not far from Salansky; hale and hearty at sixty-eight, the old fighter still keeps an eye out for stray boards and lengths of iron pipe. "They'll come in handy if we ever have to start building bunkers again."

Of the sixty-four members of the workgang engaged in disinterring "dolls" who escaped from Fort IX on Christmas Eve, 1943, only five survived the war. Three of them, including Alex Feitelson and Michael Itzchaki, emigrated to Israel. The fourth, a former Russian officer, lives in Moscow. The fifth, Berel Gempel, opened a kosher butcher store in Vancouver and later became a small-scale developer; wracked with illnesses caused by his wartime experiences, he recently retired.

Although forty years have passed, Dr. Elchanan Elkes—his bravery, his scorn for the Nazis, his warm personality—are still very much with Tory and Elstein. When the Nazis disbanded the Kaunas ghetto in 1944 and transported the survivors to concentration camps, Elkes refused an offer of the Jewish underground to smuggle him out of the city and provide him with a safe hiding-place. Instead he accompanied his people to Dachau, where he died.

In a letter to Elkes' children dated Munich, September 18, 1945, his brother Hirsch, who had been with him in the camp, wrote:

> The terrible thing began when we were sent to camp Al, near Landsberg. What your father had to suffer here physically and mentally is impossible to describe, yet he carried it all with immense dignity. "These people can never hurt me," he used to say, referring to his guards.
>
> The bitterness of our life here only served to bring the sorrows of others closer to his heart. He did not know rest. The fire he put into everything he undertook was not quenched; on the contrary, it was to consume him in the end.
>
> You know that his physical constitution was never the strongest, and that his tireless spirit did not have a worthy servant in his fragile body. Yet he would not hear of taking care of himself. Even here. No work, no service, no abuse—even of his kindness—was ever refused; and by serving others, he consumed himself. Thanks to his energy, he managed for a time to hold his equilibrium—but his strength continued to ebb, and with the deepest anguish we saw things worsen without being able to help. His will to live, too, ebbed. He awaited death as a merciful release from his spiritual anguish. "Such a life is unseemly; I cannot watch this suffering, I must be away—*Ich muss weg*." He lay on his hard bunk, very quiet, looking into the distance, accepting fate, in unspeakable pain—he lay there for fourteen days, a few teaspoonsful of water his only nourishment. He remained conscious until his last breath, and on the seventeenth of October, 1944, at 4:15 a.m., he had done. . . .

A granite tombstone bearing Elkes' name now stands in a corner of the camp over the mass grave in which he was buried. It was erected by the survivors of the Kaunas ghetto.

Gempel, Tory, Elstein, and Feitelson—indeed all the survivors of the selection in Democracy Square—cling to Elkes' admonition to his children, contained in a letter addressed to them on October 19, 1943: "Remember both of you what Amalek did to us. The Nazis callously slaughtered us, undisturbed by feelings of guilt. I observed them as I stood among them when many thousand men, women, children, and infants were sent to their deaths. How gustily [the Germans] ate their morning's bread and butter, how they mocked our martyrs. I saw them on their return from the killing rounds, drenched in the blood of our loved ones. Remember this and do not forget it all the days of your lives. Pass it on as a holy testament to the generations to come."

Appendix

According to evidence presented in 1956 at a trial in Riga, Haralds Puntulis was a platoon commander in the semi-military Latvian rural police, the *Aizsargi*. Soon after the Nazis marched into Latvia, Puntulis offered them his services, and from July 27, 1941 to the time the Russians retook Latvia he served as chief of police of the fourth precinct of the Rezekne district, in which the town of Malta was located. In the summer of 1941, Puntulis and his men rounded up all the Jews in the village of Riebina, marched them into a nearby forest, and shot them; then they returned to the village for a celebration. Later that summer he arrested the Jews of Malta, plundered their property, and forced them into a cellar where his men shot them.

In command of the neighbouring second precinct was Boleslaus Maikovskis, leader of the execution squad that massacred Riga's Jews. In December 1941, Maikovskis and his district commander, Albert Eichelis, led a raid on the village of Audrini in search of escaped Russian prisoners of war. In the skirmish that followed, three auxiliary policemen were killed and the POWs escaped into the woods. Convinced that the villagers had sheltered the Red Army men, Maikovskis requested permission from his Nazi superiors to destroy the village and its inhabitants. On January 2, 1942, auxiliary police detachments led by Eichelis, Maikovskis, and Puntulis surrounded Audrini; they burned the village to the ground and shot 170 of the village's 200 inhabitants, including children. Two days later the remaining thirty villagers were executed, and Puntulis is said to have led the firing squad and to have personally finished off the wounded with his pistol. Puntulis, Eichelis, and Maikovskis were tried on a charge of treason by the Latvian Supreme Court in Riga in 1965. The three accused were not in the courtroom—Eichelis had fled to Germany; Maikovskis had made his way to the United States and was living in Mineola, Long Island; Puntulis had found shelter in Canada—but they were represented in the courtroom by three empty chairs bearing their names. The trial appears to have been conducted with full legal rigour. A number of Puntulis's former colleagues turned state's evidence. Almost two hundred witnesses testified to the events they had seen, and scores of captured documents, photographs, and unit reports—including a description of the massacre of Audrini in the Jäger report—supported the eyewitness evidence.

Puntulis arrived at Quebec City on October 13, 1948. By 1962, when he became a Canadian citizen, he owned a successful building contracting business and lived in a comfortable suburb of Toronto. In June 1965, Canadian newspapers reported that the Soviet Union had requested his extradition from Canada. To the Soviets the request seemed straightforward, since both Canada and the U.S.S.R. are signatories to a United Nations resolution that member nations must return each others' war criminals. But in November 1965, the Toronto *Telegram* reported that "Canada has rejected Russia's demand to extradite Haralds Puntulis of Willowdale, Ontario." on the grounds that "Canada has no extradition treaty with Russia, and the charges are not substantiated."

Maikovskis did not fare as well. In 1977 the United States government initiated deportation proceedings against the Mineola carpenter for having concealed his true past "as chief of the Second Police Precinct in Rezekne, Latvia" and for having failed to inform the U.S. Immigration Service of his participation in "assaults upon and murders of Jewish and other Latvian civilians". During lengthy deportation proceedings, Maikovskis identified Puntulis as commander of the Fourth precinct and identified his picture on an *Aizsargi* identification card.

Eichelis was eventually found and tried in West Germany, and on July 4, 1980, an Ontario Supreme Court examiner, acting on behalf of the German state prosecutor, questioned Puntulis on Eichelis's role in the Audrini massacre.

Of the six Latvian precinct captains who operated under German orders in the District of Rezekne, only Puntulis was never held to account for his deeds. He died in his home, on July 4, 1982, having lived out the rest of his life undisturbed and unthreatened, sheltered by a benign Canadian government that made no effort to bring him to justice.

Chapter Notes

1 THE ARREST

The details of Rauca's arrest were learned in several telephone conversations with RCMP Staff Sergeant Glen Smith, and through records of Corporal Fred Yetter's testimony at Rauca's extradition hearing on August 26, 1982.

Rauca's attempt to identify himself with the RCMP officers is strikingly similar to Adolf Eichmann's efforts to ingratiate himself with his Israeli interrogator, Captain Avner Less. Less reports in *Eichmann Interrogated*, p. *ix*, that one day Eichmann pointed to the insignia of the Israeli police and said, "Herr Hauptmann, when I see this badge, I realize that you and I were colleagues. I was once a policeman myself."

Lawyer Ralph S. McCreath's opinions of Rauca were obtained in a difficult telephone interview in which McCreath scolded me and the press generally for prejudging his client. He objected in particular to the cover of the July 1983 issue of *Saturday Night* magazine, which showed Rauca's unretouched 1973 passport picture.

The dialogue in the courtroom is from the transcript of Rauca's first bail hearing on June 21, 1982.

2 HAUPTSCHARFÜHRER

Information on the Berlin Document Centre was obtained from Professor Henry Friedlander of Brooklyn College; Friedlander was one of the first American researchers to have access to its files. Additional material was garnered from a Reuters dispatch printed in *The Toronto Star* ("Innocuous Building Houses Explosive Papers—Nazi Records") on March 9, 1983.

Race and Settlement Office. . . . The most detailed discussion of the work of the *Rasse-und-Siedlungshauptamt* can be found in Raul Hilberg's *The Destruction of the European Jews*, pp. 46-53.

All the material on Rauca's family background, early education, career, and marriage was obtained from his R-and-S form stored in the Berlin

Document Centre. Photocopies of these forms and accompanying correspondence were included in court exhibits filed in the Rauca case before the Supreme Court of Ontario.

"When Hitler appointed Heinrich Himmler...." The description of the SS is from Alan Bullock's introduction to *The Schellenberg Memoirs*, by Walter Schellenberg, the head of Germany's counter-espionage network.

3 THE FINAL SOLUTION

"The Final Solution of the Jewish problem was the code name..." is the opening sentence in Gerald Reitlinger's *The Final Solution: The Attempt to Eliminate the Jews of Europe, 1939-1945.* Reitlinger, a British archaeologist and art historian, produced the earliest, most readable, and most authoritative books on the Holocaust.

The description of the Final Solution as a "salvational ideology" is by Lucy S. Dawidowicz, in *The War Against the Jews*, p. *xxii*.

"The anti-Semitism of reason..." comes from a letter from Hitler to Adolf Gemlich on September 16, 1919. I have taken it from German historian Joachim C. Fest's *The Face of the Third Reich*, p. 36. The quote about *Mein Kampf* and its "stench of naked obscenity" and the quote about Hitler's "insane world" are from p. 30.

"I have often asked myself why we didn't pack our belongings at once..." is from Rabbi Gunther Plaut's article "The Day Hitler Came to Power" in the *Globe and Mail*, Toronto, January 31, 1983. Plaut, senior scholar at Toronto's Holy Blossom Temple, was born and educated in Berlin.

"When faced with persecution...." For a masterly discussion of Jewish communal survival techniques, see Hilberg, *The Destruction of the European Jews*, pp. 14-17.

Kristallnacht.... The Hitler and Goebbels quotes are from Dawidowicz, *The War Against the Jews, 1933-1945*, pp. 134-135.

The telegram signed "Gestapo II Müller" was probably sent at Heydrich's direction. It is International Military Tribune document PS-3051, *The Trial of the Major War Criminals*.

"Today I want to be a prophet once more...." This widely reported speech appears in a number of translations. This one is taken from Hilberg, *The Destruction of the European Jews*, p. 257.

For the devolution of the "Führer Order" to proceed with the liquidation of the Jews, see Reitlinger, *The Final Solution*, pp. 81-82, and Hilberg, *The Destruction of the European Jews*, pp. 257-258.

4 THE MOTHER COUNTRY

For a general description of life, death, study, work, food, and language in the *shtetl* see Diane and David Roskies, *The Shtetl Book, An Introduction to East European Jewish Life and Lore*, or Irving Howe, *World of our Fathers*, pp. 5-25. For a vivid personal description of Jewish religious life in Lithuania, see Avraham Kariv, *Lithuania, Land of My Birth*.

"a jumble of houses. . . . " The quote is from Maurice Samuel, *The World of Sholom Aleichem*, pp. 26-27. The description of Kaunas is drawn from interviews with former residents and from Leib Garfunkel's article *"Vichtikste Momenten in Kovner Getoh"* ("The Most Important Moments in the Kaunas Ghetto") in Volume I of *Lite* (*Lithuania*), edited by Sudarsky and Katzenelenbogen, which I borrowed for an unconscionable length of time from the Montreal Jewish Public Library.

Material on Lithuania's geography and its history between the wars was assembled from: Arved von Taube's article "The History of the Baltic States" in *The Encyclopaedia Britannica*, pp. 670-676; Leonard Valiukas, *Lithuania, Land of Heroes*; *Jews and Non-Jews in Eastern Europe*, edited by Bela Vago and George L. Mosse; and Antanas Snieckus, *Soviet Lithuania on the Road to Prosperity*.

The estimate of the number of Jews deported to Siberia in 1940-1941 is from Reitlinger, *The Final Solution*, pp. 212-213.

5 EINSATZGRUPPEN

The best authority for Einsatzgruppen activities is the records of the International Military Tribune, *The Trial of the Major War Criminals*, Volume IV. Material on the Einsatzgruppen training course is drawn from Reitlinger, *The Final Solution*, p. 186; and Dawidowicz, *The War Against the Jews*, pp. 160-161. For a detailed description of Einsatzgruppen by a leading German scholar, Dr. Wolfgang Scheffler, see Exhibit No. 60 (36 pages) filed by the Crown at the Rauca hearing (*Federal Republic of Germany vs Helmut Rauca*, Supreme Court of Ontario, October 12, 1982).

"Six Einsatzgruppen...." The quote is from Dawidowicz, *The War Against the Jews*, p. 152.

For Heydrich's career and personality see Fest, *The Face of the Third Reich*, pp. 152-170, and Schellenberg, *The Schellenberg Memoirs*.

"...the real engineer of the Final Solution...." This apt description of Heydrich is from Reitlinger, *The Final Solution*, p. 13.

The account of Heydrich's meeting with the Einsatzgruppen chiefs on September 21, 1939, prior to their departure to Poland, is from Dawidowicz, *The War Against the Jews*, p. 154. The English version of Heydrich's teletype letter on the Jewish question in occupied territories appears in Lucy Dawidowicz's *Holocaust Reader*.

For the attitudes of German generals to the actions of the Einsatzgruppen in Poland and later in the Soviet Union, see: Dawidowicz, *The War Against the Jews*, p. 152; Hilberg, *The Destruction of European Jews*, p. 128; Reitlinger, *The Final Solution*, pp. 196-197; and Nora Levin, *The Holocaust*, p. 153. The brief quote is from Levin.

"...a queer intellectual riff-raff..." is from Reitlinger, *The Final Solution*, p. 186.

Eichmann's description of Dr. Franz Stahlecker can be found in Hannah Arendt's *Eichmann in Jerusalem*, p. 74.

"...the subordinate officers were mostly misfits...." Again it is Reitlinger, in *The Final Solution* (pp. 192-193), who most accurately describes the Einsatzgruppe leaders for what they were—men who could find success only through the Nazi Party.

"[They] were in no sense hoodlums...." This is Hilberg's evaluation in *The Destruction of the European Jews*, p. 189.

"So instead of saying, 'What horrible things...'" is from Arendt's *Eichmann in Jerusalem*, p. 106.

Himmler's Poznan speech.... The excerpt quoted is from Fest, *The Face of the Third Reich*, p. 177. Fest cites the International Military Tribune document *The Trial of the Major War Criminals*, Volume XXIX, PS-1919 as his source.

"To be harsh towards ourselves...." For a fuller discussion of the SS ethos of hardness, see Fest, pp. 183-184, in *The Face of the Third Reich*.

6 POGROM

Much of the detail in this chapter will not be found in history books; it came from lengthy interviews with Dr. Abraham Tory and Lucy Lavon (the former Leah Elstein) in Tampa, Florida on December 6 and 7, 1982. Further details were supplied by Chaim Lipman, a survivor of the Kaunas ghetto who now lives in Toronto. Helen Yermes (née Werblunsky), one of the handful of ghetto children who survived the *Kinder Aktion*, also lives in Toronto, and despite the fearsome memories it reawakened Helen gave me several long interviews. The accounts of all these informants were, incidentally, well supported by the information from captured German documents. For example, the famous Stahlecker Report to Himmler, October 15, 1941 (The International Military Tribune, *The Trial of the Major War Criminals*, document L-180), confirms their account of the outbreak of the Kaunas pogrom; Stahlecker explains how he instigated the pogrom and explains why it was important that it appear spontaneous. He also complains: "To our surprise, it was not easy at first to set in motion an extensive pogrom against the Jews."

Further material is drawn from: Joseph Gar, *Umkum fun der Yidisher Kovne* (*The Extermination of Jewish Kaunas*); Dr. Samuel Gringauz, "*Churbn Kovne*" ("The Destruction of Kaunas"), an article in *Fun Letztn Churbn* (*From the Recent Holocaust*), No. 7; and Jacob Goldberg, "*Bletlech fun Kovner Eltestnrat*" ("Pages from the Council of the Elders of Kaunas"), from the same issue. While I struggled through portions of these works in the original Yiddish, I am grateful to Ben Kayfetz of the Canadian Jewish Congress for the English translations of key chapters which appear in the brief submitted by Congress to the Federal Court of Appeal.

For a version of these same events from the point of view of the Lithuanian Activist Front, see Valiukas, *Lithuania, Land of Heroes*. For the Soviet point of view, see the heavily documented *Documents Accuse* by B. Baranauskas and K. Ruksenas, and Snieckus, *Soviet Lithuania on the Road to Prosperity*.

"...the fateful and final hour has come to settle accounts with the Jews." Authority for this quote is p. 310, *Jews and Non-Jews in Eastern Europe*, edited by Vago and Mosse.

"...the blame for the intensification of anti-Jewish hostility...." While some sources, both Jewish and non-Jewish, attribute the intensification of hostility towards Jews in Lithuania to the presence of a significant number of Jews in the ranks of the commissars who arrived with the

180

Russian forces in 1940, this is a dangerous game. First, it supports the myth that "Bolshevism is Jewish", and secondly, it ignores the equally savage anti-Semitic outbreaks that occurred in Romania, Hungary, and Croatia, states which were not subject to Russian invasion at the time.

The account of Goldberg's conversations with Bobelis and Villeisis are from Goldberg's *Bletlech fun Kovner Eltestnrat*, mentioned above.

7 "YOU MUST WITHDRAW INTO A GHETTO"

The roles played by Rauca and other SS officers were outlined by Abraham Tory in our Tampa interview.

For the attitudes and actions of the German generals, see Reitlinger, *The Final Solution*, pp. 196-197, and Hilberg, *The Destruction of the European Jews*, pp. 211-214.

The account of the first meeting of Jäger and the Jewish leaders of Kaunas is largely Tory's. He was present when the leaders reported the conversation to the community's leading Jews that same night.

"The Jews are remarkably ill-informed. . . . " The text will be found in the activity report of Einsatzgruppe A up to October 15, 1941. The report is dated January 31, 1942; its International Military Tribune file number is L-180.

The account of the selection of Dr. Elkes as Hauptjude is, again, largely Abraham Tory's, although a similar account can be found in Gar's *Umkum fun der Yidisher Kovne*. Dr. Elkes' stature as a community leader is widely recognized by historians of the Holocaust. In contrast to many Hauptjuden, who were later reviled as collaborationists, madmen, cowards, and fools, Elkes is regarded as a man of integrity who handled a hopeless situation with courage and dignity. Tory points out the vital difference: Elkes was selected by his community, while most Hauptjuden were chosen by the Germans; similarly the men on his council were appointed by Jewish leaders rather than by the SS.

"He was a man of slight build. . . . " This homage to Elkes was written by his son, Dr. Joel Elkes, Department of Psychiatry, University of Louisville, Louisville, Kentucky.

"I value all skills. . . . " This account of Elkes' grace and courage in the face of physical danger was related by Lucy Lavon (Leah Elstein), who had also been arrested and was being held with the council members at Fort

181

IX. The Gestapo, which had learned of Tory's escape from the ghetto a few days earlier, was seeking information on his whereabouts. Unable to learn anything from the council members, they released them—much to the council's surprise.

The exchange between Elkes and the SS man was more pungent than it sounds in English. *"Ich bin ein Genickschusswunde Spezialist,"* said the officer ("I am a specialist in killing with a shot in the nape of the neck.") *"Ich respektiere jeder Spezialität,"* Elkes replied ("I respect all specialties.")

8 OPERATION INTELLECTUALS

"...the very word had a soothing, ancestral ring." The quote is from Thomas Keneally, *Schindler's List*, pp. 85-86.

The major source for this account of Operation Intellectuals is the affidavits submitted to Canadian Crown attorney Christopher Amerasinghe by Professor Leon Bauminger, former director of the Yad Vashem archives in Jerusalem, and Tel Aviv businessman Baruch Direktor.

Yaacov Rabinovitch's account was obtained in a videotaped interview in his Montreal home, as preparation for a CBC documentary on the Rauca case on *The Journal*.

The conversation between Elkes and Cramer was reported by Tory and is also in Gar's *Umkum fun der Yidisher Kovne*.

On the ghetto police, see Dawidowicz, *The War Against the Jews*, pp. 316-317; Hilberg, *The Destruction of the European Jews*, p. 310; and Levin, *The Holocaust*, p. 325.

9 SILVER FORK

The introductory quote to this chapter, from Chaim Lipman, a construction engineer who helped save many lives in the Kaunas ghetto, comes from my interview in Toronto, May 1983.

The incident of the silver fork and the shooting by Rauca of its supposed owner is set out in the statement filed by Direktor with the Supreme Court of Ontario for the extradition hearing, October 12, 1982 (Court No. A-529-82).

The account of the crowd that gathered at Ältestenrat headquarters to demand *Jordanscheine* is also from Chaim Lipman, who was present.

10 THE BIG OPERATION

The description of the events of October 28 and 29, 1941, is based on interviews with several eyewitnesses—Tory, Elstein, Rabinovitch, Kupferberg, Lipman, and Werblunsky—as well as statements given to the court by Abraham Chaitowitz, Leon Bauminger, Baruch Direktor, Alex Feitelson, Rivka Peleg, and Michael Itzchaki. Their statements were checked against the Yiddish accounts published by Joseph Gar, *Umkum fun der Yidisher Kovne*, Samuel Gringauz, *Churbn Kovne*, and Jacob Goldberg, *Bletlech fun Kovner Eltestnrat*. The dilemma imposed on the Ältestenrat when called upon to distribute the *Jordanscheine* is described in Leib Garfunkel's *Kovno ha-Yehudit be-Hurbanah*, p. 72.

For a fuller discussion of the analogy of the two men lost in the desert see Irving J. Rosenbaum, *The Holocaust and Halakhah*, note 13 on p. 160.

The original German wording of the order requiring Jews to assemble at Democracy Square is preserved in Tory's diary.

11 WITNESS

Leon Kupferberg lives in Montreal but regularly visits his daughter in Toronto; I interviewed him during one of those visits, in the summer of 1982.

Chaim Lipman, whose struggle against the German and Soviet authorities deserves a book of its own, speaks some English but is more comfortable in Yiddish, Russian, and Lithuanian. Our interviews were conducted mainly in Yiddish, with occasional translations from the Russian by his nephew Norman Salansky.

Helen Werblunsky, see notes for Chapter 6.

George Kadish talked to me at some length in Tampa, Florida, on December 7, 1982. He showed me many of the pictures he had taken in the ghetto, speculated on what had happened to the people portrayed, and told me that he was willing his collection to the Holocaust Museum at Yad Vashem in Jerusalem. He also directed me to a feature story ("Hero of Ghetto of Kovno Armed With Pictures of Nazi Horrors") published in the *Easton Express* (Pennsylvania) on January 27, 1948. I have made generous use of that article.

The story of Geist and Lida was narrated to me by Mickolas Yatzkevichis, Foreign Minister of the Lithuanian Soviet Socialist Republic and himself a poet and playwright, in his Vilnius offices on July 28, 1983. After

Geist's death his effects were returned to his relatives in Germany. Among them was a diary chronicling the battle between Rauca and Geist. Several years after the war the diary came to the attention of Yatzkevichis, who immediately saw its dramatic potential; he co-authored a play entitled *I Hear Music*, with ninety per cent of its dialogue based directly on Geist's diary. The play enjoyed several successful presentations.

The account of the exhumation of bodies from mass graves at Fort IX is taken from the Yiddish works of Gar, Gringauz, and Goldberg, from court records—particularly the affidavits filed by Feitelson and Itzchaki—and from a long-distance telephone conversation I had with Berel Gempel, who lives in Vancouver. Tory confirmed the story of the young boy who escaped from the grave.

The text of Anthony Eden's December 17, 1942 announcement to the House of Commons is taken from Robert Goralski, *World War II Almanac, 1931-1945*, p. 248.

Himmler's appointment of Blobel to efface all mass burials is mentioned in Reitlinger, *The Final Solution*, p. 138 and Hilberg, *The Destruction of the European Jews*, p. 255.

12 THE LAST *AKTION*

"Elkes' pride and dignity. . . . " I have relied on Tory's account of his chief, and on the magnificent last letter Elkes sent to his children in England—a letter shared with me by his son Joel Elkes.

13 A NEW LIFE

Fuerst, who claims he saw Rauca at Auschwitz in 1944, has submitted a lengthy document to this effect to the RCMP, but he failed to identify Rauca's picture in the album of similar photographs.

Almost all the information on Rauca's post-war whereabouts is taken from his own testimony in the Supreme Court of Ontario on June 21, 1982.

"A hospital is a hell of a good place. . . . " The immigration officer remains unidentified at his own request.

Information on the *Beaverbrae* was obtained from the Canadian Pacific Railway's historical files.

"...sharing quarters with their former captors." See Abella and Troper, *None is Too Many*, p. 238.

The ship's passenger list, Rauca's application for citizenship, his oath of allegiance, and several passport applications are included in the court exhibits of *The Federal Republic of Germany vs Helmut Rauca*, Federal Court of Appeal, Court No. A-529-82.

14 THE CHASE

"By the time the leadership of the Canadian Jewish Congress. . . . " Early in April 1982, Inspector Menachem Russek, head of the Israel Police war crimes squad, telephoned Abraham Tory and invited him to come by his office: "There are some photos I would like you to identify." When Tory arrived, Russek showed him an album of about a hundred photographs of people—mostly men, and mostly in SS uniform. "Do you recognize anyone?" Russek asked. As Tory flipped the pages, he paused from time to time to say, "He looks familiar." Here and there he identified members of Einsatzgruppe A3. Some of his identifications were tentative, others more certain. On one page there were three passport-sized photos of a full-faced young man in black Gestapo dress uniform. "That's Rauca!" Tory shouted. "That's him. I've no doubt at all." Russek then showed him the picture of an elderly man walking down a city street. "That's Rauca with white hair," Tory said. "He's grown older but you can still recognize his features." Tory didn't know it, but the wartime photos were from Rauca's file in the Berlin Document Centre, while the recent photo had been taken by an RCMP surveillance team.

"They've found him in Canada," Russek confided. "The West Germans want him but it will not be an easy matter." Tory, who is honorary secretary-general of the International Association of Jewish Lawyers and Jurists, headquartered in Jerusalem, recalled that one of the association's several vice-presidents was McGill law professor Irwin Cotler. By coincidence Cotler was also president of the Canadian Jewish Congress that year. Tory wrote to Cotler on April 28, 1982, advising him of Rauca's presence in Canada and asking him to do everything in his power to see that Rauca was brought to justice. He explained that he had recently been questioned at length about Rauca by a West German prosecutor in the presence of an Israeli judge, and that Christopher Amerasinghe had also been there, representing the Canadian Department of Justice. Now that Rauca had been found, Cotler must do his bit to make sure the Canadian government did not drop the ball.

185

Cotler says he immediately wrote to Solicitor-General Robert Kaplan, advising him that he was aware of Rauca's presence in Canada and demanding his immediate arrest. For good measure, he enclosed a copy of Tory's letter. Cotler claims it was his letter that forced Kaplan's hand; without it, he says, the Solicitor-General might have dallied and allowed Rauca to slip through his fingers. Kaplan, however, insists that no letter from Cotler concerning Rauca ever reached him, and that his staff can find no record of such a letter in the log which lists every piece of correspondence received by his office.

Simon Wiesenthal . . . the peppery Nazi-hunter's admission that he had played no direct role in Rauca's arrest was made during a long-distance call I placed to his home within days of Rauca's arrest on June 17, 1982. His account of his correspondence with the U.S. Department of Justice and Canada's justice minister was confirmed in interviews with Kaplan and the former director of the Office of Special Investigations, Allan Ryan, Jr.

Kaplan's visit to Wiesenthal. . . . The gist of the conversation was related to me by Kaplan in a long interview.

The statistics on Easter German war crimes prosecutions were published in *Panorama DDR, Dokumentarische Information*, 3 II 51/1.5, *"Gerechte Strafen fur Kriegs- und Naziverbrecher in der DDR."*

The interview with Wieland was held in his offices on Monday, July 25, 1983.

For a discussion of judicial aspects of war crimes see Bradley F. Smith, *Reaching Judgment at Nuremberg*, and Hilberg, *The Destruction of the European Jews*, pp. 685-687.

"victor's justice. . . ." For the attitude of the German people to the Nuremberg Trials and the failure of mass de-Nazification procedures, see Adalbert Rückerl, *The Investigation of Nazi War Crimes 1945-1978*, particularly pp. 36-37.

Joe Salsberg's letter is quoted from Irving Abella and Harold Troper, *None is Too Many*, p. 254. For many years a leading member of the Communist Party of Canada, Salsberg had a falling-out with Khrushchev and the Communist Party over the disappearance of internationally famed Jewish writers and poets in the U.S.S.R.

"Most of the émigrés did not even bother to change their names. . . ." The quote is from John Loftus, *The Belarus Secret*, p. 91.

The information on Jäger's suicide was obtained from Adalbert Rückerl during our interview. I learned of the Schmitz suicide from Abraham Tory.

Referral to Interpol. . . . The authority for this statement is a letter dated November 3, 1977 from the State Prosecutor's Office at the Frankfurt Regional Court to the Federal Criminal Police office in Wiesbaden summarizing the Rauca case. The pertinent paragraph reads, "When an initial approach was made by the German consulate-general in Toronto, Canada, to the Royal Canadian Mounted Police . . . a reply was received stating that a request should be made through Interpol."

15 LEGAL PRELIMINARIES

Much of the material in this chapter was learned in a personal interview with Amerasinghe several weeks after the court's decision to extradite Rauca had been announced.

Jeff Ansell. . . . Neither Kaplan nor Amerasinghe would identify the reporter who had threatened to "blow the story" but Ansell confirmed that he was the one. Ansell, like all good reporters, refused to disclose the source of his information.

"Although free to leave prison on bail. . . ." Parker's explanation of Rauca's decision to remain in jail was received in a personal interview. Although Parker didn't mention it, I have subsequently learned that Rauca's house was defaced and that Mrs. Machdanz and her daughter were subjected to harassing telephone calls.

The Jäger Report. . . . A page of the report, stored in the Central Lithuanian Archives in Vilnius, is reproduced in the photographic section.

Handwriting expert. . . . RCMP Staff Sergeant Robert Gerald Fawcett's evidence can be found on pages 38-62 of the transcript of Rauca's extradition hearing. (*The Federal Republic of Germany vs Helmut Rauca*, Supreme Court of Ontario, October 12, 1982.)

The new information and complaint were sworn out by Corporal Yetter before The Honourable Chief Justice Evans on August 24, 1982.

Intervention by Canadian Jewish Congress. . . . I am indebted to lawyer Bert Raphael and to legal researcher Kenneth Narvey for most of the material concerning the legal role of the Congress in the Rauca case. The rest of the description of the Congress's role *vis-à-vis* war criminals was drawn from conversations with former president Irwin Cotler, Central

Region Director Benjamin Kayfetz, and Canadian Holocaust Survivors' Association president Sabina Citron.

16 EXTRADITION

Abraham Ric was spared the ordeal of giving evidence from the witness stand. Since Rauca's defence attorneys had announced they had no wish to cross-examine the witness, it was sufficient for Amerasinghe to read Ric's deposition into the record.

The arguments and counter-arguments on the application of the Charter of Rights to extradition law will be found in the transcript *The Federal Republic of Germany vs Helmut Rauca*, Supreme Court of Ontario, October 12, 1982, pp. 162-202.

For the transcript of the appeal see *Her Majesty the Queen and the Federal Republic of Germany vs Helmut Rauca*, Supreme Court of Ontario Court of Appeal, February 10-11, 1983, judgment delivered April 12, 1983.

Horkins' comments on Rauca's decision to accept extradition and abandon the appeal to the Supreme Court of Canada were obtained in a telephone interview on May 13, 1983 and a longer interview in his office on May 17, 1983.

17 THE ISSUE

"...more than 1,000 collaborators living in Canada...." Estimates of the number of alleged war criminals who have found shelter in Canada vary from under a hundred to over a thousand, and Simon Wiesenthal has consistently employed the one thousand figure. The truth is that at this point no one can tell with any degree of certainty. However, my own estimate suggests that if we include all those who served in SS and police auxiliary units, participated in collaborative governments, or played active roles in Fascist parties, the number is easily over one thousand.

"...110 requests for extradition...." This figure was given to me by Kaplan in our interview. He later included it in a March 14, 1983 speech at Beth Sholom Synagogue in Toronto.

For a brief but authoritative summary of the history and nature of these non-German Fascist parties, see F.L. Carsten, *The Rise of Fascism*.

"...formed their own SS divisions." The best source of material on the SS units recruited in Eastern Europe is Reitlinger: *The SS, Alibi of a Nation*, and *The House Built on Sand*.

"among the most vicious of the many non-Germans...." For an objective evaluation of the cruelties engaged in by Eastern Europeans who assisted the Nazis, see Philip Friedman, "Ukrainian Jewish Relations During the Nazi Occupation" in his book *Roads to Extinction*. For a well-documented description of Byelorussian depredations see Loftus, *The Belarus Secret*; also Wiener Library (London) Bulletin, XVI, No.1, 1962.

"...they fled to Canada after the war." See Wiener Library (London) Bulletin, XVII, No.1, 1963. Rauca's case illustrates how easy it was for people who had served in SS units to cover up their past and be admitted to Canada.

"Only forty-seven extradition requests...from Iron Curtain countries...." This number was obtained by telephone from Solicitor-General Kaplan's office.

"The Canadian Immigration Branch...did not hold the same abiding prejudice against Balts...." See Abella and Troper, *None is Too Many*; on p. 213 they quote High Commissioner Vincent Massey on his preference for Latvians. Page 226 notes, "The Latvians and Estonians are honest, ingenious and good workers." When Balts were in short supply, Canadian authorities were willing to accept Poles, but only if Polish Jews were excluded; p. 218 describes the immigration to Canada of 4,000 members of General Anders' Polish army: "To the surprise of agreeable Polish authorities, Jewish members of the Polish army were to be carefully screened out...."

"We didn't keep the documents." This admission was made by Kaplan in a personal interview.

Edward Greenspan's comments were made in an interview on the Canadian Broadcasting Corporation's *The Journal* on November 4, 1982.

On obeying orders...in *Eichmann in Jerusalem*, Arendt quotes Herbert Jäger's article *"Betrachtungen zum Eichmann-Prozess"* in *Kriminologie und Strafrechtsreform* to the effect that the Nuremberg documents demonstrate that "not a single case could be traced in which an SS member had suffered the death penalty because of a refusal to take part in an execution." Reitlinger *et al.* give specific examples of SS officials and German generals who went home rather than participate in mass murder and were not punished.

Emil Fackenheim...personal interview, summer 1982.

Sister Mary Jo Leddy...telephone interview.

Rauca's letter... parts of the letter were published in the press, but I have taken the quotes directly from a photocopy of the entire letter provided by defence lawyers Horkins and Parker.

Goebbels.... The quote is from his diaries but I have taken it from Arendt, *Eichmann in Jerusalem*, p. 22.

Ernst Biberstein... See Levin, *The Holocaust*, p. 245.

"...to see a hundred corpses...." Himmler's speech is quoted fully in Fest, *The Face of the Third Reich*, p. 177.

EPILOGUE

I overheard the remarks quoted at the Palciauskas trial in Tampa, and the first remark was also reported in the *Tampa Tribune* (page 1, section B), December 8, 1982.

Data on the number of cases under investigation by the Office of Special Investigations, the number chosen for litigation, and the number currently in court, were obtained in a personal interview with Allan Ryan, the OSI director, on August 25, 1982.

"Until recent years accused war criminals...." The quote is from *Newsweek* ("A New Hunt for Old Nazis"), October 27, 1980.

"Few of the people on Ryan's list are German...." Ryan confirmed the preponderance of Eastern Europeans during our August 25, 1982 interview.

For information on individuals on the OSI list see the Office of Special Investigations, U.S. Department of Justice, Criminal Division, annual report, "Digest of Cases in Litigation", August 15, 1982, and the Toronto *Globe and Mail*, October 20, 1976, "'Model Neighbours' Probed for War Crimes", by Ralph Blumenthal (New York Times Service).

"[Trifa] intended to apply to an easier country—Canada", see the Toronto *Globe and Mail*, July 21, 1983, "The Lax Hunt for War Criminals; Canada Powerless?" by David Lancashire.

The conversation between Kadish and Leah Elstein took place in Tampa in my presence on December 9, 1982. Information on Kadish's post-war career was obtained in an interview the same day.

The information on Norman Salansky was obtained in two personal interviews in the spring of 1983.

The information on Berel Gempel was obtained in a long-distance telephone interview, June 1983.

Bibliography

Abella, Irving, and Harold Troper. *None is Too Many*. Toronto: Lester & Orpen Dennys, 1982.

Adams, Ian. "Judgment after Nuremberg", article in *Weekend Magazine*, Toronto, November 19, 1977.

Arendt, Hannah. *Antisemitism*, Part One of *The Origins of Totalitarianism*. New York: Harcourt Brace Jovanovich, 1968.

——*Eichmann in Jerusalem: A Report on the Banality of Evil*. New York: Penguin Books, 1979.

Baranauskas, B., and K. Ruksenas. *Documents Accuse*. Vilnius, Lithuania: Gintaras Vilnius, 1970.

Blum, Howard. *Wanted: The Search for Nazis in America*. New York: Quadrangle Books, 1977.

Bullock, Alan. *Hitler, A Study in Tyranny* (Rev. ed). New York: Pelican Books, 1964.

Carsten, F.L. *The Rise of Fascism*. Berkeley: University of California Press, 1967.

Dawidowicz, Lucy S. *A Holocaust Reader*. New York: Behrman House, 1976.
——*The War Against the Jews 1933-1945*. New York: Bantam Books, 1981.

Ehrenburg, Ilya, and Vasily Grossman, ed. *The Black Book*. New York: Schocken Books (Holocaust Library), 1981.

Epstein, Helen. *Children of the Holocaust*. New York: G.P. Putnam's Sons, 1979.

Fest, Joachim C. *The Face of the Third Reich*. Harmondsworth, England: Penguin Books, 1979.

Friedman, Philip. *Roads to Extinction: Essays on the Holocaust*. New York: The Jewish Publication Society of America, 1980.

Gar, Joseph, *Umkum fun der Yidisher Kovne* (*The Extermination of Jewish Kaunas*). New York: Farband fun Litvishe Yiden, 1948.

Garfunkel, Leib. *Kovno ha-Yehudit be-Hurbanah*. Jerusalem: Yad Vashem, 1959.

Glatstein, Alexander, *et al.*, ed. *Anthology of Holocaust Literature*. Philadelphia: The Jewish Publication Society of America, 1969.

Goldberg, Jacob. *"Bletlech fun Kovner Eltestnrat"* ("Pages from the Council of the Elders of Kaunas"), article in *Fun Letztn Churbn (From the Recent Holocaust)* No.7. Munich: Central Historical Commission of the Central Committee of the Liberated Jews in the U.S. Zone, 1946-48.

Goralski, Robert. *World War II Almanac: 1931-1945*. New York: G.P. Putnam's Sons, 1981.

Gringauz, Samuel. *"Churbn Kovne"* ("The Destruction of Kaunas"), article in *Fun Letztn Churbn (From the Recent Holocaust)*. Munich: Central Historical Commission of the Central Committee of the Liberated Jews in the U.S. Zone, 1946-48.

Heller, Celia S. *On the Edge of Destruction*. New York: Schocken Books (Holocaust Library), 1980.

Hilberg, Raul. *The Destruction of the European Jews*. New York: Harper and Row, 1961.

Howe, Irving. *World of our Fathers*. New York: Simon & Schuster, 1976.

Kariv, Avraham. *Lithuania, Land of My Birth*. New York: Herzl Press, 1967.

Keneally, Thomas. *Schindler's List*. New York: Simon & Schuster, 1982.

Laqueur, Walter. *The Terrible Secret*. New York: Penguin Books Ltd., 1982.

Less, Avner W. *Eichmann Interrogated*. (Ed. Jochen von Lang.) Toronto: Lester & Orpen Dennys, 1983.

Levin, Nora. *The Holocaust*. New York: Thomas Y. Crowell Co., 1968.

Loftus, John. *The Belarus Secret*. New York: Alfred A. Knopf, 1982.

Nadasy, Steven. *The Werner Family*. New York: Vantage Press, 1971.

Poliakov, Leon. *Harvest of Hate*. Syracuse: Syracuse University Press, 1954.

Reitlinger, Gerald. *The Final Solution: The Attempt to Exterminate the Jews of Europe, 1939-1945*. New York: A.S. Barnes & Co., 1961.

——*The House Built on Sand*. New York: Viking Press, 1960.

——*The SS, Alibi of a Nation*. London: Heinemann, 1956.

Rosenbaum, Irving J. *The Holocaust and Halakhah*. New York: KTAV Publishing House, 1976.

Roskies, Diane K., and David G. Roskies. *The Shtetl Book, An Introduction to East European Jewish Life and Lore* (2nd ed). New York: Ktav Publishing House, 1979.

Rückerl, Adalbert. *The Investigation of Nazi Crimes 1945-1978*. Heidelberg: C.F. Müller, 1979.

Samuel, Maurice. *The World of Sholom Aleichem*. New York: Vintage Books, 1973

Schellenberg, Walter. *The Schellenberg Memoirs*. London: Andre Deutsch, 1956.

Shirer, William L. *The Rise and Fall of the Third Reich: A History of Nazi Germany*. New York: Simon & Schuster, 1960.

Smith, Bradley F. *Reaching Judgment at Nuremberg*. New York: Random House, 1977.

Snieckus, Antanas. *Soviet Lithuania on the Road to Prosperity*. Moscow: Progress Publishers, 1974.

Steiner, Jean-François. *Treblinka*. New York: Simon & Schuster, 1967.

Sudarsky and Katzenelenbogen. *Lite* (*Lithuania*), Vol. I. New York: Kultur Geselshaft fun Litvishe Yiden, 1951.

Vago, Bela, and George L. Mosse (ed.) *Jews and Non-Jews in Eastern Europe, 1918-1945*. New York: John Wiley and Sons, 1974.

Valiukas, Leonard. *Lithuania, Land of Heroes*. Hollywood, California: Lithuanian Days Publishers, 1962.

Von Taube, Arved. "History of the Baltic States", *Encyclopaedia Britannica* (15th ed.), 1976.

Waite, Robert G.L. *The Psychopathic God: Adolf Hitler*. New York: Basic Books, 1977.

COURT RECORDS

First bail hearing—Federal Court of Appeal, between: The Federal Republic of Germany, applicant, and Helmut Rauca. June 17, 1982. (Court No. A-529-82.)

Second bail hearing—Supreme Court of Ontario, The Extradition Act, between: Helmut Rauca, applicant, and the Federal Republic of Germany, respondent. Before The Honourable W.D. Parker, Associate Chief Justice of the High Court, Toronto, September 1, 1982.

Extradition hearing—Supreme Court of Ontario, in the matter of an extradition hearing between: The Federal Government of Germany, the requesting state, and Helmut Rauca, fugitive, before The Honourable G.T. Evans, Chief Justice of the High Court, at Toronto, commencing October 12, 1982.

Appeal against extradition order requesting that November 22, 1982 decision of The Honourable Chief Justice Evans be set aside—Supreme Court of Ontario (Court of Appeal) between Her Majesty the Queen and the Federal Republic of Germany, and Helmut Rauca. The Appeal Book, Vol. 1, 2, & 3.

Application by the Canadian Jewish Congress for leave to intervene in an appeal—In the Matter of Rule 24a of the rules respecting Criminal Proceedings of the Court of Appeal of Ontario; Her Majesty the Queen and the Federal Republic of Germany, respondents, and Albert Helmut Rauca, appellant. (Court File: 966/82.)

Appeal judgment—Supreme Court of Ontario (Court of Appeal), Justices Howland, C.J.O., Mackinnon, A.C.J.O., Brooke, Martin and Houlden J.A. April 12, 1983.

Federal Court of Appeal, between: The Federal Republic of Germany, applicant, and Helmut Rauca, respondent, "Memorandum of Argument of Canadian Jewish Congress". (Court No. A-529-82.)